I Shot a Man in Reno

I SHOT A MAN IN RENO

A History of Death by Murder,
Suicide, Fire, Flood, Drugs,
Disease, and General
Misadventure, as Related in
Popular Song

Graeme Thomson

continuum

NEW YORK • LONDON

2008

The Continuum International Publishing Group Inc
80 Maiden Lane, New York, NY 10038

The Continuum International Publishing Group Ltd
The Tower Building, 11 York Road, London SE1 7NX

www.continuumbooks.com
http://ishotamaninrenobook.blogspot.com

Printed in Canada on 100% post-consumer waste recycled paper

Library of Congress Cataloging-in-Publication Data
Thomson, Graeme.
   I shot a man in Reno : a history of death by murder, suicide,
fire, flood, drugs, disease, and general misadventure, as relat-
ed in popular song / by Graeme Thomson.
      p. cm.
   Includes bibliographical references and index.
   ISBN-13: 978-0-8264-2857-8 (pbk. : alk. paper)
   ISBN-10: 0-8264-2857-6 (pbk. : alk. paper) 1. Popular music-
-History and criticism. 2. Death in music. I. Title.

ML3470.T55 2008
782.42164'1588--dc22

                                        2008017486

Contents

INTRODUCTION

Death, wrote Elvis Costello many years ago, wears a big hat. Sometimes it does—and someday it's going to ask you to try it on for size—but the truth is that every age of man imagines its own death differently. The final farewell envisioned by the helplessly romantic 16-year-old will differ significantly from the one staring the on-duty soldier in the face, or the one politely tapping the middle-aged mother on the shoulder as she steps onto the bus after work, or the one lowering itself quietly into the chair at the bedside of the world-weary octogenarian. Not all of them, it seems safe to say, will necessarily involve over-sized headgear.

And yet within us all there is a need to have those wild, romantic, fearful, shadowy visions of death reflected back at us in a way that provides shape, sense, and meaning to our lives. For most of us, popular music will not be the first place we go looking for this. It may not even be the last. Literature, theater, opera, and film are deemed capable of tackling the really heavyweight subjects with the requisite degree of chin-stroking gravitas, leaving the leftovers—the gently crooned "babies," the screamed "oh yeahs," the sundry other trifles and fripperies—to go pop. At least, that seems to be the critical and cultural consensus.

This is at once both surprising and yet entirely understandable. Understandable because popular music is still a young genre that almost always says what it has to say quickly, concisely and relatively straightforwardly. That is simply the way it's built. Its primary function has traditionally been instant connection rather than to engage in philosophical debate, and it is, by and large, content to work within established conventions and limitations. And we, as listeners, have as often as not been complicit in this arrangement. Even today, what passes for serious comment by a recording artist would often be dismissed as nonsense if uttered by a poet or a playwright. Then again, genuinely thought-provoking ideas are often mocked as pretentious and ill-suited to the medium. The playing field isn't, and never has been, quite level.

And yet the fact that more people don't look to pop music in order to confront issues of mortality is still surprising. We are nearing the point where there will be relatively few people left alive who didn't grow up surrounded by—and often immersed in—the stuff. In theory, this should mean that our first generation of rock stars are at the stage in their lives where they should be singing songs of experience and wisdom rather than covering their eyes and flaunting their obliviousness. It follows, furthermore, that those listening in should be more receptive to hearing the message.

Partly, this holds true. Many more artists are proving that, creatively, the process of ageing holds little fear for them, and that they're willing to address the process directly in their music. It's a mistake, however, to presume that pop music progresses in a linear fashion, continuing to evolve and mature as each year passes. Thankfully, it has never conducted itself in quite such an orderly fashion, choosing instead to swill back and forth in a series of ebbs and flows. It's an even bigger mistake to simply assume that rock stars ever truly grow up. Few do. Unlike the Caesars of old, most of them don't employ someone to whisper "Remember you are mortal" in their ear. Instead, they model themselves on Peter Pan and surround themselves with the lost boys and girls.

"In a way we're in a bit of a pioneer area, because pop music doesn't really deal with [death and ageing] as a major topic," Mick Jagger told me in 2007, in the course of rather tartly conceding that the music of the Rolling Stones might not be, well, very grown up. "You're writing within certain conventions—which you can break, but you're still working with them—and you have to recognize what they are. For years the three-and-a-half-minute pop song has been an absurd convention, but we're still in it more or less. That's just one of the conventions and there are many, many others that you tend to follow. And one is that it's not conventional to write about too depressing subjects all of the time."

Note the taken-as-read correlation between death and ageing and "depressing" music. Need it be so? Not according to Anthony Wilson, the late Factory Records boss who did so much to help bring, among others, Joy Division and New Order to prominence. "*Hamlet* is about death, failure, indecision," Wilson said in 2005. "Do we think of it as depressing? No, we know *Hamlet* is among the greatest works of art and that everyone can draw a great and worthwhile experience from it. But rock and roll is a comparatively young art form. Maybe it's not surprising that certain unimaginative people think that music with dark themes, which looks at death and depression and the existential dilemma, has to be a depressing experience itself. It absolutely doesn't. I think that seeing someone genuinely test the bounds of art and create something new . . . is absolutely exhilarating."[1]

This book, then, will swim happily to and fro in these waters, with Jagger on one distant shore and Wilson on the other. As you read, I'd ask you to picture them gesticulating at each other, one clad in Lycra, prancing oddly on the sand to "It's Only Rock & Roll (But I Like It)," the other pacing along the edge of the cliff face in a greatcoat with "Atrocity Exhibition" playing on repeat on his iPod. I'll allow the reader to determine which is which.

In many ways they are arguing fruitlessly, because the reality is that death and dying crop up in popular music all the time. Some of the most loved and listened to songs in existence—from "Pretty Peggy-O" and "Danny Boy" to "Eleanor Rigby" and "Bohemian Rhapsody"—are about death. The tyrannical alliance, only now beginning to disintegrate in the face of digital technology, between the pop charts and the majority of radio stations' play lists may have conspired to convince anyone only half-listening that the world spins on its axis to the sound of moon, June, I Love You, You Love Me, and, indeed, She Loves You, and for many, many people, this is all they ever want from pop music. Good luck to them. The rest of us know that we live in a world where red roses one day become lilies and that a growing awareness of our own mortality is one of the motors that drives us to make the most of being alive.

So let's be clear. If music is a broad church then death songs require a sizeable graveyard. This book isn't just for—or about—furrow-browed young gents in black polo necks and young ladies who wear their soot-black eyeliner as a barrier against the world; death music is not merely a byword for youthful, bookish morbidity. Nor are we simply talking about hooded urban teenagers, well-schooled by their heroes in the art of sullen intimidation; for neither is death music simply about the glorification of destruction and murder; the dubious glamour of drugs, knives, and guns.

It runs much deeper and wider than that. Ask the emo kid and the gangsta rap devotee, by all means. But ask also the Pete Doherty wannabe and the self-appointed member of Generation X. Ask the Goth and the indie-rocker. Ask the teenybopper and the punk. Ask the black metal disciple and the Californian acid casualty. Ask the grizzled blues fanatic and the bearded folk fan. Ask the old time country boy and every last rider on the gospel train. Ask Laura, Tommy and the leader of the pack. Or simply ask anyone who has ever listened closely to the music of the Beatles and the Stones or Love or Ice T or the Cure or the Verve or Tupac or Leadbelly or Metallica or Violent Femmes or Nick Cave or My Chemical Romance or American Music Club or Marty Robbins or Green Day.

They are all part of this story. Over the course of the last half century we have heard tell of teenage girls weeping indulgently over their sweetheart's fatal car wreck; natural disasters sweeping whole communities and lifestyles away; the ever-evolving threat of disease, from VD, influenza, and TB to cancer and HIV/AIDS; graphic reportage of horrific murders; changing attitudes toward old age; exhortations to suicide; deeply personal laments for lost children, friends, and lovers; musical memorials for the famous; discussion of the perfect play list for our own funerals; and the thorny question of what happens to body and soul after the fat lady ceases to sing. Which means that for every "Black Angel's Death Song" there is a "Two Little Boys." For every "Folsom Prison Blues" there is a "Leader of the Pack." For every "Die in the Summertime" there is a "Do They Know It's Christmas?" For every "Cop Killer" there is "The Living Years." Death, like music itself, is a unifying force. There is something for every taste and inclination, from murderous vengeance to camp sentimentality and everything in between.

The issue isn't merely the many different ways in which popular music represents death, but that's the starting point. As a medium, it is uniquely suited to expressing the squalor and stupidity, the shocking, grubby glamour of death. It's the one art form where everyone involved wants to be a hero, sometimes shamelessly, often surreptitiously taking a tilt at glorious immortality. In this way it explicitly mirrors our own private and usually unstated desire to grab something remarkable and vaguely heroic out of the flames of death.

Most of us, I suspect, secretly hope that our demise will resemble a classic single by the Who. "I Can't Explain" seems fitting: short and sharp, exploding with meaning and a magnificent defiance, a guitar-smashing seismic tremor that will live long and fondly in the memory of others. Or perhaps something like "My Way" would fit, a self-aggrandizing slice of pure theater, the vainglorious valediction of a *capo di tutti capi* on his deathbed, the curtain call of kings. Or maybe we harbor a secret hope that it will mirror some classic, highly emotive heartbreaker in the mould of U2's "One": universally resonant, flooded with tears, agonizing but noble. A flaming Viking longship may even be invoked. Good music has the side effect of making us romanticize our own lives out of all proportion to reality, which is by no means a bad thing. But it does mean we are liable to spend much of our lives in semiconscious thrall to these heroic notions, desperately trying to stave off the realization that our passing is more likely to be a long, dull, needlessly painful affair, rather like a song-suite on side one of an early Marillion album or, God forbid, Spinal Tap's "Jazz Odyssey."

But the crux really lies in how music responds to death. As I get older I find I'm becoming more and more interested in what practical purpose music serves. I'm drawn to the notion that it should, at the very least, be useful. From an early age we are, consciously or otherwise, aware of death's presence, and while it's almost impossible to quantify or define the role that music plays in that process, looking back many of us will be able to discern where a change in our listening habits intersected with an increased awareness and understanding of our own mortality. Is music capable of passing on some vital lessons as we move through the years?

For a child, there is no song that sounds like death simply because the concept is unimaginable. The child regards death as a trap careless people fall into and simply decides it isn't going to succumb, steeling itself to be careful out in the woods. It seemed a preposterous notion, its impermanence perfectly expressed in a childhood game of Bang! Bang! You're Dead! You fall down flat on your back and then you get up again for another go. Why would anyone want to die? Why would they allow it?

Songs like "Two Little Boys" and "Seasons in the Sun" transmit a certain innate sadness, an uncomfortable jolt of something gone awry with the world, but they don't really bring death any closer. They didn't for me, in any case. I watched the TV program *Kids from Fame* and would sing along to the theme tune in the belief that the words contained some kind of universal product guarantee: "I'm going to live forever / I'm going to learn how to fly." I hurt myself flapping out of a tree. Nobody ever seemed to explain these things to me.

It's in our teens that death becomes tangible to most of us, although often—for those of us lucky enough to not yet have had any direct experience of it—primarily as an imaginative concept, something to be investigated as a means of underlining the romance of being alive and asserting our own unique individuality. Only in retrospect does it become clear that the reason so many teenagers hold death so close to their hearts is because in reality it seems so far away and untouchable, like an exotic foreign city that can't yet be visited and so instead has to be dreamed into existence.

Generations of music-makers—from Elvis Presley through the Velvet Underground and the Clash, right up to Tupac and Babyshambles—have enshrined in song, stance, and occasionally in fact the still-powerful cliché of living fast and dying young. It holds a perennial attraction to teenagers, partly because it has the effect of embalming forever a perfect time, place, feeling or individual, unsullied by the vagaries of the adult world, but also because few among that most short-termist of tribes are willing to confront the long-term consequences of the act (namely, that all the girls and boys at school might indeed think you're the epitome of cool when you're cut down in a drag race or a chivalrous knife fight, but you're not going to have much fun all alone in the graveyard on a Friday night).

Then there are the more languid teenage types, those poor, pale things "half in love with easeful Death," as Keats would have it in "Ode to a Nightingale." Fragile, borderline tubercular, and overcome with daily, near-fatal attacks of adolescent angst, what's required here isn't in-your-face tragic heroism but music itching with limpidness and melancholy. Death by duvet. Which is presumably why God invented Goth and emo. Listening to either genre is, broadly speaking, the equivalent of reading dark fables and fairytales that end badly and too soon before tucking yourself back into your cozy, suburban bed. It's easy to dismiss this as a day trip in the realm of the night tripper—as exhilarating, insubstantial, and often as amusing as a cheap horror flick—but there may be more to it than meets the eye. Only an adult—and a forgetful one at that—could argue that all that heartache, awkwardness, and anguish is a figment of the imagination and dismiss it brusquely as junior nihilism. It feels pretty damn real at the time, and it still aches more than a little looking back at it all, too. We shall see.

As a teen I had a foot in both camps. In more reflective moments I immersed myself in Van Morrison's *Astral Weeks*, which made death sound like a dream, and somehow more beautiful than being alive. Twenty years later it sounds no less beautiful, but strangely full of foreboding. And with good reason. The passing of time brings death closer, not just in reality but conceptually, too. The idea worms its way into your brain and your bones. By my panic-stricken twenties, death was absolutely everywhere and had to be chased away quickly with wine and whisky, before it revealed itself once more in the bottom of an empty glass and had to be killed again. And again. Everything I listened to back then seemed to contain all the ominous portents and ill winds of some grizzled old folk song, filled to the brim with alcohol, death, natural disaster, and disease. The few that didn't—it was the age of Boyzone and Boyz II Men, after all—made me want to kill myself anyway.

The journey goes on. Now that I'm in my mid-thirties—dull, sober, married with children—death takes the form of a sniper, usually viewed through a lens from afar but occasionally glimpsed up close in terrifying detail. I can really hear it now, and it doesn't sound like the Shangri-Las—or My Chemical Romance for that matter—although my 13-year-old self would probably have shrugged in deeply felt disagreement. It has lost just a little of that lovely romance. Unlike Jon Bon Jovi, I don't want to go down in a blaze of glory, poodle perm flapping majestically in the breeze. I want to cling on, pathetically if necessary, until the very last breath. I still want to live forever, much more than those heartless bastard kids from *Fame* could have ever realized, and yet I now know for sure that I won't.

And I need there to be some music, close at hand, to make sense of all that.

Your story, of course, will be different: different experiences, different expectations, different tunes. Different life. Different death. So what follows isn't simply going to be a list cunningly masquerading as a book. More songs about death will be omitted than included—you're perfectly welcome to fill in the gaps yourself. Instead, the idea is to rummage through a whole world of music, stopping off from time to time to talk things through with some of our most thoughtful songwriters, in order to establish links, delve into motivations, establish communities of ideas and attitudes, and dig up unlikely alliances forged through decades and across genres.

When it comes to death, most of us crave some sense of solidarity. We want to know that there is music out there that acknowledges the machismo, the shame, the guilt, the romance, the anger, the fun, the sadness, the sexiness, the horror, the horror, the exhilaration, the pain, the stupidity, the madness, the violence, and the sheer absurdity of what it means to face up to the great unknown. We want to know in our bones that this morning, yesterday, twenty-five years ago, fifty years ago, one hundred years ago, men and women were writing songs that would help us understand where we're all heading and provide warning, comfort, advice, truth, practical help, some tears, and perhaps a few belly laughs along the way.

I find something oddly comforting in recalling that Johnny Cash shot a man in Reno just to watch him die; and that almost fifty years later he sang another, even darker song, this time about the terrible toll that such actions can wreak upon the human soul. Two very different songs for two very different views of death—and I want to understand why I can't decide which one I like the best. This book, then, is something to chew on for anybody who has ached to remain alive but who finds themselves drawn to the music made by those who can't help but imagine a time when the singing stops for good. Because whoever said that the Devil has got all the best tunes only got it half right. Death has some pretty compelling ones, too.

1
DEATH AIN'T NOTHIN' NEW
From "John Barleycorn"
to "John Walker's Blues"

If it keeps on rainin'
Levee's goin' to break
And all these people have no place to stay.
"When the Levee Breaks,"
Kansas Joe and Memphis Minnie, 1929

I hate to be the harbinger of bad news this early in the proceedings, but we are all going to die. I'm no happier about it than the next man, but I do find it interesting to hear all sides of the story before I cover my ears with my hands and start humming a delirious song of denial, and that means embarking on a little time travel. There have been entire books written about old-time music's grizzled death-skull countenance. This isn't going to be one of them, but before going any further it's instructive and inspiring to look back a little further than the length of our own shadows, to crawl through the long, dark, cobwebbed tunnel connecting John Barleycorn's haystack to Charley Patton's modest Mississippi plantation house to Prince's impressive Paisley Park estate and attempt to measure what pop music has learned and lost along the way.

Just looking back is in itself a positive act of affirmation. Because it's possible, indeed it's increasingly easy, for most of us to sit in our adjustable chairs in our warm rooms in our brightly lit new world and listen to "When the Levee Breaks," written shortly after the great Mississippi flood of 1927, or Jimmie Rodgers' stark, fated "My Time Ain't Long," or almost phantasmagorical traditional songs like "The Cruel Grave," and in the course of doing so be swept away by the belief that death was so much closer to hand in some mythical *back then*. They exude a heady, exotic primitivism that seems so thoroughly rooted in the past it's easy to swallow the delusion that nowadays death is little more than a will o' the wisp, barely visible in the dimming half-light of a harsh old world that we have, thankfully, left far behind in our relentless quest for progress. After all, it's surely only a matter of time before all this money and unshakable self-belief will lead directly to a cure for dying.

This attitude is hardly surprising. With disease and extreme poverty less likely to be fatal in modern times, with technological advances significantly increasing life expectancy, with everything from automobile travel to industrial machinery to walking home in the dark considerably less risky, with child mortality rates mercifully at an all time low in the developed world, with the connection between the food we eat and where it actually comes from so easy to overlook, death has become far less culturally visible in most of our western lives. Increasingly, we're able to swaddle ourselves in the conviction that our private, personal relationship with it is a distant one, as though it were some eccentric great-aunt who occasionally writes barely coherent letters but will never visit. We can shush thoughts of our own mortality back into the furthest recesses of our minds and, in the process, regard those gnarled old-time songs as museum pieces, slices of history that have very little direct relevance in today's brisk world, concerned as it is only with matters of the ever-widening present.

But these are tough, patient songs. They don't clamor for attention or whore themselves out as ring tones to the first mobile phone that comes a-calling. They are prepared to wait until we need them. And we will. Old-time songs retain an intrinsic power because, as much as we may not like to acknowledge the fact, their core concerns never go out of fashion. In particular they remain profoundly relevant when it comes to dealing with the realities of death in any age.

You can try to ignore his entreaties all you like, but when death finally comes knocking, few recordings say it straighter than Blind Lemon Jefferson's "See That My Grave Is Kept Clean," or Son House's "Death Letter Blues," or the Louvin Brothers' "Are You Afraid to Die?" And when disease comes to camp at your house, be it on a long or short lease, "TB Blues" or "1919 Influenza Blues" still cut to the chase quicker than most. A century ago, a touch of the flu was a mortally serious business: "Influenza is the kind of disease / Makes you weak down to your knees / Carries a fever everybody surely dreads / Packs a pain in every bone / In a few days, Mamma, you are gone / To that hole in the ground called your grave." Hardly dazzling poetry, but educational. It might be worth revisiting when the much-trumpeted bird flu epidemic finally strikes.

Whether we want to hear the kind of hard, unsentimental, unvarnished truth that is these songs' stock in trade is quite another matter. Many of us would rather retreat under the covers with a trashy magazine and Michael Bolton until the fever subsides. The cold truth, surely, can't be any worse than that?

But it's when the world around us shifts or shudders significantly on its axis that the old songs really sing out loudest. When Hurricane Katrina blew in, suddenly "When the Levee Breaks" and Charley Patton's "High Water Everywhere"—"Lord, I'll tell the world the water / Done crept through this town"—didn't sound quite as archaic as they once did. They shed their incongruous exoticism and replaced it with an elemental power. That benign sepia glow suddenly burst into full Technicolor, the way great songs do when called upon for service. These songs offer a sharp rebuke, a spoonful of unflavored medicine dished out by a wizened old nanny who really does know best. They conspire to lash the modern western world—with all its imperious delusions and grand ambitions—to the ancient spectres of death and destruction falling from the sky and sweeping in from the sea. We are reminded collectively that, for all our head-in-the-sand pursuit of progress, those bad old days seemingly locked away in the past in the great songs of yore can be summoned up into the present at any time.

It's just as well they were there when Katrina struck, because nobody else was writing songs that could take their place. Bob Dylan, permanently suspended these days in some hovering fog-cloud between the past and the present, seemed to have an inkling of what was afoot. Each of his last three records contained some evidence of ominous foretelling: "I'm going down the river / Down to New Orleans," he sang on "Trying to Get to Heaven." "They tell me everything is gonna be all right / But I don't know what all right even means." Later, he wrote his own "High Water" in 2002, in open thrall to Charley Patton's song of the same name, and an eerie premonition of the devastation that would shortly follow; after the flood, he duly recorded his own version of "When the Levee Breaks" on his *Modern Times* album, without further comment.

But where were all our poet-songwriters when the Louisiana coast first succumbed to the ocean and was then so callously cut adrift from the rest of the United States—and by extension, the rest of humanity—in the summer of 2005? Where have they been in the days, weeks, months, and years that have followed? Where were our own Kansas Joe and Memphis Minnie when the world needed them not only to spell out plainly, in a manner that would strike home to every individual, the physical horror and enormous personal cost wrought by the flood, but also to serve an uncoded warning to the establishment that had, as in 1927, so badly failed its poorest citizens? "Cryin' won't help you / Prayin' won't do you no good" went the simple, ominous curse of "When the Levee Breaks," foreseeing a time when the disenfranchised underclass would rise up in response to the sustained forces of oppression, and all the existing certainties and structures would be swept away without mercy.

Well, it hasn't happened yet, and in 2005 no song was

able to articulate the sorrow, rage, and sense of loss quite so plainly and effectively, despite the fact that Katrina's long and still unfolding aftermath exposed similarly huge fissures in American race relations, as well as leaving its veneer of civility lying shockingly exposed when the tide slowly seeped back out. Kanye West stated simply on television that "George Bush doesn't care about black people," but where was the music to back him up? 50 Cent—alongside West one of the most famous and high-profile black musicians of the past decade—could only shrug that "The New Orleans disaster was meant to happen. It was an act of God. I think people responded to it the best way they can." His comments effectively summed up mainstream music's inability or unwillingness to engage, through their music, with what was actually happening down there: deathly human misery on a colossal and barbaric scale.

Ben Harper wrote "Black Rain" ("You left them swimming for their lives / Down in New Orleans") and Dr. John chipped in with the wordless but eloquent extended elegy *Sippiana Hurricane*, while Elvis Costello obliquely articulated some of the anger in the air in "The River in Reverse," the song he recorded in the city with the towering pianist, songwriter, arranger, and Crescent City resident Allen Toussaint. Apart from that? Deafening, fumbling silence. A massed rank of songwriters staring at their shoes and twiddling their thumbs.

This wasn't about a lack of compassion. There have been many fine words spoken in protest, many displays of support and solidarity, many acts of kindness, some thoroughly helpful and worthy fund-raising efforts in response to the great tragedies of the twenty-first century to date. In other words, an abundance of practical activity, but almost nothing that has fulfilled the traditional musician's role of summing up for the rest of us the deeper ache of mortal dread, barely a note that put the listener into the shoes of the man or woman or child watching their lives being swept away.

The wider implications of the feeble artistic response to Katrina is to highlight the fact that the language required for articulating the reality of death and disaster has struggled to survive translation into the pop vernacular. Katrina, not to mention 9/11 and the terrorist strikes in London, Madrid, Bali, and elsewhere, the Indonesian tsunami, the Pakistan earthquake, the ongoing conflicts in Afghanistan and Iraq, all conspire to tell an eloquent story of how the function of music has changed in the past century, particularly in regard to mortality. Verbose and articulate protest it most certainly can do, while it excels at emotive self-examination. But translating death on a global scale into simple, affecting human terms? That's an altogether more troublesome task.

Thousands of miles away, watching aghast from another continent, what I was looking for after Katrina was someone to at least recognize that what happens to people in the rest of the world happens to all of us. I wanted someone to smash the glass on the television screen and pull me through it. What I was really waiting for was an articulation of John Donne's epithet that "any man's death diminishes me / Because I am involved in mankind." It didn't happen, and through all the bluster and well-meaning acts some essential questions remained unasked, unaddressed, and thus unanswered: How does the individual face up to all this death and destruction in such circumstances? How does it feel and what does it *mean*? In the end, the fact that we are unable to digest or comprehend death on such a broad scale speaks volumes about the way we struggle to face up to our own inevitable mortality, because an understanding of the former cannot arrive without an appreciation of the latter.

Perhaps the expectation is unrealistic. By and large, pop music has always preferred to deal with what it can see two inches in front of its face. It puts its faith in sex, technology, shopping, and easily accessible emotions; above all it worships the individual. It's the music of solipsism, which is why nowadays most of us listen to it in silent retreat, the world kept at bay behind headphones the size of old half-pennies. Its birth and the growth of its popularity coincided with, and was symptomatic of, a wider disengagement and disillusion with organized religion and a diffusion of spiritual belief, as well as a lack of real respect or understanding for the world of the dead.

Broadly speaking, this is one of the genetic traits separating pop and rock music from older, more traditional musical forms: pop is generally secular in its concerns and its overall outlook. Tom Wolfe said recently that since the sixties parents have lost the ability to control their children effectively because they no longer believe in God, and thus lack the moral authority to keep their kids in line. It's an interesting, if moot, point but it is certainly clear that the widespread secularization of society ensures that music struggles to summon up the power to talk with any certainty about the realities of confronting death. Instead, it is either mired in gratuitous description or confusion—which makes for interesting listening in itself—or else simply panders to the needs of a world that has learned to parry away thoughts of mortality with bravado and ignorance, rather than meet them head-on with respect and acceptance. With half an idea that it might just be able to live forever, pop sets its gaze on the future, not the past. When it does look back, it's usually only to glance over its shoulder to see what it can steal as quickly and conveniently as possible, strip-mining cheap signifiers at a surface level and ignoring the deeper substance. The previous decade is already ancient history, ready to be plundered, repackaged, and sold on again.

This is all fine. I'm certainly not complaining. Pop music would be a grim place if all it did was pump out stark blood-and-thunder warnings of our fragile mortality—although you suspect the Sisters of Mercy wouldn't be complaining. Its entire *raison d'être* is fun, frivolity, release, and escape, and it still has no problem locating the point where maximum vacuity intersects with optimum pleasure. And yet, and yet. . . For all its valiant attempts to shut its eyes and ears to bad news and keep the party going, few other art forms are more representative of the tenor of the times that feed it. Society's subconscious awareness of death ebbs and flows according to the way the world is turning, and music is one of the most accurate barometers of what Tom Waits once slurringly called our emotional weather report. Right now, the mercury is bubbling. There is intense unease and deep anxiety in the air, so thick you can almost stir it. And so death creeps in through the shutters like a cat burglar, like it or not.

The morbid, sorrow 'n' suicide songs of emo feed the self-obsession of one-half of the teenage population but speak to no one else; rap holds a glamorous, swaggering spell over most of remainder, but says little about how they are meant to deal with the reality of death, such is its increasing fixation with swaggering fantasy depictions of machismo. At the other end of the age spectrum, Bob Dylan has become more of a hollow-laughing End Times prophet than ever before, revelling in the fact that we are all barely alive in a time of death, but his worldview has become so relentlessly pessimistic it's often difficult to squeeze any droplets of relief or enlightenment from it. And just when you thought it couldn't possibly get any more mawkish and maudlin, mainstream country has gone terminal.

Each of these artists and genres is—in very different ways—fixated with death, and we will return to them all elsewhere. Something very interesting, however, has been brewing over the past few years. The broad, majestic canon of traditional music has been in the process of magically re-inventing itself again, embarking on a popular and critical revival on a scale unprecedented since the fifties. This is no coincidence. When it comes to dealing with death, pop music, for all its flash and swagger, has little choice but to defer to the old-timers. Rather than beat the retreat from reality, folk and its kissing cousins, country and blues, act as a bridge between worlds and a point of shared feeling between communities, part of a long seam that connects the past to the present, the conscious to the unconscious—and the living to the dead. The channels between the earth and the spirit world were multitudinous and wide open in past days and communication flowed much more freely back and forth; songs would flit easily between the two, recounting the game of life in deference to a rule book that modern pop music doesn't often acknowledge or indeed even easily understand.

"In a lot of the [folk] ballads there's an afterlife and an unseen world," says Richard Thompson, who knows the twists, turns, and dark corners of these songs better than most. "Endless songs about ghosts and the unquiet dead. And there's often a moral comeuppance. Whoever perpetrated the crime is punished. Whoever tangles with the faeries, well, there is some precise consequence for upsetting the Faerie Queen. There is something satisfying about that picture of the world. It's hard to say why, but there is something satisfying about the way they deal with life and death."

Perhaps it's because these songs offer clear explanations of how we fit into the world, and how death fits too, that they are undergoing a revival in these sticky times. In a sense all subsequent death music exists in the shadow of folk music, or more accurately *within* its vast span, appearing as though from a series of Russian nesting dolls. Everything that comes after, in one way or another, owes at least a small debt of honour, and it's by revisiting the idioms of old time music that many modern songwriters are finding themselves better equipped to capture a sense of the unique tensions of the times.

Some of the best contemporary contemplations of mortality are formed from a synthesis of the old and the new, songs that merge the personal, the metaphysical, and the historical. Listen to Alasdair Roberts' *No Earthly Man* or Bonnie "Prince" Billy's "Death to Everyone" or Nick Cave's *Murder Ballads* or Tom Waits' *Real Gone* or Richard Thompson's *Sweet Warrior* or the Decemberists' *The Crane Wife* and you hear music that hunts down our fragile mortality, making no distinction between the centuries and being no less haunting and essential for all that. Mixing songs—some centuries old, some newly minted—that draw on the vast sweep of folk, country, and blues traditions, these works echo the past and yet speak eloquently and clearly for our times.

You can trace this bloodline back hundreds of years, to songs like "John Barleycorn," one of the most enduring of all British folk songs, dating back to the 1500s and offering a multi-tiered explanation of the sheer, stubborn necessity of death. Ostensibly the song is about the production of cereal crop: planted, carefully tended, grown tall, then harvested, chopped down at its fullest height to make bread and alcohol. It's a metaphor for the Christian notion of intense suffering leading to a death made as a sacrifice for the benefit of others, but it also encompasses an essentially pagan viewpoint—the vital cycle of the changing seasons; there can be no bountiful spring without the barren winter.

It is, of course, finally a metaphor for life itself, reiterating the truth that both king and pauper are equal in the eyes of death, tying the individual to the land as part of a vast cycle, each and every death nourishing the next life. The song has resonated through the centuries for artists as diverse as the Watersons, Traffic, Frank Black, and Jethro Tull. An excellent new version was recorded in 2007 by Paul Weller and Eliza Carthy, while the 2008 release *John Barleycorn Reborn: Dark Britannica* spends an entire album exploring the musical links between the land, the seasons, the spirit, and death. Separated by a whole ocean of social and musical cultures, you can hear representations of similarly cyclical patterns of life rattling around dozens of contemporary songs, from the Band's mighty "King Harvest" to Pete Seeger's "Turn, Turn, Turn," popularized by the Byrds and heavily indebted to the Book of Ecclesiastes. Even Terry Jacks' "Seasons in the Sun" pays lip-service, acknowledging that "it's hard to die when all the birds are singing in the sky." It goes against the natural order.

This philosophical view of death's essential role in the world sounds out again in one of the most popular eighteenth-century folk songs, "Tom Bowling," written in 1789 by Charles Dibdin in memory of his brother, who had died upon the seas. It ends: "Thus Death, who kings and tars despatches / In vain Tom's life has doff'd / For, though his body's under hatches / His soul has gone aloft / His soul has gone aloft." Here is cheery reassurance and solace in the traditional view of the soul and the body going on separate adventures after death. Skipping centuries, continents, and idioms, we can hear a similar worldview through the crackle and hiss of Dock Boggs' "Will Sweethearts Know Each Other There?," A. P. Carter's deathless "Will the Circle Be Unbroken?," right up to the Verve's "The Drugs Don't Work," written by Richard Ashcroft for his dying father and clinging onto the grief-stricken belief that "I know I'll see your face again."

But if you really want to hear, taste, and *smell* the overpowering sense of *timor mortis conturbat me*, then Ralph Stanley's sepulchral reading of the Appalachian dirge "O Death," also known as "Conversation with Death," is hard to beat. The song's origins are much disputed. Some folklorist studies claim to trace it back to the sixteenth century, but in its final form it may well have been written by Lloyd Chandler, a Freewill Baptist preacher from Madison County, North Carolina, in 1916. Whatever the truth, its themes certainly don't age. "O Death" unfolds as a fantastically evocative two-hander between the narrator and the Reaper.

STANLEY: *O, Death, O, Death*
Won't you spare me over til another year?
Well what is this that I can't see
With ice cold hands takin' hold of me?

DEATH: *Well I am death, none can excel*
I'll open the door to heaven or hell

STANLEY: *Whoa death, someone would pray*
Could you wait to call me another day?

DEATH: *The children prayed, the preacher preached*
Time and mercy is out of your reach
I'll fix your feet til you can't walk
I'll lock your jaw til you can't talk
I'll close your eyes so you can't see
This very air, come and go with me
I'm death—I come to take the soul
Leave the body and leave it cold
To draw up the flesh off of the frame
Dirt and worm both have a claim

STANLEY: *O, Death, O, Death*
Won't you spare me over til another year?
My mother came to my bed
Placed a cold towel upon my head

My head is warm my feet are cold
Death is a-movin upon my soul
Oh, death how you're treatin' me
You've close my eyes so I can't see
Well you're hurtin' my body
You make me cold
You run my life right outta my soul
O Death please consider my age
Please don't take me at this stage
My wealth is all at your command
If you will move your icy hand
Oh the young, the rich or poor
Hunger like me you know
No wealth, no ruin, no silver no gold
Nothing satisfies me but your soul
O, Death, O, Death
Won't you spare me over til another year?

Truly chilling. He knows it's coming all right, he's just try-ing to delay the inevitable. Death, on the other hand, is mer-ciless, impervious to any emotional bargain-pleas or bare-faced bribery. Which is how it will be. The same hard-faced bastard appears in "1919 Influenza Blues" and in Reverend Gary Davis' "Death Don't Have No Mercy," later popular-ized by the Grateful Dead and covered by, among others, Hot Tuna, John Martyn, and Mark Lanegan: "Death don't have no mercy in this land / He'll come to your house and he won't stay long / You'll look in the bed and somebody will be gone / Death don't have no mercy in this land."

You can't say you haven't been warned. Listen to these songs closely and you can start compiling a user's manual to death. They might emphasize different aspects of what it means, but they all share a willingness to hold hands with the idea of death simply as a matter of course. There are no fancy metaphors, no smart wordplay, no retreating behind fluffy concepts or sentiment. Mariah Carey, you fancy, would be lost in this world shorn of any emotional melisma.

In *You Wrote My Life: Lyrical Themes in Country Music*, the authors note that these songs "typically express an awareness of death and an acceptance of it. Death itself

occurs frequently. It is everywhere. Children die with disturbing frequency . . . but there are also songs about mothers dying and going to heaven, sweethearts passing on,
and an entire family dying. Even dogs are mourned. Death
images . . . are typically not circumscribed but direct and
sometimes even grotesque."[1]

They are referring specifically to a view of death
expressed in early country music in the American south,
but the point works just as well in broader terms: what
we're talking about is old death versus new death, awareness versus avoidance. Bony detail versus the Big Picture.
It doesn't mean that they're always all that thrilled about
the whole thing: Stanley's "O Death," rather like Bukka
White's "Fixin' to Die," is a relatively rare example of a
song from the early 1900s making a bit of a stink about
having to go up yonder and leave his wife and kids behind,
but they date from a time when it was deemed sound common sense to make your acquaintance with death in preparation of meeting it.

They also refuse to bow down to the post-Victorian distaste for discussing all matters of the flesh and the body,
the *prettifying* of death that Elisabeth Kubler-Ross, the
author of the seminal 1969 study *On Death and Dying*,
berated in a 1995 interview: "The old, old, old cultures are
also much more natural. In the more sophisticated, more
materialistic western world. . . . [T]hey put shoes on the
dead that are comfortable to wear, and silk pillows, and put
rouge on the cheeks, so they look like they're only asleep.
It's so phoney and so dishonest. . . . Things have really
deteriorated in the last hundred years, and more in the big
cities than in the country."[2]

And in pop music, where the temptation is often to sani-
tize death almost beyond recognition. The old-time songs are,
at the very least, a finger in the flooded dyke. They may be
a long way from "umbrella-ella-ella," but their spare, severe
view of death is actually deeply embedded in many aspects
of popular musical culture, so deep sometimes it's hard to
see them. They provide a template that songwriters turn to,
consciously or otherwise, over and over again in dark times.

Everyone from Led Zeppelin to Bob Dylan to Nick Cave to the White Stripes have found something to pillage from them over the years, while many other contemporary artists have covered them, updated them, referenced them, pinched a phrase, a mood, an image.

The names and specifics change, the beats might become a little crisper, the words a little sharper, the context altered, the aims a little more sophisticated—or not—but these songs form the bedrock of modern music's often faltering attempts to get to grips with mortality. It is possible to unearth unlikely connections. When Jimmie Rodgers was dying of TB he wrote "My Time Ain't Long"; when Warren Zevon was dying of lung cancer he wrote the similarly unflinching "Keep Me in Your Heart." The ailing Bill Monroe wrote his own elegy, "My Last Days on Earth," on mandolin; when Freddie Mercury was dying of AIDS he wrote the bombastically reflective "The Show Must Go On," a kind of "My Way" decked out in singlet and moustache, which may not be to all tastes but at least displayed an unambiguous awareness of what was coming "around the corner."

To provide comment on the Iraq war, Bruce Springsteen turned to the venerable American folk songs popularized by Pete Seeger to make oblique if heartfelt comment. It would be hard to think of a clearer admission of pop's limitations. That's not a criticism of Springsteen, rather a compliment to the enduring power of those simple songs to shout out way beyond their immediate reach. Meanwhile, without Alan Lomax's hugely influential collection of field recordings, you would likely as not never have heard of Moby—you can mourn or cheer as you see fit.

Once we are able to get the past into focus, the picture becomes clearer. Screw up your eyes a little and "O Death" and "It's Not My Time to Go" by Dan Hicks and the Hot Licks cover the same ground, as do "John Barleycorn" and Blue Oyster Cult's "(Don't Fear) The Reaper." Van Morrison's "TB Sheets"—a gruelling, unspeakably detailed account of the long, slow death of a friend, recorded in 1967—wouldn't exist without Jimmie Rodgers' 1931 recording "TB Blues" (which might not have been a bad thing: the moment when

Van starts snuffling at the window for fresh air is usually the time when we reach for the off button).

Without the Watson Family's "The Triplett Tragedy" or "The Long Black Veil" there would be no Violent Femmes' "Country Death Song" or Nick Cave's "Song of Joy." Without the traditional "Avondale Mine Disaster" or Vernon Dalhart's 1924 recording of "Wreck of the Ol' 97"—which sold over a million copies—there would be no Bee Gees' "New York Mining Disaster" or Gordon Lightfoot's "Wreck of the Edmund Fitzgerald." Without Dave Van Ronk's "Talking Cancer Blues," there may not be anything quite like Jack the Ripper's blunt yet defiantly jaunty "I Was Born a Cancer": "Beneath the Capricorn / My captain said 'You have a cancer of the lungs' / I said amen to the smoke of tobacco." Or, indeed, the recent subgenre, or should that be subspecies, that has become known, less than thrillingly, as cancer-country, popularized by Tim McGraw's "Live Like You're Dying," Rascal Flatts' "Skin"—sample lyric: "Between the red cells and white / Something's not right," which isn't a line you'd ever have heard Ralph Stanley singing—and Craig Morgan's "(I Thought That I Was) Tough." The suspicion here remains that the subject is simply yet another means for modern country music to wring the maximum volume of sentimental tears out of its audience; for all their adolescent romanticizing of death, My Chemical Romance's cancer concept album *The Black Parade* is at least a much more direct account of life in the grip of the disease.

It's not all stark and po-faced. Not then and not now. Dig out "Terrible Operation Blues" by Big Bill Broonzy as a hilarious example of an old-time parody of all that shotgun shack suffering, or Regina Spektor's "Chemo Limo"—about a cancer sufferer making the choice between paying for cancer treatment or living the high life ("And on any given day I'd rather ride a limousine")—for a more modern, more knowing take on spotting death in the rearview mirror. Even the rash—if that's the right word—of early-twentieth-century sexual disease songs, like "St. James Infirmary" and Woody Guthrie's "VD Blues"—"Well, I got disgusted and I sailed down on a spree / When I got back home, I had that old VD"

—remain pertinent at a time when STDs are at "epidemic" proportions in Europe and the US and a bigger threat to public health than any time in the past few decades. It's easy to laugh, but who else is writing about it?

✔

Death may change its methodology as the years pass, but its ultimate function and purpose is firmly fixed. Society, on the other hand, is in a state of constant flux. The old-time songs were written before television, twenty-four-hour multimedia, feminism, telephones, motor cars and airplanes, nuclear technology, chemical weaponry, space travel, electricity, and fast food . . . the list is hardly exhaustive; indeed it barely scratches the surface. Culturally, it sometimes seems that songs like "O Death" and "Death Don't Have No Mercy" might as well come from Pluto; they're like an ancient map for a version of a city that no longer exists.

Biologically and emotionally, however, these hardy, atavistic songs strike a chord somewhere deep down inside us. They simply have to be bent into shape; they have to be *made* to sing to the tune of the times. Which is harder than it looks. Often it's the small, personal point of connection within the big picture that is the hardest part to pull off. It isn't necessarily hard to write a song stating that war or terrorism or society's numerous ills are a "bad thing" —and, God knows, many artists do. That kind of thunderingly declaimed last rites on our culture talks a language that the twenty-first century can really understand. Nearly seventy years after Essie Jenkins sang "Influenza Blues," for example, Prince sang "Sign O' the Times" about, among other things, the emergence of another deadly contemporary disease, AIDS. They are both songs about the Big Bad Wolf knocking at the door. For Jenkins, it's her own front door. For Prince, it is the door of the western world, somewhere *out there*. His song is a (rather fashionable) litany of very modern ills—AIDS, crack, nuclear meltdown, space tragedy—with a detectable whiff of the apocalypse about it. "In France a skinny man died of a big disease with a little name

/ By chance his girlfriend came across a needle and soon she did the same." He makes crisp poetry out of it, and he captures the sense of a world so dangerously drunk on its own achievements it's unaware that the skies are darkening, but he doesn't make us really fear or feel the rapid rat-a-tat-tat at the window.

It's hardly Prince's fault that most pop singers are now absurdly well rewarded for their gifts and have become privileged members of society in a manner that would have made Essie Jenkins's head spin clean off its moorings. It makes for no less compelling art, but this authorial distance may explain why there have been, relatively, precious few worthwhile, empathetic musical reactions to the great humanitarian catastrophes of recent times. Perhaps it is too soon. Maybe as humans we have lost all our ability to empathize—as we see more and more depictions of death on television and computer screens, we appear, perversely, to understand it less and less. More likely, popular music has lost the instinct and confidence to speak quite so simply and truthfully about things it no longer experiences firsthand, particularly when the stakes are so high. And particularly because, when it presumes to do so—Phil Collins' "Another Day in Paradise" springs immediately to mind—it so often gets it hopelessly, insultingly wrong. Pop music is still struggling to construct its own lexicon of death, its own way of approaching the subject in order to make some sense of the changing times. The big, grandiose gestures get in the way: it gets too heroic, or too mawkish, or too gory, or too didactic.

The truth is, music's role as town crier is all but obsolete. We no longer need to hear the news in an age where we eat, sleep, and breathe it. Instead, we want to be told how we're supposed to *feel* about it. It's the difference between a court report and an op-ed column. In terms of the effect this has on the way music deals with loss on the scale of Katrina or 9/11, it has largely meant a shift away from the up-close, nose-against-the-glass ruminations of personal mortality that so concerned our forebears. Stoic, black-and-white reportage telegraphed in plain language, or conversing with Old Death himself, trying desperately to make running repairs to the bond between the body and the soul, simply doesn't fit with such fragmented times. We all exist in our own bubbles of communication, while pop music has become so overwhelmingly a medium of self-expression and opinioneering that it's easy to forget that the notion of the pop star as an artist is a relatively new concept. You might want to bring it up with Bob Dylan the next time you bump into him.

In this way, death becomes just another metaphor, rather than the natural and inevitable end it really is. And as a result, we end up with music, such as Paul Simon's *Surprise* or Bruce Springsteen's *The Rising*, that is inspired, if that's the right word, by events like 9/11, incorporating the impact of the event into the writer's existing worldview rather than placing the writer within the events themselves. It is fuel for the fire rather than the fire itself. Unlike Kansas Joe and Memphis Minnie, Elvis Costello doesn't literally tell the story of the destruction wreaked by Katrina and his own experience of much reduced circumstances in "The River in Reverse." He doesn't do it because he wasn't there, because he knows that we all watched it unfold on television, and because he presumably knows there are songs like "When the Levee Breaks" that still resonate on a purely gut level.

Instead, he does something else with all that death, despair, disease, and destruction. Which, in this case, is tie the tragic events into a broad, impressionistic but undoubtedly furious narrative about the realities of modern-day, Bush-whacked America, where the flood is barely literal at all, but rather symptomatic of something much bigger and even more deadly: "Are your arms too weak to lift? / Another shovel on the graveyard shift / Here comes the flood if you catch my drift / Where the things that they promised are not a gift / What do we have to do to send / The river in reverse?"

It's a wider-reaching, more sophisticated response for a wider, more sophisticated audience. And brilliant—as are parts of *The Rising* and *Surprise*—on its own terms. But it doesn't crack open the actual experience and let us crawl inside in the way, say, "High Water Everywhere" does. Songwriters now veer toward the big picture because they are no longer news-bringers talking to their own community. They have much louder voices which carry much farther than Mississippi John Hurt's or Dock Boggs' ever could. When it comes to communities and social issues, it's no longer "I," but "you," "they," and—sometimes—"we." But does this approach make us empathize on a deeply personal level? Does it make us understand that death, whether in New Orleans, New York, or the New Forest, is always present, buried within? Not really.

The truly great modern day songs that extrapolate death in its abstract, mass form and make it fit right into the palm of our hands often require a novelist's light touch, or perhaps the gift of a great character actor. It takes a fearless, intuitively attuned songwriter to inhabit events outside his or her own experience—whether on a global or a local level —convincingly and report back from inside them in a way that makes it real for the rest of us. Significantly, the very few songs that have truly tried to get under the skin of the major events of our times hark directly back to the language, imagery, and first-person narrative style of the folk ballad tradition.

Outside of rap, which will be considered in detail later, and which in reality has a surprisingly narrow social focus despite fulfilling the Webster's dictionary definition of folk as "music that is an expression of the life of the people in a community," most of the artists who succeed in bringing to our front doors the reality of death writ large draw on the language and skills of the old death songs. Instead of illustrating how death drips into and subtly affects their own worldview, they instead subsume their own character and throw themselves into death's own territory. Above all else, they understand the one true gift that old-time music has handed down: that what is required is not proselytizing from a pedestal but a more humbling immersion in the language of empathy.

Only a handful are able to speak that old dialect fluently enough to communicate clearly to by-standers the human center at the heart of catastrophic events. Steve Earle has taken us to the electric chair—as both the condemned man

("Billy Austin") and the prison guard ("Ellis Unit One")—and in doing so has revealed the sheer inhumanity and moral cowardice of the death penalty, but his greatest achievement in this field is "John Walker's Blues." It's perhaps one of the most important and extraordinary songs of recent times, and popular music's only notable attempt at articulating the thought process that drove US citizen John Walker Lindh to fight for the Taliban forces in Afghanistan before his capture late in 2001: "I'm just an American boy / Raised on MTV / And I've seen all the kids in the soda pop ads / But none of them looked like me / So I started looking around / For a light out of the dim / And the first thing I heard that made sense was the word / Of Mohammed, peace be upon Him."

In writing the song, Earle dug up some uncomfortable home truths about 9/11 that few other songwriters would have been able, or willing, to bring out into the light. "We came to fight the Jihad / And our hearts were pure and strong / As death filled the air we all offered up prayers / And prepared for our martyrdom." What Earle was telling us, in his own way, echoes the dark warning of "Cryin' won't help you / prayin' won't do you no good" in "When the Levee Breaks." This is what you and we are up against. Don't underestimate it. The rules of life and death have changed. And casting blame is a dangerous game.

That the sectors of society most frightened by John Walker Lindh's very existence were the ones least willing to listen to the song says plenty about why these kind of undressy first-person accounts of the reality of death are no longer a subject near the top of most songwriters' agendas. Better to offer up vague platitudes, political tub thumping, or sentimental arias to those who have gone than look at why someone is prepared to kill and be killed. Earle was roundly attacked for glorifying and sympathizing with a "traitor," when what he was trying to do—and he succeeded, brilliantly—was to get into the mind of the kind of people that the US and much of the west now fear the most: suicide bombers, fundamentalist terrorists, people who take their cues, however distorted, from a culture that looks upon death very differently than the one in which pop music usually swims. "I'm trying to make clear that wherever he got to, he didn't arrive there in a vacuum," said Earle.[3] Implicit in that comment, and that song, is that we are all capable of being seduced by death, and of creating the circumstances where it thrives.

But if we as a society are ill prepared to look at our own deaths with a clear, cold eye, we are unlikely to see something like 9/11 or Katrina, or the almost unaccountable carnage of modern warfare, clearly and dispassionately either. Richard Thompson dived into the petrified skin of an Allied Forces soldier recently on "Dad's Gonna Kill Me," his soldier's-eye-view of what it's like to be in combat in Iraq, out in the desert with "Old Death a-Walkin'" constantly alongside, just as he has stalked the terrain of a hundred old songs since time immemorial.

"It's important that people hear their entertainers talking about the Iraq War," says Thompson. "And the most devastating consequence of . . . war is that someone you know has died. It's just a natural thing for me that a song would have that subject matter—coming from the folk tradition, it's all over the place. To me, the song is a clarification of the war for the audience. It's saying, this is what politicians say about the war, and this is what the war is really about. It's clearly two different things."

It's not a particularly pleasant task to point out the difference between a heroic death and an unnecessary one, to articulate the gap between the blanket assumption of chisel-jawed bravery projected upon soldiers and the grip of debilitating fear they have to confront on a daily basis. The song has met with praise from troops, who recognize and embrace the familiar yet usually unexpressed version of death portrayed in the song, but is less palatable to the families of those fighting, who understandably need to believe that death in warfare has some greater, higher purpose.

The 21-year-old Illinois soldier in Tom Waits' transfixing "Day After Tomorrow," a gentle, swaying ballad—as old as the hills, as fresh as paint—of devastating emotional power, sings from the same place, both geographically and emotionally. Borrowing a little from PJ Proby's "Today I Killed a Man I Didn't Know," the expression of the fear and confusion of dying here comes with more sadness, nostalgia, and regret than outright anger. "Tell me, how does God choose? / Whose prayers does he refuse?" Waits asks, "Who turns the wheel? / And who throws the dice?" This, ultimately, is the very human articulation of the sheer disorienting terror of being caught up in events that most of us only ever see through a screen from many, many miles away.

However comfortable our chairs, however warm our homes, when cataclysmic events occur, whether on a global or personal scale, they act as a harsh reprimand for modernity's lack of respect for death. Songs like "Day After Tomorrow" and "John Walker's Blues" acknowledge that events like 9/11, Katrina, and the indiscriminate waging of war can and should be used by songwriters to remind each of us that there is no escape from the realities of our history and geography. They tread very deliberately in the footprints made by countless venerable old-time songs, music that truly understands the link between the present and the past and forces us to recognize that there is no escape from our responsibilities to each other, no hiding place from the fast truth of our biology, and no slipping the leash of our own destiny. Death don't have no mercy, and we are all going to die. How we deal with the news plays a big part in how we live, and how songwriters deal with that news is, in the end, a big part of what makes them artists rather than entertainers.

2
TEENAGE WILDLIFE
From Sob to Suicide

It doesn't matter if we all die . . .
The fear takes hold
Creeping up the stairs in the dark . . .
Waiting for the death blow
Waiting for the death blow
Waiting for the death blow
The pain
And the creeping feeling . . .
Aching inside me.

You might well have been picking flowers to the sound of
"Walking on Sunshine," but that's what *I* was listening to
when I was 14. The Cure's "One Hundred Years," an almost
pathologically depressing song from an album that sounded
like it was made by a man with his head caught in a mincer:
you can have any color you want as long as it's black, black,
black. I still have a great deal of affection for the Cure's
psychedelic pop forays and fluffier feline moments, but
nowadays I don't really receive much emotional sustenance
from any song that begins "It doesn't matter if we all die."
I find it a juvenile thought that says nothing to me, and

indeed makes me itch slightly with the half-remembered embarrassment of youthful despair, just as thinking of the tortured poetry I earnestly scribbled in scores of notebooks can still, twenty years on, make me want to bite my own knuckles in shame.

But back in those dread teenage days "One Hundred Years" and many other songs of a similarly woebegone hue *mattered*. They spoke loudly and clearly to me, and though it's almost impossible to recall exactly why this music resonated at that time, it's important to at least remember that it did. Adults rarely display anything other than equal measures of disdain, discomfort, and ignorance when it comes to their understanding of teen tribes and their strange rituals and obsessions, but the fact is most of us have been there. Could it partly be the shameful recollection of the intensity of our own past passions that encourages us to gaze down upon each new wave of teenage angst-mongers with just a little more disdain than we afforded the last?

In 2006, the *Daily Mail* ran a feature under the heading EMO CULT WARNING FOR PARENTS: "Although the look is similar [to Goth] the point of distinction, frightening for schools and parents, is a celebration of self harm," part of it read. "Emos exchange competitive messages on their teenage websites about the scars on their wrists and how best to display them. . . . Although it is invariably described as a 'secret shame', there is actually a streak of exhibitionism about it. The internet has many sites dedicated to Emo fashion (dyed black hair brushed over your face, layering, black), Emo bands (Green Day, My Chemical Romance), Emo conversation (sighing, wailing, poetry)."

I particularly like the "sighing, wailing, poetry"—as though these were in some way *bad* things. But it was ever thus. The dawn of the internet age has shone a far-reaching searchlight upon the murky world of our more introspective teenagers, a world that once existed only in scribbled notes hidden under pillows and in intense conversations conducted in dark, airless bedrooms—and, it is often forgotten, buried in our own memories. The web has arguably bred a greater sense of theater in our teens, an awareness of playing to the gallery, but little has really changed. Lingeringly intense thoughts about death, suicide, and doomed love are a mainstay of this particular strand of teen consciousness, and they have always been amply reflected in song and tut-tutted at by adults.

It's worth recalling that, in 1960, the BBC banned both Mark Dinning's "Teen Angel" and Ricky Valance's version of "Tell Laura I Love Her," deeming the subject matter of these "death discs" too morbid for their intended audience. "It sounded grotesque to adults, who knew the subject was hardly casual, and innocent to the young, who thought it the ultimate statement of enduring love," says BBC broadcaster and music historian Paul Gambacinni. In 1956, Edith Piaf's "Les Amants D'un Jour" told the tale of a doomed couple found dead in their little Parisian apartment, their poor young hearts overcome by the force of their passion. Scrape away the lame scare-mongering so beloved of publications like the *Daily Mail* and you find in emo the bedrock of all previous teen pop tribes: angst, morbidity, self-absorption, a strict group ethos dressed up as individualism, innocence, and naiveté passed off as experience and world-weariness, and the desire to shock taken to Olympian levels.

Creating art at the nexus of teen romance and youthful tragedy is hardly a novel concept. Young love has a long literary history of being prematurely struck down, its demise fetishized into something gloriously tragic. It's nothing new. It's a central pillar of Chaucer's *Troilus and Criseyde,* Shakespeare's *Romeo and Juliet,* and dozens of other ancient, enduring, often incestuously interwoven works of art, each one stacked on top of the other like Jenga pieces. The death of love's young dream puts the seal on an enduring, eternal bond that the adult world can neither fully understand nor sully.

The singer of "Come Away, Come Away Death," for instance, one of four songs from *Twelfth Night,* is drowning in a self-pitying broth of unrequited love that would positively thrill the skinny jeans off of your average emo kid: "Not a flower, not a flower sweet / On my black coffin let there be strown / Not a friend, not a friend greet / My poor corpse, when my bones shall be thrown." The lover unravelling in the song, dead from a broken heart after being cruelly spurned by a fair maiden, yearns to be buried in a secret place so no other "sad true lover" will chance upon the grave and be disabused of his or her own dreams of pure, innocent love. In the folk staple "Barbara Allen," a boy dies of unrequited love for the cold Barbara, who observes his passing dispassionately. Afterward, she is crushed with remorse and quickly surrenders to death. A briar grows from her grave and a rose from his until, finally, they entwine and grow together.

So beautiful. So sad. So young. Clearly the arrival of rock and roll did not denote Year Zero of the archetypal teenage mind set. The Adam and Eve of the drive-in age did not arrive on the scene in 1955 in a puff of smoke, hand-in-hand, quoting James Dean, listening to Alan Freed, and swigging from glass Coke bottles.

British writer Jon Savage recently wrote an excellent, weighty history of the cultural origins of the teenager that began its journey in the late nineteenth century and *stopped* in 1945. Savage unearthed proto-Goths in Paris, something very close to punk in Hitler's Germany, and a spoiled, gloomy, self-obsessed (sound familiar?) budding teen-diarist called Countess Marie Bashkirtseff. He called in on Anne Frank, Arthur Rimbaud, and an infestation of young, bookish, faintly precocious kids almost everywhere. What is Prince Hamlet, after all, if not a troubled teenager profoundly pissed off by the actions of patronizing adults, the first stirrings of existential dread, and a bumpy relationship with a young lady that inevitably ends with both of them lying in the cemetery? In 1600 this was sufficiently rich material with which to stitch together one of the world's enduring, ageless artistic statements. By 1960 it had, a little more humbly, at least all the classic hallmarks of a hit single. And in 2008, too. The emotional motor driving the creative act remains broadly the same; the means of expression, however, changes—often profoundly, as you'd expect —with each new generation. Today, teen death is all about ending "my days with you in a hail of bullets." In 1960, on the other hand, it involved a killer shark.

For evidence of how truly innocent the teen death song once was, you need only dip your toe into the murderous depths of "The Water Was Red" and instantly submerge yourself in an altogether less troubled age. It's hard to believe that it was less than fifty years ago that a teenage couple met and kissed on a "lonely beach," returning whenever they could to take a dip in the sea. Their hopes and dreams of a future together, however, were comprehensively chewed up and spat out between the teeth of a feral shark. It could happen to anyone. "And the white fin came into sight / The shark had struck and disappeared / And left his sweetheart dead." The boy then avenges his lover's death by plunging back into the water "with a tear in his eye and a gleaming knife in his hand" to kill the beast and bring its fin back to shore, as a memento presumably, for his dead sweetheart lying on the silver sand.

"It was about this young couple who went out swimming," recalls the song's author, legendary pop writer Jeff Barry, who also wrote "Tell Laura I Love Her," "Give Us Your Blessings," and "Leader of the Pack." "She went out into the water and got killed by a shark, so the water was red, and then he took his knife and dove in and killed the shark, to make the water red again. It turned out when I saw *Jaws*, the opening of that film is what the whole song was about." Steven Spielberg couldn't be reached for comment.

It would give us all, I'm sure, intense joy if I could report that the popular phrase "jumping the shark"—pinpointing the moment when a dramatic storyline becomes just too ridiculously implausible to take even remotely seriously, marking an unrecoverable nadir in a TV show, movie plot, or musical genre—stems directly from this ripe source. Alas, it does not. But "The Water Was Red" adequately highlights the problem many of us have with the sob songs of the sixties: they are regarded as camp, ridiculous—and often very funny. Viewed from our culturally superior vantage point, "The Water Was Red" seems like an outlandish slice of melodrama. You might even imagine that if you listen very closely you will hear the distinct sound of pop music scraping the last few remnants from the bottom of a barrel that was once filled to the brim with a commercially potent brew. But when it was recorded by the splendidly named Johnny Cymbal in 1961, it simply took its place in the lineup alongside any number of like-minded songs. Between 1960 and 1965 pop music was plagued by a rash of similarly unfortunate, untimely and truly bizarre deaths, leaving behind a generation of wailing girls, scarred forever, as they witnessed young men called things like Terry and Tommy ascending to heaven on the fenders of their buckled drag racing cars and the husks of their twisted motorbikes, never to be forgotten. What on earth was going on?

There was, Jeff Barry points out helpfully and entirely sincerely, nothing intentionally funny or exploitative about these songs at all. He regarded them as "teen dramas, little visual shows. It was never calculated. It was all so innocent to me. There was never any intention other than to entertain." This is no doubt true, but while the subject of young men and women preoccupied with death is as old as the hills, the emergence of the teen death song is significant in itself. It was the first time pop music truly grasped the glamour of a well stage-managed death, and it learned the lesson fast. It was also the clearest indication that, for the first time, pop music was writing specifically for the emotional needs of a pre-adult audience.

There had been death songs in the pop charts before 1960, of course, but they were a decidedly odd assortment. Among their number were no less than four versions of "The Ballad of Davy Crockett" ("The king of the wild frontier") in 1955 alone, novelty songs like "The Battle of New Orleans" and "Bad Man's Blunder," a doggedly silly version of a violent old tune called "Little Sadie," and venerable murder songs like "Tom Dooley," given disconcertingly brisk treatments by the Kingston Trio. There were country songs that crossed over into the pop charts, like "The Three Bells" by the Browns, an odd affair charting the birth, marriage, and death of Jimmy Brown in three brisk stanzas, emphasizing the unchanging physical landscape and the fact that life rolls on and on even amid death.

"El Paso" by Marty Robbins—the most successful of his numerous "Gunfighters Ballads"—and Johnny Cash's "Don't Take Your Guns to Town" were both in the classic gun slinging tradition, essentially aural versions of the cowboy B movies that were so popular at the time. Cash's song is a cautionary tale of an over-eager young cowboy—"A boy filled with wanderlust who really meant no harm"—who finds himself out of his depth in a saloon bar and pays the ultimate price. Robbins' song also takes the moral hard-line familiar to many traditional folk and country songs—it's the staunch tale of a man who kills another and must return to the scene of the crime to take his punishment. An eye for an eye. Man's stuff.

Most of these songs have their roots in traditional music and an old, masculine, gnarly version of the world. They are invariably set in some undefined past. They represented the status quo at a time when pop music as we now know it was bursting out of the chrysalis but didn't yet quite know what it was. It wasn't rock and roll, which came barrelling out of the South in the early fifties, as yet unnamed, with Jackie Brenston's "Rocket 88," wriggling from the waist down and still a little too raw and uncivilized for most mainstream tastes. And yet it wasn't quite the sophisticated, ultra-clean, parent's idea of what pop music should be either, all Doris Day and Patti Page's "How Much Is That Doggie in the Window?"

Instead, it made its bed on a plot of land somewhere between the Brill Building and Memphis, Tennessee, marrying northern restraint to a diluted approximation of the southern rhythm and setting itself the task of building its own empire. Teenagers were, for the first time, central to the pop plan—as ever, it all largely came down to the power of the purse. It was a time of improving prosperity and a freeing of inhibitions. In the UK in particular, World War II and the years immediately afterward had been a time of privation and austerity; the young had been greatly constrained by rationing, a lack of funds, and National service, which required every healthy man between the ages of 17 and 21 to serve in the armed forces for eighteen months, and remain on the reserve list for a period thereafter. National service ended in Britain in 1960; John Lennon and Ringo Starr avoided it only by a matter of months. How different musical history might have been.

In the States, where the teen phenomenon was most pronounced and influential, there was a post-war boom of consumerism: cars, radios, telephones. Eisenhower was president between 1952 and 1960, during which time the economy was strong, the feel-good factor was high, and there was greater time to devote to leisure pursuits. Given the hardships of the previous decade, parents on both sides of the Atlantic were prepared to give their children a little extra leeway. By 1959, the average US teenager had the modern equivalent of $400 a year to spend entirely on him or herself (compared to an annual average of $230 over forty years later). It was sufficient to buy their own records, watch their own choice of movie, drive their parents' car, and buy their own Cokes, cigarettes, and beer. The teenager was now a consumer in its own right, and an increasingly powerful one at that.

With money and freedom comes aspiration. It is a quirk of human nature that the sense of comfort and stability that allows such economic freedom also brings a scratchy desire for something *more*; you are able to glimpse a bright new world beyond the picket fence of conformity and you want to jump over and roll around in it. The British playwright Shelagh Delaney perfectly described her teenage self as like a tethered horse that was suddenly cut loose; it's this sensation of unfettered opportunity that typifies the youthful mood of the late fifties.

For the first time, teens began to spend most of their spare time with people their own age, forging the idea that they were a race apart. There was a burgeoning sense of shared experience. Cinema was key in helping shape a distinct teenage consciousness: films like *The Wild Ones* and *Rebel Without a Cause* (both 1953) and, a couple of years later, *Blackboard Jungle* and its cash-in follow-up *Rock*

Around the Clock rubbed shoulders with the rise of Elvis Presley to create the phenomenon of the rebellious teenager that burst into popular consciousness in the fifties. By 1956 it was already being acknowledged—and lightly lampooned —by the Hollywood establishment in *The Girl Can't Help It*. And once society puts a label on you, you feel the need to act out the part, to mark your territory clearly. You do it with distinctive dress, coded language. And most of all, you do it with music.

Quite quickly, death became a hallmark of teen rebellion. James Dean had died in a car crash in 1955, at 24 the first martyr of the rock and roll era. Subsequent songs about handsome, fated young men perishing in car accidents played up to this dark romance. The generation who had just witnessed and survived the horrors of war, on the other hand, did not view their mortality so lightly. They regarded songs that reduced life and death to a smudgy teen melodrama as highly distasteful. Little wonder it became one of the points where the generational battle lines were drawn.

"From the late 1950s to the early 1960s, songs about adolescent romance ending in death were abundant," found the 1993 study "Death as Portrayed to Adolescents Through Top 40 Rock and Roll Music." "This was an age of social innocence in the United States, when an adolescent subculture, with a distinct identity, was emerging. To some extent, these findings may be explained both in terms of adolescent interests and the cultural environment."[1]

The crucial elements of the teen death song fell into place almost instantly: high school sweethearts, bound together and never to be parted. Their time is short, but a needless death somehow proves to all the dissenting onlookers and scornful head-shakers that this was a pure, true, enduring love. This was a heady mix of speed, love, rebellion, and tragedy, in many ways playing out the same scripts in song as those being played out on screen. "[These songs] were of appeal to a teenage audience and were romantic ballads that expressed love in extreme terms," says the BBC's Paul Gambacinni. "The lover was willing to die, and often did, for his beloved, or a surviving girl wailed of her dedication to her deceased boyfriend. Teen . . . mortality was nothing new. What was new was that death for love was expressed in pop music."

Although light-hearted "historical" death songs like "The Ballad of Davy Crockett" didn't wither and die immediately —or indeed, completely; variations on this kind of silliness have continued to make sporadic assaults on the pop charts through the years, and a good thing, too—quite quickly they became entirely redundant to a young audience and culturally irrelevant. It literally became Goodbye Cowboy, Hello Chevrolet.

"In the original lyric of 'Tell Laura I Love Her,' instead of saying he saw a sign for a stock car race, he saw a sign for a rodeo," says the song's writer Jeff Barry. "He got gored to death by a bull! But the publisher said, 'No-one can relate to that,' so I changed rodeo to a stock car race. He got gored to death by a Chevy!" It would be hard to conceive of a more wonderfully illustrative and literal cultural gear change, signifying the passing of the old to the new.

"Tell Laura I Love Her," the tale of Laura and Tommy's doomed love, became a number-one US single in June 1960 for Ray Peterson, and is perhaps the quintessential teen death song of the era. It wasn't the first, however. Mark Dinning's "Teen Angel," a hit in the first month of 1960, was the moment when pop, finally, starting writing its own mass-market obituaries for its own audience. It was preceded at number one by Johnny Preston's "Running Bear," a song documenting another star-crossed love affair heading for the graveyard, with the help of every Native American cliché in the universe and a handy historical setting. But where "Running Bear" was a look backward, crucially "Teen Angel" was a contemporary song. This is here and this is now. It is an unashamed weepy, a dirge that tells the sorrowful tale of a girl out driving with her boyfriend. The car stalls on a railroad track and he pulls her out to safety. Driven by some overpowering passion, she runs back to the tracks, where a train hits the car and she dies. When her body is recovered, the boy's high school class ring is found clasped in her hand. This, tearful young girls will whisper to each other at school the next day, was the priceless memento for which she ran back. And later that night, which of them didn't lie in bed and silently pray for the chance to experience a love that pure, that powerful? If death was the price to pay, so be it.

For teens at the time, this was genuinely emotionally affecting stuff, but musically "Teen Angel" was rather insipid. Dinning would follow it with "The Pickup," about a girl who jumps from a bridge and kills herself because her date is too embarrassed to see her again. Perhaps the implied arrogance grated, because it bombed and Dinning's career also fell crashing from a great height, but the baton was swiftly picked up by others. Indeed, before 1960 was over the country singer Bob Luman was singing, on the wonderful "Let's Think About Living," "If we keep on losing our singers like this I'll be the only one you can buy!" Suddenly you couldn't move for teenagers being cruelly cut down long before their prime.

In an age defined by movies, the songs all shared a cinematic quality. They were narratives in short acts that could be visualized by anyone, but other than that the songs cut across the musical spectrum; some are far better than others. "Last Kiss" by J. Frank Wilson and the Cavaliers tells broadly the same story as "Teen Angel" but is a far superior song, somehow more grown up and the emotion more plausible, its sense of conviction pulsing out from the steady roll of its rhythm. Jan and Dean's "Dead Man's Curve" remains one of the greatest song titles of all time, but this single-song foray into the surf-death genre never quite lives up to its promise. The Deltones' "(All I Have Left) Is Johnny's Hubcap," on the other hand, does.

In the aftermath of Buddy Holly's death in a plane crash early in 1959, not even the skies were spared the attentions of the sob song. "Ebony Eyes" by the Everly Brothers is a genuinely somber, substantial piece of work: that beacon light from the control tower whipping through the dark skies remains an enduring, haunting image, and you get the distinct sense that Phil and Don know a little bit about this death business.

"It was the first song that I remember as a kid dealing with death in a pretty direct way," recalls Will Oldham, the American songwriter who has often tackled mortality working as the Palace Brothers and Bonnie "Prince" Billy. "I was 4, 5, 6 years old, and I listened to the Everly Brothers over and over again, acting out all the songs with the little plastic figurines that I'd gotten for my birthday, and that was the last song on the record. I thought it was just a really wonderful story. So well told. I don't think it make me think of death at that point, but I could tell that it was a sad song. I just didn't have any idea how sad."

This is how death sneaks onto the unsuspecting child's radar—on the wings of a haunting tune and strange, sad words that hint at a terrible absence. For me, many years later, "Two Little Boys" by Rolf Harris had a similar affect and, improbably, still retains a deeply melancholic power.

There are literally hundreds more teen death songs dating from the early sixties, from maudlin doo-wop weepies like the Mystics' "Star Crossed Lovers" to the slightly sleazy jazz of Paul Hampton's "Two Hour Honeymoon." The modern tendency is to lump them all together and dismiss them as camp, tongue-in-cheek, even vaguely exploitative. According to Jeff Barry, the intentions of his own songs, at least, were always honorable. "It certainly wasn't tongue in cheek," he says. "It was never intended to be anything other than serious." A trawl through comments left on internet sites like YouTube confirms that they are certainly still capable of moving people, but although Barry, who was born in 1938, claims with a certain degree of plausibility that teen death songs marked the moment when "young people for the first time started writing songs for young people," deep down this isn't the sound of teens expressing themselves. Instead, it's the sound of young adults observing teenage preoccupations and expressing it for them. And subtly skewing the message.

The teen death songs of the sixties are significant in the sense that for the first time in modern musical culture youth equates with introspection and unhappiness, a harder concept to deal with for most parents than the more straightforward rites of passage of cutting loose and going a little wild. On a basic level the songs are pure theater; almost every death song treads that path to a certain extent. In common with teenage death songs ever since, exploring mortality is used as a shortcut to expressing a sense of sadness, a way to swoon into the arms of really big emotions, to try them on for size and see how they feel. It is cathartic and revealing.

Looking back, however, it's clear that the underlying thrust of these songs is deeply conservative. Not simply because there is no attempt to really grapple with the reality of death and its aftermath, but because the deaths in these songs hold a deeper symbolic meaning. At a time when rock and roll was loosening inhibitions, belts, and bra straps, what this nascent death music was *really* preaching were the joys of chastity and true love forever. It was holding determinedly onto the certainties of the fifties as the sixties came rushing in.

Eventually, left to their own devices, teen lovers like Tommy and Laura would inevitably succumb to base human impulse and commit the dreaded deed. How, then, to preserve them from the grubby influence of this dazzling new world of pre-marital sex, pregnancy, drink, and drugs? How to maintain the status quo? A reckless, accidental death was used as a function by songwriters to maintain the purity and innocence of teen romance, unsullied by the complications of sex. They couldn't employ anything as harsh as murder. It couldn't very well be natural causes. What better than a car crash, a train wreck, or indeed a shark attack—let fate striking the intervening blow, an untimely death ensuring that this innocent affair remained an eternally pure love. Break them apart and, conversely, you keep them together forever.

"'Tell Laura I Love Her' is a song about two people very much in love," says Jeff Barry. "None of it has anything to do with sex, which is how it should be. It ends badly for the lovers but it ends well for love. It doesn't say she is doomed to be alone, but will Laura forever love Tommy? Yes." On the cusp of the era of the Pill, free love, and greater social and racial integration, these songs mark some of society's final attempts at keeping its teenagers in line. Perhaps *that's* why they sound so outmoded and silly now.

As the sixties bore down, this kind of innocence was bound to perish. Already, death didn't seem quite such a seductive, faraway dream. By the time the Shangri-Las recorded "Give Us Your Blessings" in 1965, a true gem of a song, thunder-cracks and all, there is a newfound defiance in the relationship: yes, Mary and Jimmy want to please her parents, but if the parents don't give approval they are going to run away and be together anyway. Death here is used as a warning: step out of line, succumb to temptation and recklessness, and there will be moral consequences. Though once again written by Jeff Barry and his then wife Ellie Greenwich, Barry attributes the change in attitude to the influence of cowriter and producer George "Shadow" Morton, who "was much more James Dean than I ever was!"

Shadow was simply reading the mood of the times. While the marvellous "Leader of the Pack," also cowritten with Morton and released in 1964, dared you to laugh at its arch, corny brilliance, its good girl/bad boy dynamic was another sign that things had moved on. "Leader of the Pack" came so close to parodying itself it's somewhat surprising that anyone bothered writing a take-off; nevertheless, the Detergents did a sterling job in 1965 with "Leader of the Laundromat" ("Tenderly I kissed her goodbye / Picked up my clothes, they were finally dry"). The sob song had become ripe for an unambiguous laugh. In the same year, Jimmy Cross' "I Want My Baby Back" took the genre to its logically absurd conclusion. Driving home. Bad weather. Car crash. His "baby" dies. So far, so textbook. However, this time the ensuing months of sorrow and heartache end with a spot of late-night grave robbing. To the sound of coffin doors creaking and muffled underground rejoicing, Cross finally gets his baby back.

This, symbolically, marked the end of the first and most innocent wave of the teen death song. Occasionally down the years the thread of light, dreamlike pain has been picked up again, but there has been no attempt to conceal the joke: Jimi Hendrix's "Wait Until Tomorrow," the Ramones' "7/11,"

Blondie's "Susie and Jeffrey," the Avengers' "Car Crash." All performed with a nod and a wink. Morrissey, a keen student of kitsch sixties pop, was well aware what he was doing when he wrote "Girlfriend in a Coma," a classic deathbed song that switched the traditional gender roles and kept its tongue wedged firmly in its cheek. The Smiths had already covered "Golden Lights" by the British girl singer Twinkle, who had a hit with "Terry" in 1964, a rare British-bred example of the teen death song. By and large, though, pop music had weightier, more pressing matters at hand.

3

Take a look at my life, all black
Take a look at my life, all black
Take a look at my life, all black
I used to see red now it's just all black.

Ye gads. Welcome to the teen death song, 2008 style: "All Black" by Good Charlotte. Or if that doesn't float your boat, how about "Bury Me in Black" or "Rapid Hope Loss" or "I'll Follow You into the Dark" or "Anthem of Our Dying Day"? How did sweet Laura end up here, with all these intense boys in black clothes shouting along to bands called things like Dashboard Confessional, My Chemical Romance, and Jimmy Eat World?

The golden age of the sob song made death a valid subject matter in the mainstream, but for a while popular music didn't know quite what to do with it. The teen death song took a beating in the latter half of the sixties and much of the seventies. Death had become a political issue: civil rights, war, drugs, inner-city life. Pop music, having infiltrated the heart of mass culture, reflected this. On the occasions where it approached death, the existential condition of its 14-year-olds wasn't considered to be of as much importance as the state of the wider world: songs like "Freddie's Dead" or "Ohio" or "Billy Don't Be a Hero" defined much of the decade and beyond into the seventies; songs of social protest, where every death echoed far and wide. Even Elvis Presley got in on the act with "In the Ghetto."

In any case, the best music of the seventies was, at heart, an intensely theatrical experience, an attempt to slip the limitations of the self. Much of the rest was distinctly adult-orientated and cloaked in self-conscious, overblown poetry. There was plenty in the work of David Bowie, for example, for the alienated teen to chew over, but very little direct expression of empathy or clear association.

As the decade wore on, the sense of isolation was exacerbated by the nature of the times. In the UK, the three-day week, the winter of discontent, and general economic turmoil had made the seventies one of the century's bleaker decades. Globally, the harsh, greedy, "no-such-thing-as-society" ethos of Thatcherism and Reaganomics played its part, as did the escalation of the Cold War to the point where nuclear combat seemed more of an inevitability than a looming fear. The baby-boomers were hitting their thirties and beginning to feel the pace, negotiating the fall-out from Vietnam, an uncertain financial future, and the comedown from all that heady idealism and optimism of the sixties. Many were burned out. Others had yet to relinquish their claim on youthful hedonism and struggled to cope with the responsibilities of parenthood.

Their offspring certainly felt the effects of this chill wind. The early eighties marked a vast upturn in the suicide rate in 15-to-24-year-olds, particularly among males, and an almost perceptible widening of the generation gap. At the same time, the teenager was being publicly objectified and re-invented again in a manner and scale unprecedented since the late fifties. Following the upsurge of punk, teens were able to turn on the TV and see themselves everywhere. MTV hit the air in 1981 and specifically targeted the youth audience. The much-maligned "yoof TV" began in the UK shortly after. Films like *The Breakfast Club* and *Pretty in Pink*—movies with an almost total absence of parental figures—provided shallow, Hollywoodized versions of teens struggling for independence and undergoing turmoil in a world that didn't understand them. Independent movies like

River's Edge told a more complex story of the strange allure of death among high school kids.

Songwriters reacted in two ways. Some embraced the ethos of the age and danced in the shadow of the mushroom cloud, determined to raise themselves above the drab and the ordinary: the New Romantic movement was a glamorous, hedonistic reaction against the gloom of the times, while Madonna became the material girl, the ultimate consumer's pop star. On the other hand, punk and its immediate legacy —forking into post-punk, new wave, indie, and especially US hardcore and later alternative rock—brought things back down to earth with a bump.

Taking its cue from a scattering of previous howls of youthful discord—from "the world's forgotten boy" of the Stooges' "Search and Destroy" to Alice Cooper's "I'm 18"—punk pushed disaffection and nihilism right to the forefront of teen music, with song-statements such as "Endless Vacation," "No Future" and "Blank Generation." But while much of the ire of punk was of the manufactured, commodified variety, with one foot in the art school/bohemian ethic that harked back to the sixties, the US hardcore movement, which coalesced in localized scenes in 1980, reflected a genuine sense of raw, miscreant alienation. Where mainstream pop was determinedly bright and outward-looking, hardcore was deliberately austere and stripped down. "Hardcore comes from the bleak suburbs of America," wrote Steven Blush in *American Hardcore: A Tribal History*. "Parents moved their kids out of the cities to these horrible suburbs to save them from the 'reality' of the cities and what they ended up with was this new breed of monster."[2]

It was backyard music, powered by the dead ache of the urban hinterlands. Many of its foremost writers—Henry Rollins, Paul Westerberg, Ian Mackaye—were teens themselves and could feel which way the wind was blowing. They recognized that the emotional landscape of youth had changed beyond all recognition; they were, indeed, wrestling with the same questions as their audience regarding the standing and value of young individuals within society.

The average, the routine, and the banal became legitimate subjects. Introspection, realism, boredom, and disaffection were all the rage and, crucially, liberated by punk, young blue-collar singers were able to pick up a guitar, form a band, and articulate their own dissatisfaction rather than rely on the words of others. The DIY ethos was a huge part of the attraction. The results were very masculine, often sexist, homophobic and broadly idiotic, but the best of it had the devotional power of a new religion and its unadorned, diary-style lyrics, barked out over a fusillade of short, sharp, ugly, thrilling guitars resulted in what Jon Savage once described as "a rush of claustrophobic nihilism" that formed the foundation stone of much of the thinking and feeling behind subsequent young death music.[3]

It is a sound defined by the lexicon of violence and rage at recurring teen problems—pressure at school, bullying, dead-end jobs, parental issues, alcohol and drugs, lack of adult compassion or understanding, misfiring relationships, a grim world waiting outside—usually articulated in defiant, romantic, and often very violent fantasies. "Death Comes Ripping" by the Misfits, "Dead End" by the Dead Kennedys, "I Love You" by Black Flag, or Minor Threat's "Seeing Red," with its palpable sense of defiant outsiderdom: "You see me and you laugh out loud / You taunt me from safe inside your crowd / My looks, they must threaten you / To make you act the way you do."

The aggressively articulated confusion at the heart of US hardcore fed into the great wave of independent alternative rock in the eighties: from the original phalanx of Washington, D.C.'s "emotional hardcore" bands—Rites of Spring, Embrace—from which the twenty-first-century incarnation of emo takes its name, to Hüsker Dü, R.E.M., and later Nirvana, Rage Against the Machine, Nine Inch Nails, Green Day, Dashboard Confessional, and My Chemical Romance. Crucially, the fealty is primarily to a mind-set rather than a specific sound. The lyrics from Mission of Burma's "That's When I Reach for My Revolver"—"Tonight the sky is empty / But that is nothing new / Its dead eyes look upon us / And they tell me we're nothing but slaves"—would slip easily into scores and scores of emo songs.

Released in 1984, the Replacements' "Sixteen Blue" ("Your age is the hardest age") is one of the great songs of disaffected teen empathy, a beautiful, tender cry of solidarity for adolescents struggling with their sexuality, their parents, their peer group. But it's "The Ledge" ("I'm the boy they can't ignore / For the first time in my life, I'm sure") by the same band that, two years on, moves the protagonist of "Sixteen Blue" onto the rooftops, staring down at the emptiness of his life. He was by no means alone. Spread across a variety of niche genres, by the mideighties suicide had become the primary emblem and dramatic motif of the teenage death song, and has remained so ever since.

*

Teenagers invest a vast amount of time and energy asserting their independence from other teen tribes; the smallest things take on the greatest significance. In the past they have undergone many striking transformations—a variety of brave haircuts, strange shades of makeup, tight clothes, loose clothes, tight jeans, baggy jeans, new drugs, old drinks, loud, quiet, sexy, asexual—but underneath the camouflage each new wave of recruits share similar core concerns: it's no coincidence that the classic teen novels—*L'Etranger, The Bell Jar, Catcher in the Rye*—resonate for generation after generation. Many of them feel vulnerable, lurching between actual and self-induced depression or making their first forays into alcohol and drug experimentation. They are negotiating puberty, love, sex, exams and, while withdrawing from the world, looking for empathy, points of association, and reassurance. It's often not provided by parents or teachers; it has to come from somewhere else. The music being earnestly shared in the privacy of bedrooms and, increasingly, bounced around internet chat rooms and MySpace or Bebo sites, the names being scrawled inside the schoolbooks and inked onto the backs of jackets, will never again ring out quite so potently or be so greedily consumed.

For all the tendency to get bogged down in the specific superficialities and codified membership rites of each new teenage trend, be it Goth, nü-metal, industrial, emo, or any other, most teenagers like both a little light and a little gloom. It's not an either/or situation. Some teens—like some adults—react to the quirks of their age by gravitating to straightforward pop: an energized celebration of being young, and in love, and having sex, filled to the brim with the promise of the bounty life will bring. But just as a gambol around in a summer meadow can be life-affirming, a walk through the graveyard in the dead of a rain-slicked night can be powerfully uplifting—and cleansing—too.

And lest we forget, and we often do, the teenage years are the time when we most willingly buy into the self-destructive mythology of rock and roll. When it comes to the darker side of life, teens tend to gravitate toward music that can be best described as emitting a kind of romantic, heroic nihilism. Teenage songs—acutely attuned to the needs of their audience—continually revisit these same sentiments, expressed through the filter of the changing times and in the form of different, nominally alternative musical genres such as hardcore, indie, metal, and emo.

Suicide is simply the most powerful signifier of the ingrained sense of disaffection driving many teens. Suicide is there in the first wave of hardcore, plastered on the cover of Black Flag's *Family Man* album, and buried in the grooves of the Dead Kennedys' "Straight A's"; it's there in grunge, in Nirvana ("All Apologies"), Soundgarden ("Like Suicide"), and Pearl Jam ("Jeremy"). It's certainly there in the grittier works of heavy metal and hard rock: Metallica's "Fade to Black," Pantera's "Suicide Note Pts. 1 & 2," up to Evanescence's "Tourniquet" and the Foo Fighters' "DOA." And it's still there in the more recent examples of mainstream pop-punk, in Jimmy Eat World's "Pain" and even Avril Lavigne's "Take Me Away."

Entire albums are fixated with death and decay, most notably Nine Inch Nails' *The Downward Spiral,* a suicide concept album that graphically describes the act in the title song ("Problems have solutions / A lifetime of fucking things up fixed in one determined flash") and the great emo masterwork *The Black Parade,* by My Chemical Romance, a rampantly over-the-top death-opera for disgruntled high school freshmen.

They are all coming from the same place, aimed broadly at the same age group. Again and again teens embrace the stylized idea of suicide; they play with the idea of it. For most, simply contemplating death is enough, a release valve to their emotions, as well as a means of developing a stance, a philosophy of life, of involving yourself in the adult world of big ideas. It's also a way of getting noticed: talking suicide is a sure way of gaining attention, a trump card for a group unaccustomed to being taken entirely seriously.

"Very young people, I think, feel pushed around and ridiculed—*and are*—simply because of their age," said Morrissey recently on his website. "The world can seem to be full of officious meddlers who like to tell others what to do—and, as a matter of fact, that's *exactly* how the world is! So in my voice, I think young people hear someone who understands the . . . excavations of the heart."

Not just *his* voice, but a huge variety of others making an array of very different noises. Most 14-year-olds who hurl themselves at the mercy of Metallica's "Fade to Black" would likely hear the Smiths' "There Is a Light That Never Goes Out" or "Asleep" and spit with disdain at its pallid sensitivity, but these songs are, deep down, trying to soothe the same itch, articulating the same sense of inner turbulence. They capture a feeling that resonates beyond a mere sound. There is an allegiance to a shared emotional vocabulary that transcends the choice of a pair of trousers, or a hat, or a haircut, or a band, though few teens would be willing to admit it.

As the foremost and most vilified of the current emo crop, My Chemical Romance have simply taken alternative guitar music's historical affiliation with teenage unrest to an extreme, and some might say, rather obvious conclusion. They have effectively become a death theme band: "Cancer," "Dead," "Kill All Your Friends," "The Ghost of You," "Blood," "Drowning Lessons," "Cemetery Drive"—the prevailing message is that life (and love) is hard and short and then you die. Other groups have signed up to this limited manifesto. "All Black" by Good Charlotte, for example, is so ruthlessly on-message it's practically parodic: "Take a look at my life, all black / Take a look at my clothes, all black." Many emo songs specialize in offering the young listener a glamorous, fetishized view of death and suicide: "Anthem of Our Dying Day" and "Until the Day I Die" by Story of the Year; Linkin Park's "Breaking the Habit" or Better Than Ezra's "A Lifetime" or "Not Now" by Blink 182 or "Demolition Lovers" by My Chemical Romance, a Bonnie and Clyde romance writ anew. Death Cab for Cutie's "I'll Follow You into the Dark," which in many respects is a beautiful song, claims that the pair of young, romantically doomed lovers have "seen everything to see."

From an adult perspective, it's easy to get tricked into thinking that this music contains a message of troubling, barely earned world-weariness for songs aimed at such a young audience, not to mention a terrible paucity of ideas expressed in a limited lexicon: it's all darkness, confusion, black, and cold. Then I think back to the Cure's tirade of gloom, "One Hundred Years," and realize that emo is just addressing the same urgent needs, only wrapped up in a new skin.

A less interesting skin, admittedly. Although emo is often regarded as an extension of Goth, its spiritual baby brother, the two share little in common other than the fact that they are easily ridiculed and caricatured and share a fondness— along with most of the rest of rock and roll—for black.

Goth in its true and original incarnation is the anomaly of the teen death genre in that it is capable of surviving the transition into adulthood. Musically it is equal parts David Bowie, post-punk, the Doors, the *White Album*, and Wagner. Culturally, it picks up on Mary Shelley, Sylvia Plath, paganism, the Blue Meanies, Romanticism, Goethe, and Hammer Horror films. It has an artistic curiosity and genuine intellectual fascination with death that predates the Victorian era, but it also indulges—at least theoretically—the schoolboy impulse to be unpleasant to animals. It snuggles up beside both Camus and *Dracula*. Goth in its first wave—Siouxsie and the Banshees, the Cure, Bauhaus—is intense, ethereal, and dreamlike, a European fairy tale, a walk in the woods at dusk, Lewis Carroll in monochrome. Much of it also has an overt sense of humor and a fluffy, fuzzy sexiness.

That's not to say that some of it—the Cure's *Faith* and *Pornography* spring immediately to my mind—isn't relentlessly bleak, and that it has often toppled into self-parody, courtesy of bands like the Sisters of Mercy and Fields of the Nephilim. More often than not, however, it combined substance with a playful streak: for every "Hanging Garden" there's a "Let's Go to Bed." Emo on the other hand, with its factory-formed, cookie-cutter guitar shapes, identikit band names, and connect-the-dots vocabulary, has little of the *juice* of Goth. Much of the humor and sex and depth has been squeezed out. What it shares is its utter self-absorption. It places the miserable teenager right at the center of the universe, exactly where they belong, and is entirely disinterested in engaging with the world politically in the way that punk or hardcore did.

There are undoubtedly cultural reasons for emo's pervasive grimness. It thrives at a time when teenagers are far more worldly than they were fifty years ago—they live in a much more psychologically complex universe in many ways, and they are vulnerable to many more influences. Innocence is terribly hard to cling onto. More prosaically, what can acceptably be said in a mainstream song is far greater than it was even twenty years ago.

Each generation of teens wants to up the ante on the one that went before, and since rap went overground in the nineties, all rock music—nü metal, alternative and emo in particular—has been trying to compete with that undiluted visceral thrill. Heightened emotional realism is at a premium. In this sense it is ruthlessly target-driven music. Emo bands know their audience well enough to be aware that they are drawn toward dark rooms, a daily contemplation of doom and gloom, just-so scratchy guitar shapes, and the thin, impassioned whine that seems to be the authentic voice of noughties suburban teen dissatisfaction. So that is what they get. This approach naturally allows for a degree of exploitation and writing-to order. Listen to "Teenagers" by My Chemical Romance—a manifesto for 14-year-olds written by Gerard Way, a man in his late twenties—and you hear an artist who is able to balance a degree of personal catharsis with a big dollop of commercial nous. All pop and rock music, however, stands guilty on that count.

Emo has simply gained greater notoriety than Goth or hardcore because it has carried its juvenile grudge so deep into mainstream territory. Emo and its various scions may be just yet more variations of angst-ridden guitar rock aimed squarely at the teen market, but emo has perfected a formula: shocking enough to annoy the parents, but not sufficiently so to prevent it selling hundreds of thousands of copies. And it's certainly not happening in a vacuum: hugely popular teen shows like *Buffy the Vampire Slayer* and *Angel* have made the spooky, offbeat, and deathly sexy. In this way songs of young death have invaded the charts in a manner not seen since the sixties, and suicide has also become a staple subject of nu-metal and "alternative" mainstream pop-punk songs and even country, with Blaine Larsen's "How Do You Get That Lonely?"

The dark side has become the cool side, and a personal association with death lends a sense of gravitas and social kudos. It may be unpalatable but that's just the way it is. Trawl through the web or talk to teens and many will say they love a particular song because a friend recently died or committed suicide. Whether this is true or not, the subtext is: "I understand. I look young but I'm dealing with some major issues. Don't underestimate me." It's at once a disassociation from teenhood and about the most teenage thing anyone can do.

Given that the link between teenagers and suicide is a real and troubling one, depicting, describing, contemplating, or even recommending the act in song is always guaranteed to raise the hackles of certain elements of the media, not to mention parents. Most contemporary evidence, however, suggests that letting teens explore these feelings head on or even simply allowing them the opportunity to wallow in their pit of despair is the best possible response—advice of the pull-yourself-together variety, or a reaction that doesn't approach the problem with sufficient respect or seriousness, simply closes the gates of communication and is liable to increase rather than soothe the sense of alienation and depression. Despite much media hysteria, there has been little evidence of a risk of "suicide contagion," a phenomenon first recognized shortly after the publication of Goethe's *The Sorrows of Young Werther* in 1774, a novel that featured a young man who killed himself over unrequited love and, it is said, inspired a spate of copycat suicides across Europe. This, contrary to the gist of the *Daily Mail*'s headlines, hasn't happened in the wake of emo.

Thus the smart argument says that *not* addressing the subject in teenage music is less helpful than bringing it out into the open. Beyond the obvious criticisms of the objective adult observer, for the teen listener these songs offer a real sense of catharsis. And for every one that flirts with the beauty of dying and seems to exploit the lure that death has always held for the young, there are songs like "Hold On" by Good Charlotte or "The Truth About Heaven" by Armor for Sleep, that preach caution and, finally, life.

It is a delicate path to walk, between empathy and glorification, but there is a clear sincerity of purpose among the more accomplished of emo's writers, such as Gerard Way and Dashboard Confessional's Chris Carrabba. For all the posturing, they appear to be more in touch with their inner teenager than many of us, and are aware that singing about death and suicide gives release to their fans. Better, after all, to drown in the song than drown in the river. "There is a fortitude that is gained from dealing with death and it completely changes who you are," says Way. "It either turns you into a person who feels sorry for themselves for the rest of their lives, or you find this new kind of strength and you learn how not just to deal with that death, but everything in life. I find that's a really interesting subject."[4]

And anyway, teen suicide songs are hardly without precedence. Considering that the earliest examples of songs in the death pop genre encompassed everything from fatal shark attacks to being hit by a train, it's hardly surprising that there were a few notable suicide songs back in the innocent early sixties, although it wasn't really a speciality of the house. Mark Dinning's "The Pickup" flopped, but

Pat Boone's "Moody River"—"more deadly than the vainest knife"—was more successful, reaching number one on the Billboard chart in 1961. The singer goes down to the riverside, where he finds his love's discarded glove and a note telling him she has been cheating on him and "no longer can I live with this hurt and this sin."

The following year the deadly river claimed another victim. The sweet-sounding "Patches," "darling of the old shanty town," and Dickie Lee's boy-hero were to be married in the summer, until his parents stopped him seeing her because of her lowly status. We're back in traditional sob song territory here, except the solution is even more drastic than usual. Knowing not why her beloved has stopped coming to see her, Patches gives herself to the water. When he hears the news, Lee's bereft boy sees no other option. Dickie Lee, incidentally, didn't have much luck romantically. In "Laurie," he discovers he is dating a ghost. Perhaps it's Patches, returned to find her old lover. We can but hope.

The central refrain of "Patches"—"It may not be right / But I'll join you tonight / Patches I'm coming to you"—is simply the message of a song like "I'll Follow You into the Dark" cooked on a lower flame: "The time for sleep is now / It's nothing to cry about / Cause we'll hold each other soon / The blackest of rooms." Which, in its own thoroughly modern, moody way, is saying the same thing as "Gloomy Sunday," the venerable, luxuriously doom-laden "Hungarian Suicide Song" written by Rezso Seress in 1933 and made famous by Billie Holliday in 1941: "Would they be angry if I thought of joining you?" All recognize the allure of suicide; all acknowledge that it transgresses acceptable behavior. It is possible, then, to draw a line from the thirties through 1960 and onto into the noughties. It's not a straight line; it's faint and crooked like the ones that score our palms, but it provides a timely reminder that misery has long been proudly worn as a badge of otherness, particularly by the young.

Tolstoy's *Anna Karenina* begins "All happy families are happy alike; all unhappy families are unhappy in their own way." Substitute the family for the teenage tribe-member and you have a neat explanation of why publicly declaring your own specific brand of unhappiness—through your clothes, your hair, your makeup, above all through your choice of music—remains the inalienable right of every teenager. Since rock and roll first began it's one that each successive generation has exercised, each one believing that it's inventing the idea for the very first time, which is as it should be. "The thing about being young," Nick Cave once said, entirely correctly, "is that you think you're the final product in evolution."[5]

Lest we forget, and we often do, teenagers tend not to be anywhere near as stupid as we think they might look; daily reports of their descent back into the primeval swamp serve only to make adults look ill-informed. They know better than most that this music is meant as entertainment. The more their favorite bands and their clothes are hated and derided, the more fun they are likely to be having. They understand that these songs are about fleeting moments, capturing seconds of joy, despair, beauty, loss, panic, hatred, utter desperation. But the moment passes—tears are shed and life moves on. Despite the patronizing implication, specifically teen-orientated music does prove, by its very definition, to be "just a phase" for most of us. Songs like "Tell Laura I Love Her" or "One Hundred Years" or "Teenagers" hardly supply a template or philosophy that can survive the passage into adult life.

A phase it may be, but adolescence is a fiercely personal experience, the most intense period of many of our lives. Those old Cure albums may not have much to say to me in 2008, but they pack a Proustian punch that few other of the records and tapes and CDs littering my home can replicate. They recall that time when I felt the highs and lows of life so exceptionally, *deliciously* keenly that it's still possibly to feel the phantom pains today. And I'm glad I can. It means I can detect a faint, distorted, rather ghostly version of my shamed teenage self reflected in an otherwise alien and culturally and socially detached tribe. And as my eldest daughter starts to creep toward those dread teen years, it's instructive to be reminded that embracing the darker, harder, more difficult parts of the teenage experience through funereal songs of despair is nothing new. And it is not, by and large, the end of anybody's world.

BLOOD ON THE FLOOR
Music, Murder, and Morality

They cut his throat from ear to ear
His head they battered in
His name was Mr. William Weare
He lived in Lyons Inn.

Hardly poetic, but undeniably strong on detail. When the
London solicitor and high-stakes society gambler William
Weare was shot and stabbed by John Thurtell and his two
accomplices in Radlett, England, in 1823, news of his sensa-
tional murder and the rather seedy underworld events leading up to it were the talk of the town, chewed over endlessly
in the penny broadsheets. A contemporary ballad called
"The Hertfordshire Tragedy" told the whole gory story,
right down to mentioning the stones that dragged Weare's
body to the bottom of the pond where he was finally discovered, as well as musing upon Thurtell's chilling detachment: "Although his hands were warm with blood / He down
to supper sat / And passed the time in merry mood / With
drink and songs and chat." The fiend! One theater production of the tale promised to display the carriage in which
Weare traveled to his fate, as well as the very table at which
Thurtell "down to supper sat."

It may be true that popular music loves murder and the language of extreme violence almost as much as it loves sex and money, but we can't lay all the blame at the door of tabloid newspapers and gangsta rap. Since time immemorial songs, ballads, plays, and poems have been knocked off almost instantaneously in reaction to hot-off-the-stove current affairs, the more grisly and gruesome the better. They routinely spared few details and they sold faster than Sweeney Todd's meat pies. "The Five Pirates of the Flowery Land" shifted three thousand copies in one hour following the London execution in 1864 of five sailors "for the willful murder of George Smith upon the high seas." In the days before reality TV, public hangings—surely our ancestors' equivalent of *Big Brother*—routinely attracted substantial crowds, but this event fired the public's imagination to an even greater extent, inspiring some bright publisher in London's seedy Seven Dials to seize the opportunity to make a fast buck. The song, rather tame as these things go, eventually sold ninety thousand copies, commemorating those "sailors from distant foreign nations / Suspended on a dreadful tree." They're the kind of sales figures that in this day and age would take a song to number one in the UK on virtually any week of the year.

Away from the sinful city, up in the Appalachians, deep in the Scottish lowlands, and even in well-heeled New England, similarly bald, unflinching accounts of local difficulties were being passed around, sometimes orally, sometimes in written form, ultimately in both, and often in many different versions. The case of Lizzie Borden, tried and acquitted (but not *quite* convincingly enough for public satisfaction, it seems) for the brutal murder of her father and stepmother in Fall Rivers, Massachusetts, in 1892, bequeathed a famous children's rhyme—"Lizzie Borden took an axe / And gave her mother forty whacks / And when she saw what she had done / She gave her father forty-one"—and has inspired ballets, operas, and novels, as well as giving at least two minor rock and roll bands their name.

Even more enduring is the case of Tom Dula, a Civil War soldier who returned to his home in Wilkes County, North

Carolina, in 1865 only to discover that his childhood sweetheart, Ann Foster, had married another. He in turn took up with her cousin, Laura Foster, and when she fell pregnant they decided to elope. On the night of May 27, 1866, Laura was seen leaving to meet Dula but never returned. Her body was found three months later, mutilated by multiple stab wounds. Dula fled to Tennessee but was captured—with the aid of a Colonel James Grayson—and returned to Wilkes County, where he was hanged in 1868.

Dula's role in the murder, however, was never made convincingly clear; many locals implicated his former lover Ann Foster, now Ann Shelton, although Dula's testimony exonerated her. The mysterious, gruesome nature of the murder, not to mention the intriguingly entwined sexual relationships that lay behind it, ensured that the trial gained national coverage in the press. Shortly after Dula's execution, a ballad telling the tale was written by local poet, Thomas C. Land. The first recorded version of "Tom Dooley" (a phonetically accurate rendering of the local pronunciation of "Dula") was made in 1929, but it was the version released by the Kingston Trio in 1958 that became the most popular, selling over six million copies and effectively launching the "folk boom." The spoken introduction to their version suggests a love triangle, but instead of women making up two of the three sides, the song implicates James Grayson as Dula's love rival, which was not, in reality, the case.

An entire book, meanwhile, has been written about the origins of "Stagger Lee," the most famous and versatile murder song of them all. Why this particular murder ballad has proved so enduring is something of a mystery given that the crime, committed in St. Louis, Missouri, in 1895, is as depressingly unremarkable as most murders, both then and now. Lee Shelton was a 30-year-old gambler, pimp, and leader of a local gang called the Stags. An all-purpose neighborhood hoodlum-hero, he fell into an argument with William Lyons in Curtis' saloon on Christmas night, 1895, which escalated to provocative hat-snatching—hence the mention of the "John B. Stetson hat" in many versions—and which ended in Shelton shooting Lyons dead. Shelton, also known as "Stag" Lee, was eventually sentenced to twenty-five years in 1897 and died in prison in 1912. The earliest known recording of "Stagger Lee" (also called "Stagolee" and "Stack-o-Lee") dates from 1923, but the song had certainly been in circulation since the early part of the twentieth century. It has since been recorded by everybody from Neil Diamond to the Clash, white dance bands to black convicts, Nick Cave to Huey Lewis and the News.

On one level, then, it is simply a standard, a gripping little story, there to be sung, enjoyed, and passed around. Tragic tales involving sex, love, and murder make compelling narratives in any medium; they never lose their currency. Virtually all murder songs, from Skid Row's "18 and Life" to Eminem's "Kim," operate on a titillating, grubbily glamorous level, and if they throw a little reflected menace and swagger back on the singer, all the better. Every artist of a certain stripe believes they exist somewhere just beyond the law, self-legislating themselves to go where others aren't allowed to follow. It's hardly surprising, then, that so many of them are attracted, both in song and often in the way they portray themselves, to the outlaw persona —the righteous gunslinger, the cold-blooded killer, the morally justified equalizer, the half crazed passion-player. Some musicians have even played those roles for real, among them Leadbelly, Son House, Spade Cooley, Bertrand Cantat, Varg Vikernes, Jim Gordon, and Big Lurch.

The purely commercial lure of murder remains strong. When two albums of blood-curling old Calabrian folk songs were released a few years ago as *Il Canto Da Malavita: La Musica Della Mafia*, they got the kind of publicity—and sales figures—few collections of nineteenth-century tarantella can match. Why? Because when you mix our perennial fascination with the Mafia with lyrics like "Whoever took the liberty to neglect their duties / I'll slaughter him like an animal" then people invariably start to pay attention.

In 1919 local New Orleans composer Joseph John Davilla wrote "The Mysterious Axman's Jazz (Don't Scare Me Papa)" to cash in on the fact that a jazz-loving serial axe-killer—yes, really—was stalking the city. Davilla's rag was written to ward off the demon, who had contacted the local paper saying he would kill again that night at a quarter past midnight, but that he would spare anyone in any place where a jazz band was playing. Hence "The Mysterious Axman's Jazz (Don't Scare Me Papa)." The cover of the sheet music depicted a cartoon of a family—the father's head is bandaged—doggedly playing ragtime with terrified looks on their faces, but the levity hardly reflected the terror abroad in the city between 1918 and 1919, when the axeman's victims included a pregnant woman and a baby.

Add murder to the mix and you can sell almost anything. On another level, however, the relish with which songs like "Tom Dooley" and "Stagger Lee" have been sung, repeated, altered, embellished, and exaggerated for over a hundred years suggests a more fundamental need for successive generations to revisit the terrible deeds they describe. In part, these songs act as a kind of incantation to ward off evil spirits, a self-inflicted dose of poison to aid immunity from the full disease.

"The function of these songs is to get it out there, so that it's been sung about as a real thing that has happened," says Richard Thompson, talking about "Tom Dooley." "Whatever the society is, Appalachian society in this case, they need to deal with this subject matter, to get it out there and sing it. They need to look at these things, and so they look in the guise of entertainment. It makes it easier to deal with. You sing about your hard times at work, your happy times like weddings, and you [also sing about] the local problems, the dark things that happen locally. That's the arena where it's okay to bring that stuff and sing about it on a regular basis in the guise of a good tune. In that way society is dealing with the problem of what you do with someone in the community. Something like 'Tom Dooley,' it's the ballad functioning as a newspaper. In societies where people didn't particularly read or there wasn't a radio or TV, that was the way the news was carried."

Thompson has written his own murder mysteries, songs such as "Did She Jump or Was She Pushed?" Thom Yorke recently visited the same territory in "Harrowdown Hill," his song about the death of the British biological warfare expert David Kelly, caught up in the crossfire of a battle between the government and the media during the Iraq War: "Did I fall or was I pushed? / And where's the blood?" asks Yorke. Thompson argues that the function of these song isn't to provide answers—either literally or intellectually—but simply to "ask moral questions" of those listening.

"The audience like to deal with these kinds of subjects. In a song often you're dealing with things below the spoken desires of the audience. They are below consciousness, these things that are slightly troubling, and as a songwriter you look for them. You turn them into songs and sing them and sometimes it can be unsettling for the audience, especially the ones that deal with serious subjects, but because it's entertainment you can do it and the audience will go through that process. They almost like to be unsettled. It's part of the job of a songwriter, and its part of what the audience expects—from me, anyway."

It would be hard to find a more astute or accurate distillation than the one Thompson provides of the continuing appeal of the murder song to grip an audience beyond mere titillation. That these songs, with their deeply planted roots in society, have survived hundreds of years of use to burrow their way into the twenty-first century says something about our enduring taste for indulging in a little vicarious violence and social transgression, but it's also a testament to an eternal human desire to bring dark subjects out into the light and examine them in the hope that somewhere amid all this chaos and confusion, blood, guts, and gore, something will start to make some *sense*.

There is perhaps a greater need than ever for pop music to fulfill this kind of meaty function. It may no longer perform the role of the local newssheet, but in a world arguably growing desensitized to the emotional reality of murder through its over-exposure on television, films, computer games, millions of internet sites, and tabloid newspapers, it is still better equipped than most other mediums to make us confront some hard realities.

The most remarkable recent example of a song opening

up a whole community's can of worms is the Smiths' "Suffer Little Children," the first lyric Morrissey ever showed to Johnny Marr as they embarked upon their songwriting collaboration. The song is an explicit and provocatively beautiful excavation of the notorious "Moors murders" that took place between 1963 to 1965 in Manchester, during which time five children aged between 10 and 17 were abducted and savagely killed by Ian Brady and Myra Hindley, before being buried on Saddleworth Moor on the outskirts of the city. First released on the Smiths' 1984 debut album, "Suffer Little Children" caused a minor outrage at the time; *The Sun* called for it to be banned, although after consultation between Morrissey and some of the children's families, the motives of the song were deemed to be beyond question.

That much is clear from the most cursory of listens. "Suffer Little Children" articulates a desire for the souls of the children to find peace: when the song was written in 1982, only two of the five bodies had been found, hence the dead child's cry of "Oh, find me, find me, nothing more / We are on a sullen misty moor." The same sad cry—"Be sure to find me / I want you to find me"— runs through Tom Waits' "Georgia Lee," written after the murder of 12-year-old Georgia Lee Moses in 1997. Unlike the Moors murders, the crime remains unsolved. As Waits said: "I guess everybody was wondering, where were the police? Where was the deacon? Where were the social workers? And where was I? And where were you?"[1]

The motivation behind writing such songs is far from simple. By facing up to horrific events that haunted both the local communities and the writers themselves (Morrissey, between the ages of 4 and 6, was living in Manchester when the Moors murders took place; the body of Georgia Lee Moses was found near Waits' home in northern California), they aren't attempting to find justice in the traditional sense, and there is certainly no desire to titillate, no attempt to overplay the emotions. Instead, the songs are written out of a compulsion to confront monsters, the way you might force yourself to walk the long, dark way home for no apparent reason.

Partly it's an attempt not so much to exorcise as at least to acknowledge local demons, to square up to the fact that certain horrific events can alter forever how you perceive a place and your place within it. Morrissey often admitted that he felt the Moors murders had left a malevolent pall hanging over the city ("Oh Manchester, so much to answer for") made all the darker for largely going unspoken. As in the Auteurs' "After Murder Park" and "Unsolved Child Murder," where we learn that "people 'round here don't like to talk about it," "Suffer Little Children" and "Georgia Lee" are airings of events that have come to be regarded as the local society's secret stash of dirty laundry.

On a more personal level, the songs are a way of reminding the writers—and whoever else is listening in—of something compelling and deeply unpleasant about the true nature of man. "Suffer Little Children" establishes the timeless elemental imagery denoting natural order—the "fresh lilaced moorland fields"—and then rips it up to reveal the horror lurking below. Whatever superficial beauty lies on the surface—of nature, of humanity—the real, dark, true stuff lies in a shallow grave not far below.

At heart, it is a late-twentieth-century version of a traditional murder ballad. The debt is obvious: the narrative isn't fixed, the singer shifting perspective to speak as the children, then as the killer, then the children's parents, then moving back to the children again. And it ends with the promise of a haunting: "We will be right by your side / Until the day you die." Those tugging, ghostly voices that speak from beyond the grave, pleading for peace and an end to the prospect of eternal torment, are a hallmark of numerous old-time songs.

But then murder songs, more than most others, are full of old ghosts. Ghosts of the dead and ghosts of old familiar characters. The most famous ones are all about archetypes: the same faces show up over and over again, hiding behind new names, shapes, and forms. You can find the spirit of Bonnie Parker and Clyde Barrow, for instance, running amok through everything from Bruce Springsteen's "Nebraska" and Bob Seger's "East Side Story" to My Chemical Romance's

"Demolition Lovers." There are also several different songs —most notably by Merle Haggard, Serge Gainsbourg, and a terrific mod-jazz single by Georgie Fame, which ends with probably the best pop shoot-out of all time—that celebrate the murderous exploits of the original duo.

Then there is the Jesse James anti-authoritarian fugitive killer, forever running for the border with the bounty hunter and his posse at his heels, unsure who to trust and doomed to die for his sins: he's there in much of Marty Robbins' and Johnny Cash's songbook, in Woody Guthrie's "Pretty Boy Floyd," and in "Indiana Wants Me" by R. Dean Taylor, in "I Shot the Sheriff" and "Cop Killer." His romanticized legacy formed the ethos of the whole Outlaw Country movement.

Jesse is a close relative of "Stagger Lee," except Stag has no great quest for justice to pursue, no moral hinterland: he is just plain *bad*. That's his purpose. He has hardened over time into the ultimate badass, the nerveless, merciless sharp-shooter who roams the world looking for trouble, brandishing his .44 through numerous bars, streets, and bedrooms. A repeat offender throughout countless murder blues, he has become synonymous with anyone characterized as true evil: he is the "Midnight Rambler," "Bad, Bad Leroy Brown," and both of the "Natural Born Killaz." As we shall see further on down the line, he has also become rap's number one original gangster.

Tom Dooley, on the other hand, has become the everyman figure for the backwoods bad man; he is more mercurial, the type who takes his lover a-walking through the hills and along the riverbanks, whispering sweet entreaties into her ear, before leaving her for dead, her blood slowly draining into the water, her hair entwining with the grass. How often through the centuries has this shadowy, morally impenetrable figure appeared in classic murder ballads? He's there in "Pretty Polly," "Knoxville Girl," "Down in the Willow Garden," "Psycho," and "The Banks of the Ohio," right through to Neil Young's "Down by the River" and Nick Cave's "Song of Joy" and "Where the Wild Roses Grow."

There is no moral dressing in the majority of these songs. There is no explanation. Nothing beyond the description of the mere act, the aftermath, and the inevitable conclusion is spelled out. Partly this is because many of the popular, twentieth-century versions of songs like "Tom Dooley" and "Knoxville Girl" are taken from older, much longer folk songs (in the case of the latter, the seventeenth-century ballad "The Cruel Miller," which became "The Oxford Girl" and then "The Wexford Girl"). Over the years several verses fulfilling a narrative function and explaining matters in a little more detail have been excised in the interests of brevity. But in neither "Knoxville Girl" nor any versions of "The Wexford Girl" is any clear purpose for the girl's murder given. She has agreed to marry the boy; they go for a walk. He beats her to death. At the end, he still "loves her so well."

Occasionally we catch a glimpse of a motive, like a deer speeding away through the trees—jealousy, the pain of rejection—but all the while there is something else looming into view, something more troubling concerning what Nick Cave has called "murderous male attention and nefarious transferred erotic desire."[2] "All beauty must die," he sings in his original murder ballad "Where the Wild Roses Grow," as he applies a rock to the skull of Kylie Minogue, singing as Elisa Day, a.k.a. the Wild Rose, a.k.a. the Knoxville Girl in yet another of her thankless incarnations. There is a message buried within these songs concerning atavistic male attitudes to women that is quite profoundly disturbing. It is beyond simple misogyny. It is, rather, the tragedy of Othello. The desire—however fleeting—to destroy the thing you purportedly love the most in order to fully possess it is one that most of us will understand on some level; and it is this over-riding compulsion, this dreadful, inexplicable date with destiny taken to an impulsive and eternal conclusion, that rises like stream off songs like "Knoxville Girl."

"It's weird, you hear 'Knoxville Girl' and it's just chilling, beating this woman to death beside a river," says the Canadian songwriter Ron Sexsmith, a self-confessed fan of the murder ballad. "It's crazy. I don't know what people thought about those songs back then. He gets arrested at the end but it's almost like they want you to feel sorry for him."

The killer's remorse is usually spelled out in the final verse, moral and legal justice is dispensed, but the lack of any real reason is the part that nags and troubles and makes us stop and think long and hard about our own darker instincts. Why? Because we know that this is *exactly* how terrible things happen in the real world. Murder doesn't seep in through the pores; it starts from within, and it can catch you by surprise. If these songs seem somehow senseless, if we struggle to find a real clarity of purpose behind their composition, then that should not necessarily be regarded as a negative. In fact, it's their triumph. "It is time for writers to admit that nothing in this world makes sense," wrote Anton Chekhov in 1888. "If an artist decides to declare that he understands nothing of what he sees—this in itself constitutes a considerable clarity in the realm of thought, and a great step forward."

The key line, I think, on music's relationship with murder is buried deep in a parched, sinister elemental blues, written in 1992 but harking back to the previous century. Tom Waits' "Murder in the Red Barn" was inspired by the real-life events of 1827, in which the English woman Maria Marten was murdered by her wealthy lover William Corder and buried in a shallow grave in the red barn of a farm in Polstead, Suffolk. A hugely popular broadside ballad called "The Murder of Maria Marten" recounted the act, as told by the murderer; Waits does not stick to the detail—he appears to move the story to the US and the characters are unrecognizable—but he clearly knows the original tale. And halfway through comes a line that never fails to stop me dead in my tracks: "For some murder is the only door through which they enter life."

It nods, of course, toward the odd kind of celebrity status that murder can bestow upon both victim and perpetrator, both then and now, but it also hints obliquely at the purpose behind many of these songs, to explore not just our inner fears but also the darkest areas of the human condition. The Waits line ties in with Nick Cave's epic "O'Malley's Bar." It starts like a joke—man walks into a bar—and it *is* a joke in many ways, in all its cartoonishness, its bloodthirsty relish and pathetic execution of power, as our anti-hero slaughters what seems like the entire town (actually, it's thirty-seven people by my count). We are almost in Tom Lehrer territory. The lavishness of the violence invites comparison with songs like "Rickety Tickety Tin," in which the daughter murders all the members of her family in bizarre, macabre, and hilarious ways.

"O'Malley's Bar" is a black joke, but by walking through that saloon door with murder on his mind, Cave's killer is also walking through the door Waits is talking about: the act of destruction is a search to find some kind of greater meaning to his life. "There was something about a guy walking into a bar and blowing everyone away that I found quite interesting at some point," Cave said. "Now, I find it an act committed by someone who lacks imagination and moral commitment. However I think our society is such that I can understand people committing acts like this. In its way, it's a legitimate spiritual quest, a way of getting a bit of quality, a bit of meaning into their lives. It's the by-product of a doomed world."[3]

"O'Malley's Bar" came out less than two years after Joel Schumacher's 1993 film *Falling Down*, another contemporary attempt to plug into this idea of murder as the ultimate protest against an inexplicable world. But never mind Michael Douglas, really we're into the world of Dostoevsky's Raskolnikov and Albert Camus' Meursault, murder as an existential act, committed as part of the search to carve out a personal moral code. In his afterword to the 1955 edition of *L'Etranger*, the French-Algerian author muses on Meursault, the murderer who murders for no discernible reason: "He says what he is, he refuses to hide his feelings and society immediately feels threatened. For example, he is asked to say that he regrets his crime, in time-honored fashion. He replies that he feels more annoyance about it than true regret. And it is this nuance that condemns him."

Alongside the likes of Jesse James and Bonnie and Clyde, Meursault also appears as an archetype in many modern murder songs as the socially transgressive individual whose calamitous actions appear to be randomly deployed and motivated only by an attempt to show that the moral parameters set by society actually mean nothing. In one shot all the external religious and empirical structures are destroyed. Death, after all, is random, inexplicable, painful, inevitable, and—often—seems utterly meaningless. The murderer-in-waiting in Talking Heads' "Psycho Killer" is struggling to "face up to the facts"; murder gives the illusion of taking control and gaining power. The Cure, famously, translated Camus into the language of brittle post-punk on the snaking "Killing an Arab": "I can turn and walk away / Or I can fire the gun. . . . Whichever I chose / It amounts to the same / Absolutely nothing."

Meursault's troubling lack of remorse is echoed by the teenage killers in Springsteen's "Nebraska": "I can't say that I'm sorry / For the things that we done / At least for a little while, sir / Me and her we had us some fun." And again on the Boomtown Rats' "I Don't Like Mondays," written just days after the 16-year-old Brenda Spencer killed two adults and wounded eight children and one police officer in a shooting spree at Cleveland Elementary School in the San Carlos section of San Diego, California, in 1979. When asked why she did it, Spencer replied: "I don't like Mondays. This livens up the day. I had no reason for it, and it was just a lot of fun. It was just like shooting ducks in a pond."

Johnny Cash wrote "Folsom Prison Blues," in which he famously shot a man in Reno "just to watch him die," because he was "trying to think up the worst reason a person could have for killing another person. And that's what came to mind."[4] It's this line, a masterpiece of economy, that makes the song more than just a barely rewritten version of Gordon Jenkins' "Crescent City Blues." It forces us to contemplate a truly amoral act, an act of sport, and why it was committed.

Richard Thompson, who has lived in Los Angeles for over twenty years, isn't alone in finding "Folsom Prison Blues" alive with resonance fifty years after it was written. "It's a wonderful song, very simple but it tells it like it is—a real slice of real life. Mindless acts: America is the place for that. American prisons are just jammed packed full of people who are there forever for [killing people who were just] passing in the street. It's gotten very, very dark in America, and it will get darker."

Everyone in these songs is brought to justice in the conventional sense but, the Folsom convict aside, they are not changed. Their minds do not surrender to the law imposed upon them. They don't even display any real recognition that they have done anything wrong. This terrible, off-hand banality, more than the bloodstains and bullets, is the really scary thing about murder ballads. Deep down we know it's the truth.

🖎

If Meursault is another murderous archetype then so is Joe, the woman-slayer of "Hey Joe," the song made famous by Jimi Hendrix but written by Billy Roberts in 1962, although it appears to have its origins in much earlier traditional songs. Joe pops up in "Delia's Gone," "Blood on the Floor," "Careless Love," "A to Z Blues," "Murderin' Blues," "I'm Gonna Murder My Baby," "Cocaine Blues," Tom Jones' "Delilah," Willie Nelson's "I Just Can't Let You Say Goodbye" and "Red Headed Stranger," Uncle Tupelo's version of "Lilli Schull," even Michael Jackson's "Smooth Criminal" and the Beatles' "Run for Your Life," as well as scores of other songs. The invariably "mean" women done her man wrong and he has shot her down, or words to that effect. Many of the narratives—such as that of "Delia's Gone"—have their roots in real-life events that occurred in poor, black neighborhoods around the end of the nineteenth century, often involving mere teenagers, and are therefore no laughing matter.

Their historical roots, combined with the sheer number of songs that deal with men despatching their unfaithful woman in a variety of brutal fashions, suggest that this is more than mere posturing. The force of murderous passion on show in these songs should not be mistaken for a measure of love. It is about asserting power, enforcing gender stereotypes, and maintaining status in the local community. Indeed, Robert Nighthawk's menace-heavy "Murderin' Blues" premeditatedly states he'd rather wear prison chains than have his woman cheat and lie; the thuggish machismo and misogyny on display in these songs would simply be funny were it not for the fact that a disgustingly high number of women continue to die violently at the hands of men. Outside of rap—which will be discussed elsewhere—you don't often hear this kind of thing written anew in popular song anymore; certainly not in anything remotely near the mainstream, though there are plenty of songs by bands called things like Cradle of Filth, Dismember, and Cannibal Corpse that make a career out of grisly depictions of violent female death.

Guns 'N Roses' "Used to Love Her" ("but I had to kill her") is a high-profile exception. A "joke" song about burying his woman in the backyard from their *LIES LIES LIES* album, the album cover featured a mock-tabloid paper with numerous sensationalist headlines, including "Wife-beating has been around for 10,000 years." In which case, presumably, it's perfectly okay for a heavy metal band with a history of violent, stupid, sexist lyrics to pass the subject off as a joke in a song.

The even less edifying tone of the old murder songs, however, seems to be regarded as somehow more acceptable today by virtue of the time that has passed. A dubious distinction, but at least the men involved generally get their come-uppance. A long stretch in prison—or worse—is deemed an acceptable price to pay for keeping your woman in line, and thus retaining your masculine credentials.

The same kind of justice is rarely dispensed when the gender roles are reversed. Most songs that portray the woman as the violent perpetrator tend to suggest that there is some moral justification for the crime. "Frankie and Johnny" is *the* great woman-scorned murder ballad, and another that has its origins planted firmly in reality. As reported in the *St. Louis Post Dispatch* on October 20, 1899, 22-year-old dancer Frankie Baker stabbed her 17-year-old lover Albert

Britt in her home, having found him with another woman, Alice Pryor. Most of the limited available evidence suggests that Baker was eventually acquitted of murder on the grounds of self-defense and lived on until 1950, by which time the song written about her exploits was fast becoming a standard, much to her discomfort.

"Frankie and Albert" appeared shortly after the events of 1899 as a means of spreading the tale among the local community and beyond. Over time the stabbing changed to the more sonically exciting shooting—"the gun went off, rootie-toot-toot"—and Albert morphed into Johnny, possibly in some way related to the use of the term "john" as a prostitute's customer. Other than that, at its core the song is real-life reportage, the story simple enough to incorporate several dramatic augmentations by the many artists who have performed it over the past hundred years.

The tale was recorded under both the "Albert" and "Johnny" titles by many early blues artists, including Leadbelly and Mississippi John Hurt, and has since been covered by everyone from Sam Cooke to Bob Dylan. The lyrics come in many differing versions, but the vast majority are skewed in sympathy toward the killer, seeing her as the wronged party. The song often starts: "Frankie was a good girl / Everybody knows / She paid a hundred dollars / For Al's one suit of clothes." Already, we are being groomed. A common conclusion, used in Van Morrison's recent version, is: "This story has no moral / This story has no end / This story only goes to show / That there ain't no good in men." Ah yes, no moral indeed.

In a few versions Frankie is hanged for her crime, but more often than not the actions of the "evil woman" in murder songs tend to be justified by mitigating circumstances or else played strictly for laughs. The eponymous killer in Aerosmith's "Janie's Got a Gun," for instance, wreaks vengeance on a sexually abusive father, while Wanda, the heroine in the Dixie Chicks' "Goodbye Earl," poisons her rotten husband after years of domestic abuse in an odd song that is both played for laughs but also strives to be empowering: an ethical, uplifting murder ballad. In Garth Brooks' "The

Thunder Rolls" the man is heading back from somewhere "he never should have been" and gets his just desserts. Julie Brown's "Homecoming Queen's Got a Gun," a 1984 sob song pastiche in which the good girl gets crowned and then goes on a killing spree, is simply a joke; "Nightmare," an excellent slice of sixties girl-group camp by the Whyte Boots, is a rare case of girl-on-girl murder, but the fight to the death between high school love rivals is, naturally, over a certain Bobby and, again, has a high giggle factor.

In all these songs, the woman's feelings are either portrayed as a joke or she gets off scot-free with her crime. Again, gender politics are at play: female rage can either be laughed off or else "permitted" as a reaction against male cruelty. In both cases, there is no doubt that the patriarchs are still running the show.

The old-time songs, intriguingly, are far less chauvinist in their depiction of murder by a maiden's hand. Women are allowed the courtesy of being just plain bad, from "The Cruel Mother" to the killer of "Little Sir Hugh." In "Lord Ronald," a venerable traditional song recently revisited by Alasdair Roberts on *No Earthly Man*, a wonderful album that deals entirely with traditional songs of death, the young man's true love feeds him poisoned eels from his "father's black ditch," which sounds rather unpleasantly Freudian. But we never do find out why she did it. And on Nick Cave and PJ Harvey's tremendous version of "Henry Lee," a traditional murder ballad based on the ancient tale *Young Hunting*, the woman won't let her man return to the girl he loves "far better than thee," and instead plugs him through and through with her penknife. Not exactly commendable, but a gesture that confirms that—when it comes to sexual equality—you have to take the rough with the smooth.

♠

Let's edge away from the deep, dark truthful mirror of personal contemplation and allow the unarticulated, primal horrors bubbling within our breasts to subside. Our crimes and misdemeanors are, thankfully, usually played out on a less terrible and dramatic stage than the ones these songs describe, and even when they're not, culpability is not always so cut and dried. Pan away from the act of murder and it's possible to see it as a mere cog within a much more complex mechanism that, once you know how the parts fit together, can be dismantled piece by piece through song.

Bob Dylan, particularly in his earliest work, often plundered real-life murder cases to critique a society content to see only what it wanted to see and find, as quickly as possible, the nearest, most convenient, and least powerful scapegoat. Written within a year of each other, "Who Killed Davey Moore?," "The Lonesome Death of Hattie Carroll," and "Only a Pawn in Their Game" explore communal and political complicity through the act of murder in its most broadly symbolic sense.

In "Davey Moore," Dylan uses the death of the boxer after a bout against Sugar Ramos in 1963 to examine the conscience of all those who had a connection with the event. Who has the most blood on their hands: Is it the referee? The crowd? His manager? The gambling man? The boxing journalist? The other fighter? "Not me!" they all shout in reply. It's an exercise in rhetorical game-playing that gives momentary pause for thought, but the target is too specific to make a connection much beyond the immediate context of boxing.

Within months, however, Dylan had written "Only a Pawn in Their Game," which follows exactly the same tack, but this time the stakes are higher. Taking as its inspiration the assassination of civil rights activist Medgar Evers in Mississippi in June 1963, Dylan looks beyond the killer's trigger finger to direct his scorn at the ingrained system of institutional racism that allowed, indeed encouraged, the murder to happen, and that furthermore allowed Evers' killer to remain free for many years afterward. It's a brave, thought provoking song, eschewing righteous condemnation of the act itself for something more considered. Indeed, there were those who thought that Dylan made far too little of the human angle, the role of individual responsibility, in making his wider point. The Clash's "Somebody Got Murdered"—a commendably anti-glamour murder song that attempts to remind us all that every violent death leaves an ugly stain and a great big hole in the world—takes the thought behind Dylan's big picture view to task: you can bemoan the ills of society all you like, but the buck has to stop somewhere close to home: "I been very hungry," it says. "But not enough to kill." Which isn't always a fashionable statement.

Dylan had his eye fixed on the big fish, however, rather than the small fry. "Hattie Carroll" again uses a contemporary murder case, still smudgy with newsprint, to espouse civil rights issues and highlight social iniquities. One of Dylan's greatest songs, it examines the morality of a judicial system that protects the interests of the rich, white, and well-connected murderer over the poor, black, menial worker victim. In doing so, it must be said, Dylan plays fairly fast and loose with the facts, but he is merciless in his determination to get to the heart of the matter, and utterly, ruthlessly persuasive.

Using media accounts of acts of murder only as launching points, these songs are partly purely technical exercises, Dylan shifting his stance with all the skill of a practiced debater, channeling Bertolt Brecht and seeing where it will take him; and partly they reflect genuine, heartfelt indignation. This was back when, lyrically speaking, Dylan owned up to possessing a conscience; he quickly discovered it was a burden and has rarely displayed one since. It's hard to imagine that he held a particularly strong opinion on the moral rights and wrongs of boxing, but he is clearly still in love with the work he did on "Hattie Carroll," judging by the frequency with which he revisits it on stage. The emotion in the original version, meanwhile, is impossible to fake.

And like Jesse James and Tom Dooley, Hattie Carroll, the innocent victim struck down by the forces of the powerful establishment, has too become an archetype in the murder song. The difference is that she's a plot device rather than a central character—it's the wider social ramifications of her death that really matter, which sounds callous but that's the way these songs work. She is there again in Peter Case's "Million Dollars Bail," which also uses a murder to ponder the means by which the system chooses to punish the rich: "There's two kinds of justice everybody knows / One for folks up on the hill, the others down below." And in the Dead Kennedys' version of the old Bobby Fuller classic "I Fought the Law," rewritten in light of the events of 1978, when San Francisco City Supervisor Dan White brutally shot and killed the city mayor George Moscone and supervisor Harvey Milk, but was convicted of voluntary manslaughter and served only five years of a seven-year sentence. Reflecting a widespread sense of local outrage at the leniency relative to the crime, the Dead Kennedys changed the lyrics of Fuller's song and entitled it "I Fought the Law (And I Won)." Meanwhile, Billy Bragg adopted the melody of "Hattie Carroll" for his own "The Lonesome Death of Rachel Corrie," a tribute to the US aid worker who was killed in the Gaza Strip in 2003 while attempting to obstruct a bulldozer operated by the Israeli Defence Forces.

Later, Dylan was still seeking justice through murder, still shifting perspectives. "Hurricane" barrels into earshot with all the scene-setting urgency of a screenplay—"Pistol shots ring out in the bar-room night!"; instantly we're right there, amid the neon and blood—but then expertly guides the listener away from the murder scene, massaging our sensibilities like an expert defence lawyer until our sympathies lie not with the dead, but with the living, in this case the man convicted of the murder, Rubin "Hurricane" Carter, "an innocent man in a living hell." The song played its part in the wave of public disquiet that helped Carter win a retrial in 1976, at which he was re-convicted of murder. His conviction was finally quashed in 1985 when all charges were dropped and he was released eighteen years after entering prison for a crime he didn't commit.

So it goes. Winston Churchill once said that the manner in which a society treats criminals "is one of the most unfailing tests of the civilization of any country." The manner in which a society flings around the assumption of guilt is similarly revealing. Bruce Springsteen's "American Skin (41 Shots)" comes closest in modern times to fulfilling the critical role of a song like "Only a Pawn in Their Game," looking beyond the simple, devastating, irretrievable act of taking another man's life to uncover some uncomfortable truths about where we all are at the beginning of the twenty-first century.

Inspired by the shooting of an innocent black man, Amadou Diallo, by four plain-clothes police officers in the Bronx in 1999, "American Skin" was widely reported as an "anti-police" song when it was first aired in concert in June 2000, but in reality the lyrics, though critical of the NYPD, present a far less conveniently cut-and-dried examination of the forces that drive four white men to pump forty-one bullets into a young, unarmed African immigrant. "I was just setting out to basically continue writing about things that I'd written about for a long period of time, which is, who we are," said Springsteen later. "What does it mean to be an American? What's going on in this country we live in? It was asking some questions that were hanging very heavy in the air. . . . And it was an extension of . . . a lot of my other work."[5]

A song tackling race, identity, and complicity by using such a specific, emotive, and thoroughly contemporary shooting, coming from an artist as high profile as Springsteen, was guaranteed to stir up a hornet's nest—which, you suspect, was exactly the point. All four police officers were eventually cleared of any wrongdoing, but the underlying impulse of the song was not to apportion blame to specific individuals, but to make all of us look around before, hopefully, looking inward. "Here is what systemic racial injustice, fear, and paranoia do to our children, our loved ones, ourselves," said Springsteen. "Here is the price in blood."[6]

Which is what Nick Cave is getting at when he says, "There are worse things than murder."[7] Murder is the symptom, not the disease. The realization that civilization—whether on a global or national level, or simply on an individual basis —isn't innate but is instead a man-made concept, a painfully fragile artificial barrier built on shifting moral and legal foundations that merely act as a defence against the threat of the full savagery, fear, and confusion of human nature bursting through. What happens when—as in "O'Malley's Bar" or "Folsom Prison Blues"—we choose to pay these artificial constructs no heed? Well, then we get a full taste of our own worst instincts. It's *Lord of the Flies*. And we are forced to ask ourselves: what would *we* do if we allowed ourselves to go to these deep, dark places?

It's this huge, gaping hole between what we think we are, what we strive to be, and what we really are that explains the unceasing power of songs of murder to both entrance us and yet trouble us greatly. We listen to the grave deeds recounted in these songs and we wait for neat answers and pat explanations. But they never come. Instead, they force us to question our own morality. The best, most savage murder song screws up the listener's shock and contempt—my God, how *could* you?—and throws it right back in his face, accompanied by a question of its own: look into your own dark heart and see what's the worst you can find. It won't be pretty. As Steve Earle sings in "The Truth," a song sung by a murderer languishing in his cell: "The truth is it doesn't matter what you do / 'Til you gaze in that mirror with an eye that's true / And admit that what scares you is the me in you."

4
HOW DOES IT FEEL?
Death in the Sixties

It's 1966. "The Green Green Grass of Home" and "Snoopy vs. the Red Baron" are gracing the charts with their less than gritty musings on certain mortal truths, yet elsewhere pop is finally extracting itself from its fumbling teenage clinch with the Reaper long enough to get its hands dirty. That the greatest leap in music's dealings with mortality was made by the biggest band in the world was hardly surprising given their growing thirst for innovation, but the Beatles' "Eleanor Rigby" still reverberated with the shock of the new when it arrived. "Death is a subject normally avoided in pop music," wrote Ian MacDonald in *Revolution in the Head*, his in-depth study of the Beatles' songbook. "Where acknowledged it is either sanitized with heavenly choirs or treated as a black joke. Consequently, the downbeat demise of a lonely spinster in 'Eleanor Rigby'—not to mention the brutal image of the priest 'wiping the dirt from his hands as he walks from the grave'—came as quite a shock to pop listeners in 1966."[1]

It retains some of that ability to provoke even today, remaining one of the toughest, most honest, least sentimental pop songs ever written about death, perhaps all the more so for having been composed by the same man who had recently written "And I Love Her" and went on to record "Mary Had a Little Lamb." There is no room for escapist fantasy here; no cartoon japes or carefully measured acts of rebellion; no displays of hollow bravado or camp corn. No over-the-top saloon bar slaughters. No farmyard animals. To the accompaniment of a plain, sparsely unforgiving string arrangement, a lonely old lady dies her lonely death, her only funeralgoer the equally lonely priest who buries her. No angels. No heaven. No sense of nobility or redemption or of a life particularly well lived. No one mourns and no one is saved because, frankly, we're entering a world that doesn't believe in those kind of pat, one-size-fits-all ideologies anymore.

The spare, matter-of-fact horror that "Eleanor Rigby" described didn't arrive by accident. Seeking comfort in the stiff embrace of the traditional western religious belief system didn't reflect the way the weather vane was pointing in 1966. McCartney's song marks a deliberate and conscious attempt to swim in the wider countercultural currents, chipping away at the comforting facades that society draws down over death. The "face" that Eleanor Rigby "keeps in a jar by the door" could hardly speak more clearly of a growing desire to strip away the masks of conformity to discover what lurks beneath.

Some of the most ground-breaking popular music of the sixties came closer to touching the essence of death and, in particular, the process of *becoming* dead and the state of *being* dead than in any period since. It was simply as though, for a few moments, music was somehow more attuned to the vast network of interconnections that make up the world as perceived by each individual consciousness, and thus became more alive to the possibilities of exploring them. Though rainbow-colored on the outside—and history, by and large, is happy enough to keep things that way—as it wore on the decade's music developed an underbelly that was often black as pitch. Imagine the sixties as a 45 single: the A-side is commonly held to have produced the most joyous, sun-dappled, life-affirming pop music to date. Flip it over, though, and you find a long, somewhat experimental B-side that spent much of its allotted time contemplating the End and attempting —at least as much as the constraints of unfocused eyes and the wearying demands of all that free love would allow—to look into the abyss.

At the dawn of pop music's first and most emphatic Great Imagining, nothing was off-limits. So began a rather brief but awfully big and interesting adventure. If the fifties was about making the most of the rock and roll fad while it lasted (which wouldn't be long, according to most commentators), by the midsixties the relative longevity and diffusion of ideas and styles had lead to a significant expansion of ambition. Singers became songwriters (and vice versa) and realized that they belonged to the same extended family as poets, actors, playwrights, artists, and directors. Not only did pop music awaken both socially and sexually, it also located its pseudo-spiritual side. Suddenly, or so it seemed, it became aware of its umbilical link to the Cosmos. It began reading the stars, listening to the rhythm of the earth; it became aware of the world not just around but within.

It was hardly a scientific study. More often than not it deployed a random, pick-n-mix approach to ancient lore, obscure cultures, bizarre beliefs, old myths, and Eastern religions. This heady, messy broth of Buddhism, Hinduism, alchemy and magick, Zen, Satanism, paganism, Scientology, witchcraft, the occult and the ritualistic, Cosmology, Shamanism, and Theosophy ushered in at least as much confusion, distress, and downright insanity as it brought enlightenment but, superficial and unfocused as much of it was, it certainly cracked open pop's chrysalis and allowed a very colorful new species of butterfly to emerge.

It became altogether routine for pop stars to toss around names like Michelangelo Antonioni and Jean Luc Godard, Lenny Bruce, Ken Kesey and Timothy Leary, Jack Kerouac, Alesteir Crowley and the Dalai Lama, Sophocles and Andy Warhol. Or to name-check the working-class authors of northern England and the civil rights leaders of black America in a single breath. It was *de rigueur* to attach yourself to a spiritual guru; a mantra was as essential to one's well-being as possessing a nose. Pop stars were alternately pushing and being pulled by the dizzyingly swift changes in countercultural currents, as well as taking lots and *lots* of drugs, getting steamed up about a variety of political and social issues, asking reams of tricky questions and generally believing they might be able to supply some of the answers too. Over and above all that, the popularity—and potency—of LSD in particular, widely regarded as offering a shortcut to spiritual transcendence, converged with fashionable classic texts such as the *I Ching* and the newly burgeoning trend in self-expression, introspection, and confidence. It all paved the way for heady and occasionally dangerously intoxicating examinations of the self.

Little wonder that death was firmly on the musical agenda. Almost uniquely, the sixties was a time when musicians not only wrote about death, but also attempted to approximate and re-create the imagined experience of dying and the state of being dead through the sounds and textures of the music. Not just "She is dead" or "Death is sad." But also "What does being dead feel like?" "What does death sound like?" "What does death *mean*?" At a time when pop music sometimes seemed like one big, high-stakes poker game, each new creative leap seeming to spur another, even more dazzlingly bold one, there was no shortage of contenders who considered these questions and thought, "Well, let's see if we can find out . . ."

This great awakening, accompanied by a desire to make heavier, more expressive music that locked into whatever mood or message the song propounded, quickly toppled over into bellowing self-importance and resulted in the formation of rock music, whereupon death started to become largely a matter of playing to the gallery rather than philosophical exploration. But for a while, roughly between 1965 and 1968, pop didn't really know or care what it was supposed to be, and consequently created some of the most beautiful, haunting, disturbing, and bizarre attempts at answering those essentially unanswerable questions, in the process travelling a whole universe away from the tragic narratives of past sob songs or the leaky sentimentalism to come.

"Eleanor Rigby," the second song on the Beatles' seventh album, *Revolver*, is very much a part of this great suite of uncommonly substantial death songs that offers a counterpoint to the carefree primary colors of the summer of love, yet its very sense of ordinariness, its determination to be firmly grounded in reality, marks the song out as unique, an anomaly in its execution if not its subject matter. Compare it to "See My Friends" by the Kinks, released a year earlier in July 1965, which, with its trancelike melody and drone, a staple of Indian music, marked pop music's first significant eastward glance. The Beatles and the Byrds would soon follow its gaze to discover where that seductive, mysterious noise was coming from.

Written as a lament for Ray Davies' sister, who died when he was 13 (buried almost unnoticed in the middle of the song is the heartbreaking line "She is gone / Wish that I'd gone with her"), the true wonder of "See My Friends" lies in the hypnotic drag of this new, spiritually weighty *sound*. The words weave in and out like a mantra, the emphasis falling on "she is gone" and "across the river," but they are at the beck and call of this dreamlike death-journey, evoking some ancient and mythical crossing between the world of the living and the dead. This is the music of loss that works upon the realm of the senses rather than relying on our ability to make a straightforward reading.

"Eleanor Rigby," on the other hand, like McCartney's similarly cool, detached "For No One," is a truly literal, literary piece of work: the language is lean, perfectly weighted, and strikes the imagination with all the whittled-down precision of a short story, rather than opting for sensory overload. Even when he had one foot in the nursery slopes of the Himalayas, McCartney made sure that the other was firmly planted in the flowerbed of some municipal park in the northwest of England. He has always felt an instinctive pull toward the ordinary people and ordinary lives that surrounded him as a child.

"I know exactly what prompted me to write that song," he told me at the end of 2007. "When I was a kid I was very lucky to have a real cool dad, a working-class gent, who always encouraged us to give up our seat on the bus for old people and this led me into going round to old pensioners' houses. It sounds a bit goody-goody, so I don't normally tell too many people. There were a couple of old ladies locally, and I used to go round and say, 'Do you need any shopping done?' Consequently, I'd hang out with them a little bit, and I always really liked their stories about war time and stuff. As a kid, all those things really fired my imagination. These lonely old ladies were something I knew about growing up, and that was what 'Eleanor Rigby' was about—the fact that she died and nobody really noticed. I knew that this went on due to my connection with lonely old ladies."

The same sure footing in the routine wasn't shared by many of McCartney's contemporaries, who—aside from Davies, perhaps—rapidly allowed themselves to be spirited away in the fast-lane to nirvana. Their number included some of his fellow band members. Two other songs on *Revolver* approached the subject of dying in a much looser way, more interested in capturing death as a full-blown sensory experience in which the writer *takes part*, rather than a detached, literal, intellectual one.

"Tomorrow Never Knows"—which according to most Beatles commentators was originally called "The Void"—is less a song in the traditional sense (it hangs its hat on only one chord and heroically keeps it there as the wind whips all around) than a cross between a meditation and a daredevil expedition into the unknown. The lyrics are cribbed from the dedicated tripper's user manual of the day, Timothy Leary and Richard Alpert's *The Psychedelic Experience*, which is itself a partial translation and rumination on *Bardo Thodol*—commonly known as the *Tibetan Book of the Dead*—the ancient funerary text of the Buddhist lamas that seeks to guide the reader through the experience of death, and their consciousness of death during the point between dying and being reborn. It's not, perhaps, a text in which you could imagine 50 Cent or Nikki Sixx scribbling notes in the margin.

Lennon wrote the genesis of the song during his third acid trip, conducted alone with the intention of embarking upon a rather scholarly journey of self-discovery. Taking its cue from Leary and Alpert, the song equates an LSD trip with an embracing of death itself—"Lay down all thought / Surrender to the void"—making explicit the fashionable belief that consistent tripping would result in release from your baser self and usher in the much-desired "death of the ego." This would free the individual and allow him to see himself and the world around stripped of all artifice, and thus experience a much deeper, truthful representation of consciousness. It was, essentially, a route to destroying the artificial self and discovering what really lies beneath. A haphazard and potentially wounding undertaking, particularly when pursued via unmodulated doses of psychotropic drugs.

According to Nick Bromell, author of *Tomorrow Never Knows: Rock and Psychedelics in the 1960s*, "the famous 'death of the ego' was experienced sooner or later by anyone who tripped—and some trippers never recovered from this experience, never regained their precarious grasp of the 'normal' way of being in the world. . . . Yet precisely because it was so terrifying, for those who did survive it the death of ego was a tempering experience. It was a vision quest in which the seeker, having passed through a hell fire that annihilates the ego, emerged on the far side more reconciled to the fate of being without a genuine self. The tripper saw that this is how it is: *no one* has a genuine self, and everyone must somehow go on nonetheless."[2]

Adherents to this school of thought, and there were many, believed that we are all imaginary constructs, continually undergoing a series of deaths that reveal ourselves in increasingly fragile yet more truthful guises. The experience of "ego death" is, in theory, about as close as it's possible to get to experiencing the psychological sensation of being dead while still being alive, and allowing the participant to carry the memory of his own death perpetually within him.

How close psychedelic drugs could come to replicating a state that takes a lifetime of solid dedication and study for Tibetan lamas to even get near remains a moot point, but if the transportative effect described in the words is open to debate, aurally "Tomorrow Never Knows" doesn't disappoint;

after all, there would have been little point in going to all the trouble of killing your ego and then singing about it over a tune that resembled "Octopus's Garden." Thankfully, the Beatles, George Martin, and Geoff Emerick pulled out their most visionary and limit-stretching production job to date in order to soundtrack Lennon's journey into the beyond. Even forty years on, tuning in from an age whose technological advances makes the world of the sixties seem as distant as the Middle Ages, the experience of listening to "Tomorrow Never Knows" is still akin to being sucked into a dark, endless vortex, built around Ringo Starr's vast, thunderingly hypnotic drum pattern, topped off with Lennon's eerily treated voice and a series of bizarre sampled sounds that give the impression of someone having a very macabre last laugh.

Even shorn of any lyrical content, it is clear that this is cosmically profound music. Working purely sensually, it brings death into focus on an intuitively personal level (I always feel myself riding atop black, swirling water, racing with increasing rapidity under an overly bright sky filled with murderous crows; you?) in the same manner as the furious guitar pyrotechnics of Hendrix's "Star Spangled Banner" brought the blood and guts of the Vietnamese jungle bursting out through the valves, or the way that the flickering threat of imminent violence, like flames licking up the walls, encapsulated in the guitar introduction to the Rolling Stones' "Gimme Shelter" made manifest the countless violent episodes occurring around the world in 1968.

Jagger describes "Gimme Shelter" as "an-end-of-the-world song." It certainly sounds like it; the Stones never were much given to solemn introspection, and when it came to death their Liverpudlian comrades were generally of a far more soul-searching bent. Lennon revisited the subject of surrendering to "the void"—again, on *Revolver*—with "She Said She Said," inspired by another, earlier, less beatific brush with acid. Hanging out in Los Angeles with the Byrds in 1965, a tripping Lennon became increasingly agitated when the actor Peter Fonda dropped in and told him about the time he accidentally shot himself as a young boy. He had technically "died" three times on the operating table, he said, and therefore knew "what it's like to be dead." Freaked out, Lennon screamed that Fonda was making him "feel like I've never been born" and eventually ordered him to be removed. In other versions of this well-aired tale, Fonda claims that Lennon said, "No, no, you're wrong" to him.

Whatever anecdotal embellishments may have been added over the years, the song is a classic slice of a drugger's death-trip paranoia and a fine example of Lennon's contradictory nature. He doesn't *really* want to know what it's like to be dead, thanks very much. At least not while he's stuck in someone else's house, and in *someone else's* version of death, a long way from home with a bunch of people he barely knew; those kind of soul-scraping expeditions were to be made under more controlled conditions, in solitary confinement, hence the later trip that inspired "Tomorrow Never Knows." Nevertheless, "She Said She Said" convincingly captures all the nervy, jittery energy bouncing haphazardly around a suggestible mind that, since it has been reminded of the subject, now *can't help* thinking about what it would be like to be hurtling toward the other side.

In his panic, Lennon casts his mind back to memories of more innocent days: "When I was a boy / Everything seemed right." He was far from alone in fixating upon this retreat into the bosom of childhood (in reality, things had hardly been "right" when he was a boy, but he returns to it often in song). The sixties preoccupation with the death-state wasn't always a projection into some great future wilderness, but often a regression into a romanticized child-state, and often beyond into a pre-birth consciousness. In many ways, much of this music isn't so much about being dead as being unborn.

The Beach Boys, or more accurately Brian Wilson, dived into the same precarious waters as Lennon and swam even farther out. Wilson described his second acid trip, a great wallop of a dose taken toward the end of 1965, in the manner of a regression back into the womb. The trip begins with the sound of sirens from nearby fire trucks. Soon, he experiences the sensation of being consumed by flames and experiencing total obliteration: "I was bathed in flames, dying, dying, and then the screen inside my brain went blank. I visualized myself drifting back in time. Getting smaller and younger. . . . I continued getting smaller. I was a baby. An infant. Then I was inside the womb. An egg. And then, finally, I was gone. I didn't exist."[3]

In light of this terrifying-sounding experience, a little later Wilson wrote "Let Go of Your Ego," a.k.a. "Hang on to Your Ego." The uncertainty demonstrated within the two differing song titles says it all about the ambivalence of his ego-death experiences: a glimpse of death brings the promise of huge self-knowledge, but it's a painful submission and one that doesn't always supply a return ticket. Better perhaps just to continue along life's way, barely skimming the surface? In the end Wilson wasn't sure of the answer and, pressured by the other Beach Boys, he rewrote the song, all references to ego excised, and released it as "I Know There's an Answer" on *Pet Sounds*, an album positively saturated with the sound of a man looking for a warm, safe retreat from reality.

He didn't find it. Paul McCartney once said that he delayed taking LSD because he was scared that he might never be able to get "back home"; in Wilson's case, seeking ego-death constituted a dangerous journey far away from home, and one that left him permanently stranded. After his third trip he talked to friends about dying, seeing the Clear Light—a phrase popularized by *The Psychedelic Experience* —and then being reborn. He vowed to approach his music differently and immediately began reworking "Good Vibrations" with the intention of creating the ultimate religious experience through music. Inevitably, it didn't take long for the whole experience to cripple him both psychologically and creatively, to the point where the childlike state became not so much figurative as literal.

Upon this axis of death, drugs, childhood, and self-discovery much of the most fascinating music of the sixties was spun into life. Little wonder the words of Lewis Carroll and Edward Lear, dark nursery rhymes full of sex, confusion, death, and disturbingly distorted views of familiar things, worked so powerfully upon the collective imagination. Lennon was in thrall to nonsense verse, while Jefferson Airplane's "White Rabbit" famously pilfered Carroll's *Alice's*

Adventures in Wonderland and *Through the Looking Glass*, using its topsy-turvy childhood imagery to reflect a sense of contemporary, drug-induced displacement that still gives off some powerfully bad vibes. The words are all very acid-friendly—"When logic and proportion / Have fallen softly dead"—but like "Tomorrow Never Knows," it is the music that suggests something more unnerving, particularly that slow, sinister bolero rhythm that keeps twisting further and further into the subconscious, until it climaxes in a rather expertly portrayed disorientation of the senses. In Hunter S. Thompson's *Fear and Loathing in Las Vegas*, it's at this culminating point in the song that the chemically deranged attorney, Dr. Gonzo, demands that Thompson throw the plugged-in tape player into the tub where he is bathing, and thus send him blasting right through the goddamn wall and into some lip-smacking great beyond. "Just tell them," says Gonzo, "I wanted to get higher."

There is nothing quite like the power of suggestion. Just as the eyes rather than the mouth provide the window to the soul, there is nothing so wonderfully magnetic as a song where everything is implied, not simply through the words but through the nuances and textures of the music. You could listen, for instance, to Massive Attack's "Safe from Harm" with all the lyrics magically excised and its sense of urgent urban threat and claustrophobia would still leap up at your throat. Similarly, the music of the Blue Nile's "From a Late Night Train" is so richly redolent of quiet desolation, reflected melancholy, and a weariness at the transience of all things that it really requires no further articulation.

It is this quasi-synaesthetic linking of sound and meaning that is so implicit in many other of the key songs and albums of the sixties, attuned as they are to the spirit of an age largely defined by mood rather than words. Love's *Forever Changes*, released in the US in November 1967, seeds the spectre of death in the listener's mind without having to make the connection too explicit. Aside from the still-arresting announcement, made on "The Red Telephone," that Arthur Lee is "sitting on a hillside, watching all the people die / I'll feel much better on the other side," there is hardly any direct mention of death on *Forever Changes*, though arguably this startling couplet tells us quite enough. And yet the whole album reeks to high heaven of decay, its lush acoustic guitars and elegant string arrangements conjuring up a dreamlike, claustrophobic edge that perfectly bears out Lee's later statement that "I thought I was going to die at that particular time, so those were my last words. I'd always had this thing about when I was going to die, man, or physically deteriorate, and I thought it would be about 26, something like that. I just had a funny feeling." *Forever Changes* is his funny feeling made beautiful, terrible flesh. "[It] was to be my last words to this life. And it's like death is in there, so it's definitely forever changes."[4]

They weren't Lee's last words, as it happens, but he was another who never quite made it out of the sixties intact. As it might be possible to discern from his less than coherent explanation, drugs played their part. The sickly sweet, euphoric womb-warmth of heroin and the intense introspection of acid combine in *Forever Changes* to make music that is as blissful as a mouthful of candyfloss but leaves a deeply bitter aftertaste. It's a peculiarly LA-sounding record, the scorching sun all but obscured by that smog; the fixed smiles masking the barely suppressed threat of violence. In other words, "for every happy hello there will be goodbye."

Like something that had been left out in the sun too long, the hippie dream had begun to curl up at the edges, leaving dark black blotches disfiguring the picture. *Forever Changes* pokes around in the ashes. Putting the needle down at the beginning of "Alone Again Or" still feels like opening a particularly large can of worms: Manson, Vietnam, the King and Kennedy murders, and Altamont are among the grubs audibly wriggling free. *Forever Changes* is not so much an exploration of death as a premonition of it, and one that greets the prospect ambiguously to say the least. Life is a bad, weird dream; death will finally wake us all up.

The music of the Doors cast the same kind of long, velvety shadow over the Californian idyll. Their debut album in particular, released at the very beginning of 1967 but recorded in the late summer of 1966, is full of invitations and invocations to death: "Break on through to the other side"; "Take a highway to the end of the night"; "This is the end"; "Picture what will be / So limitless and free." One of the reasons—aside from Jim Morrison's frequent descents into drunken, bellowing lunacy and his penchant for over-ripe poetry—that the Doors remain a band that attracts plenty of respect but little residual love is the fact that, for all the sometimes ridiculous Byronic posturing (which, admittedly, wasn't quite so hackneyed in 1966; Morrison's antics have become more clichéd with time, for which you can blame everyone from Iggy Pop to Ian Astbury and Bobby Gillespie), their music genuinely made people feel odd and sometimes deeply uncomfortable. Lyrically, they delved into subjects and imagery that frequently unsettled; musically, they were a band capable of writing thrilling three-minute beach-pop songs who could also make music that sounded like the darkest heart of the forsaken American night. "The music of The Doors, the things they chose to sing about and the way they went about it was frequently larger than life and that was uncomfortable for people," said Jac Holzman, the man who signed them to Elektra. "It put them on edge."[5]

No song more so than "The End," their rewriting of the Oedipal myth, where Morrison declares his desire to kill his father and fuck his mother. "The first time he did the Oedipal section of 'The End,' it was at the Whisky-A-Go-Go [in Los Angeles]," recalls Doors keyboardist Ray Manzarek. "That was absolutely mesmeriszing. The entire place just, little by little, came to a stop watching [us] invent it for the first time. There were sections in 'The End' which were always open to improvization, and this time it started: 'The killer awoke before dawn and put his boots on / He took a face from the ancient gallery . . .' And I thought, a *face*? Ah, a dramatic mask. The ancient gallery? Greek. Oh shit, I know where he's going! He's going to do Oedipus Rex. And sure enough, he says, 'Father I want to kill you. Mother I want to fuck you,' screaming it out. Underneath, I'm just doing a droning style Indian bass line, and when I saw where he was going I was almost going to stop him, and then I thought . . . 'Why?' We weren't singing about peace and love. We were about deeper Freudian and Jungian things. Morrison's words are loaded with symbolism. It's definitely not, 'If you're going to San Francisco / Wear some flowers in your hair.'"

This is a band, it's easy to forget, who within a few months would be appearing on *The Ed Sullivan Show*—whose music was reaching the very center of mass pop culture. It's no coincidence that "The End" was used at the beginning of Coppola's *Apocalypse Now* to signal to the audience exactly where we all are, emotionally speaking. This is Vietnam, late sixties. Another world. A world defined by death. And, ah yes, here's "The End," rising up into the flames like a be-charmed snake, hissing and coiling its way across the screen: "This is the end / My only friend, the end / Of our elaborate plans, the end / Of everything that stands, the end."

The brighter the sunshine, the deeper and darker the shadow. The Rolling Stones' "Paint It Black"—also cut in 1966—made this alternative, negative print of the sixties story explicit. Over a seasick rumba, all rattling minor keys and zinging sitar, we learn that the singer's love is dead and, as a result, the whole world has been dramatically drained of color. It's modish, and flirts with the glamour of the vaguely Satanic with a typically Stonesy lip-smacking relish, but "Paint It Black" remains at heart a thoroughly devastating and disturbing account of the impact that grief can have upon an individual, the way it seeps into every little corner and fundamentally changes your place in the world.

The combination of the driving minor-chord raga and sheer all-encompassing nihilism is still overpowering. "I look inside myself and see my heart is black," sings Jagger, and for once he sounds entirely sincere. It's arguably more powerful, in its depiction of an individual who sees death in every petal of every flower and every cuticle on every fingernail, than "Sympathy for the Devil," which is a vast Bayeux Tapestry of a song, painting death on a historical scale with audible excitement, verve and driving enthusiasm. Once again, the music is crucial to the attitude, a propulsive samba spurred on by those exuberant woo-woos; if anyone was in any doubt about the fact that death holds a certain sexy swagger, "Sympathy for the Devil" provides the antidote.

The song was inspired by Jagger reading Mikhail Bulgakov's *The Master and Margarita*, the classic Russian novel written in the thirties but only published in 1967, featuring a suave devil as its central character. The narrator in the song, however, sounds less like the devil than death itself, sauntering down the centuries as though embarking on some bloodthirsty Grand Tour, proudly talking us through some of his greatest hits: the Crucifixion, the Hundred Years' War, the Russian Revolution, the Second World War. Events are brought up to date with the acknowledgment that the present is no more civilized than the past, working in the death of Bobby Kennedy, who died while the song was being recorded in the summer of 1968. In the end, of course, we are all implicit: "You shouted out, Who killed the Kennedys?" sings Jagger, "When after all, it was you and me." Each one of us harbors his own personal devil, and when it comes to the profound social upheavals of 1918, or 1968, or 2008, casting up blame and seeking absolutes is always more complicated than it might look.

☠

It wasn't just California and London. The feeling of actively chasing the shadow of the sun, worrying away at this dark flip side of the honey-toned sixties, was on the wind and in the grooves elsewhere. Out on the east coast, the Velvet Underground's whole oeuvre conjured up the flight of the black angel through a "ghost bloodied country all covered with sleep." Given the choice, says Reed, we should "choose to go." The coruscating, savagely beautiful noise the Velvets made on "The Black Angel's Death Song" and much of the rest of their first two albums of 1966 and 1967 is well documented; but for me it's the slow, sad, narcotic drag of their eponymous third album, recorded in late 1968, that really evokes the seductive lure of foggy, eternal nothingness: "I saw my head laughing / Rolling on the ground / And now I'm set free to find a new illusion."

Just around the block, death roars through Dylan's "Like a Rolling Stone," all trussed up like Napoleon in rags, waiting to collect the girl who once convinced herself she would never have to face such routine humiliations: "Go to him now, he calls you, you can't refuse / When you ain't got nothing, you got nothing to lose / You're invisible now, you've got no secrets to conceal." Death here takes the form of social obliteration, a rubbing out of status. Its teeth marks are perhaps even more evident a year later, in the blitzed, blanked-out solo recordings from Dylan's 1966 tour, on the endless whispered dreamscape of "Desolation Row" and "Visions of Johanna." Welcome to life after the hard rain has fallen, Dylan guiding us by the hand through the charred post-apocalyptic landscape of a world that will never hold quite so many certainties again.

The sense of profound loss echoes down to Tallahatchie, Mississippi, expressed via the tight, stabbing, airless blues of Bobbie Gentry's "Ode to Billie Joe," a huge national hit in 1967 that positively throbs with humid dread. It speaks of the unnamed horrors lurking just beneath the surface of small-town normality, touching on suicide and, perhaps, infanticide.

The mysterious and terrible events that take place above the dark currents of the Tallahatchie River do not, however, happen in a cultural vacuum. These waters have already witnessed some dark episodes of American twentieth-century history. They have already brought misery and devastation by bursting and flooding the surrounding area, a tragedy recorded in Mattie Delaney's "Tallahatchie River Blues" in 1930. More damning, however, were the events of twenty-five years later, when the body of 14-year-old black youth Emmett Till was fished out of its waters. Having already been beaten, shot, and brutally disfigured by a group of white vigilantes spurred by racial hatred, Till's body was then submerged in the river using a cotton gin fan tied around his neck with barbed wire. Dylan wrote a song about it, but the event was most vividly brought to life by the Staple Singers in 1965, on the title track of their superb, live-in-church album *Freedom Highway*: "Found dead people in the forests, Tallahatchie River and lakes / Whole world is wondering, what's wrong with the United States?"

The Tallahatchie had already felt the tragedies of America ripple its waters before Billie Joe McAllister turned up. Once we're aware of this, his demise has a horrible inevitability about it. Listeners have often wondered what exactly the doomed Billie Joe was throwing off the Tallahatchie bridge that day. A dead baby? Bloodied clothes? Perhaps. But it sounds to these ears like a bag full of the nation's lost hope and innocence, dropping into the muddy waters with barely a sound and slipping slowly out of view.

And from Mississippi to Belfast, also weighed down by an awareness of its own unique, ravaged history. The title track of Van Morrison's 1968 album *Astral Weeks*—"I ain't nothing but a stranger in this world / Got a home on high"—is simply a more direct articulation of the idea that sighs through the Beach Boys' "I Just Wasn't Made for These Times," the sense of being out of place and out of step with the conscious world around you. Of refusing to view death as an enemy but regarding it instead as an accomplice in the search to find your true destiny.

The album's sparse farewell of "Slim Slow Slider," meanwhile, combines ancient Celtic folk imagery ("horse she rides is white as snow") with the blunt, prosaic starkness of a classic blues ("your brand new boy and your Cadillac"), while name-checking contemporary London landmarks like Ladbroke Grove. The result is to create a timeless landscape, neither now nor then, that will forever hold the girl he "knows [is] dying." But then *Astral Weeks* is an entire album lost in the mists of some unspecified, internalized dreamland, situated somewhere between the conscious and the unconscious, the past and the present, the country and the city, the child and the man; a place where, if we are lucky, we are still able to convene with those we have loved and lost, over and over again.

Superficially it's a long way from "Paint It Black," but these songs are all linked by a shared consciousness, a common explorative attitude, a sense of the pioneering spirit and a kind of naïve fearlessness. Taken as a piece, they offer conclusive proof that death need not be dealt with in a depressing, nihilistic, jokey, or violent way. This is, almost without exception, uncommonly beautiful music, which also confirms that a serious contemplation and evocation of death can find a home right at the center of mainstream culture if the times and the music are in harmony: all of these songs—and many more that share similarities of tone and content, such as Tim Buckley's "Song to the Siren" and the Byrds' "Everybody Has Been Burned"—were released in a period spanning a mere three or four years.

It is music that puts faith in the listener's ability to go beyond literal interpretations and trust our own instincts about what we are hearing. It shares a respect for, a depth of feeling toward, and a willingness to understand death that is highly uncommon in most pop music both before or since. It has at its heart the desire for a consciousness of our own death to become a part of our waking state, to embrace death not just philosophically but also sensually.

This is an echo of an ancient song, filtered through a highly contemporary cocktail of utopian ideals, half-assed ideologies, reckless drug experiments, and a heightened awareness of the numerous ills battering at the world's door in the mid-to-late sixties. The combined result is a type of music collectively defined by abstraction and dreaminess, its view of death at once childlike and yet highly evolved. Unashamedly self-absorbed, it has little time for bald pronouncements or the kind of stark realism that often accompany ruminations upon mortality in many other songs rooted firmly in the here and now: there are few words of comfort, few acts of brave stoicism, few wise warnings. The warnings came later, in the expressionless eyes of Brian Wilson, the mental disintegration of Syd Barrett and Roky Erickson, the derangement of Arthur Lee, the deaths of Brian Jones, Jim Morrison, Janis Joplin, and Jimi Hendrix. It is possible to see and feel—or think you've seen, and believe you've felt—

too much. Although many of these musicians put their faith in the childlike belief that they could immerse themselves in death and then climb back out of the water without getting wet, a big part of the thrill on all sides was the knowledge, made implicit in the songs, that they were half in love with the idea of going under for good. Many never resurfaced.

Though moving, joyful, often very silly and occasionally pregnant with real significance, the sound I hear reverberating through most of this music is the deep and sometimes disturbing ache of sadness; a desperate, inevitably doomed desire to regain lost innocence. Growing up and shedding our childhood skin is the most painful "death" many of us will experience in a lifetime, and here is the music that makes us feel it most keenly. This, in many ways, is the real soundtrack to the teenage experience, written as childhood recedes from view, never to return.

The fact that it was created in the sixties is no accident. One of the most piquant tragedies about living through a period of such rich creativity and bountiful promise is that it offers the engaged creative mind sporadic, tantalizing glimpses of something close to paradise. Some inevitably seek to live there all the time. But before the corpses and casualties began stacking up, this wonderful, rogue strain of death music hummed and buzzed with a naïve wonder, a lovely, liquid-like sensuality that poured out and spilled over the boundaries separating and compartmentalizing the living and the dead, in the process making us just that little bit more aware of how fragile and impermanent true consciousness really is. And also how vivid life can be.

By the time the Who's "The Seeker" comes along, released early in 1970, the moment has passed. Though the idea of exploring death as a source of enlightenment and release from the constraints of human bondage remains—"I won't get to get what I'm after / Till the day I die"—the sound is bombastic and heavy, as though the previous decade's intention to slip underneath the doors of perception like ghost music has been replaced by a desire to pummel them down using sheer, ugly, brute force. There is, too, a weary disappointment that, though arguably entirely justified, shudders through the song. "I asked Bobby Dylan / I asked the Beatles / I asked Timothy Leary / But he couldn't help me either." It sounds suspiciously like a spell being broken.

The dream was already on its last legs. Paul McCartney, there at the beginning, was a complicit party. Listen carefully and you can hear something other than the officious teacher expiring in the middle of "Maxwell's Silver Hammer" on *Abbey Road*—just after the second "bang bang!" if my ears don't deceive me. George Harrison carried on the spiritual sound quest on songs like "Art of Dying," but soon we'd be into the midseventies, wading knee-deep through cod-philosophical musings such as Emerson, Lake and Palmer's "Great Gates of Kiev/The End," which concludes "There's no end to my life, no beginning to my death / Death is life!" against the churning backdrop of a "progressive" adaptation of the music of Mussorgsky. Or the extended silliness of Led Zeppelin, where death is invoked like some primal Norse God simply to further aggrandize music that is already intoxicated with nothing other than its own over-inflated sense of significance.

The shift may also have had something to do with changing drug trends—cocaine, buzzing with an empty, chattering self-importance, had barged into the spotlight and began to supersede psychedelics, the drug that more than any other tended to encourage a more layered, explorative view of an individual's personal, private relationship with his or her environment.

Listen closely, however, and you can still hear echoes of this brief, strange episode of conjoined exploration. It's there in the early music of Pink Floyd, in Brian Eno's *Spirits Drifting*, in the music of Spiritualized, Galaxie 500, the Cocteau Twins, and My Bloody Valentine. It courses through Talk Talk's extraordinary last pair of albums, *Spirit of Eden* and *Laughing Stock*. It's there in Scott Walker's most recent solo works, *Tilt* and *The Drift*, where he eschews the demon-melody altogether, off to explore some blasted internal landscape of noise that summons up nothing but cold dread.

Perhaps most obviously it re-emerged again when dance music went overground in the eighties and beyond, helped by the explosion in the use of ecstasy, a speedier relative to LSD. Simultaneously a reaction to the soulless eighties —the impact of a decade of Thatcherism in the UK, the reign of Reagan in the US—and an increasingly hedonistic, drug-induced retreat into the realm of the senses, in its trancelike rhythms and its rising tidal wave of sound, dance music at least paid a degree of lip-service to the notion of opening up ancient portals of communication to the great beyond through a combination of the power of rhythm and the push of psychotropic drug use.

This kind of Shamanic quest for transcendence, a glimpse of an understanding of the deathlike state by stimulating the senses with sound, rhythm, and substances is a central tenet of many ancient belief systems, and although the dance music boom lacked the intellectual and cultural context that the sixties provided, it still brought moments of profound beauty and carried along with it the core idea of never being so alive as when nearest death—and vice versa.

Death needn't always be spelled out in music; it's a picture that need not always be painted with words. Nowadays, this kind of unspoken, sensual death music constitutes an engaging minor tributary, a diverted underground current. In the sixties, it was an ocean.

APPETITE FOR SELF-DESTRUCTION
Oblivion Songs

The day Pete Townshend sat down with his distressed Rickenbacker and articulated the wish to shuffle off stage before he got old, bald, and be-slippered, he tapped directly into one of rock's great articles of faith: the rather thrilling promise that our pop stars could at any moment dive head first, and willingly, into oblivion. From the extracurricular explorations of Lord Byron and Samuel Taylor Coleridge, through the activities of louche, proto-punk Parisian poster boys like Arthur Rimbaud and Paul Verlaine, right up to the Beats and the hippies, the notion of making artistic discoveries through pain, danger, intoxication, misery, self-harm, and breaking on through to "the other side" of consciousness has proved a seductive one. It has bled into popular music, to the extent that the greatest, most potent rock and roll myth of them all is that, as a medium, it requires of its truly committed participants the ultimate sacrifice of self-destruction.

This is one reason why death is so much an integral part of popular music, rarely far from any aspiring rock god's thoughts. Why else would a band call themselves the Wannadies? Or Suicide? Or the Killers? It's partially attributable to good old-fashioned peer pressure. The first of the three-acts of a rock and roll career is largely dictated by the rules of the school playground. One-upmanship, posturing, and bullying is rife. "Either take a drink, motherfucker, or get off my stage," Paul Westerberg once told his Replacements band-mate Bob Stinson, who had just successfully completed three weeks of a court-ordered rehab program for alcoholism. "It was the first time I'd seen Bob cry," recalled his ex-wife.

Some, like Stinson, who finally died in 1995 after years of self-abuse, are unable to pull back from the brink. The list of rock stars who have departed the scene early through substance abuse and suicide is as depressing as it is dull, and need not be repeated here. This is not a book about "the stupid club," as Kurt Cobain's mother accurately called it. And anyway, relatively speaking, most musicians are able to survive the worst excesses of their death-or-glory behavior to sing their songs, often the ones fondly recounting such reckless exploits, well into the third act. This late staging post is the scene of much friction as rock and roll heads toward its bus pass: aged sixty-something, do you keep pretending you're teetering forever on the edge of glamorous self-destruction? Or do you own up to your back pain and reduced taste for narcotics and morph into something a little less obviously, well, dangerous?

Most often the impetus to auto-destruct is played out not in reality, but in a virtual, parallel world where both artist and audience get to indulge rock's pronounced sacrificial streak without any need for an undertaker. From the star's point of view, when you are adored by tens of thousands, when your most banal pronouncements are given extraordinary weight and prominence, when you are looked upon by —mostly, but not always—the young and impressionable to provide solutions and guidance far beyond your remit, when you are objectified beyond mere flesh and blood, then the tendency is to regard rumors of your own mortality with a large sprinkling of salt. You push your luck, and many want to see and hear you push it as far as possible.

From an audience's perspective, the desire to see a rock star perform the ultimate act of martyrdom is at times almost overwhelming: it provides a neat ending, demonstrating a Messianic act of devotion to the ultimate rock and roll cause. Die young. Stay pretty. In an industry increasingly obsessed with constructing and protecting legacies, our desire for our favorites to stay the way they were when we loved them best is a strong one. Even those of us who live long enough to get beyond such essentially immature notions can still be heard to say things like "It's not as good as the last one." Or "I wish R.E.M. had stopped making records after *Automatic for the People.*" Or "Why did the Velvet Underground/Sex Pistols/Led Zeppelin ever re-form? It ruined *everything.*" It's simply the middle-aged version of the die young/stay pretty cliché, a polite death wish lacking the courage of its own convictions.

Most rock stars, acutely aware of their status and standing in the eyes of their fans, understand why writing about a sudden leap into oblivion strikes a chord. It is a symbolic gesture in recognition of what, deep down, an audience really wants. David Bowie made this dynamic explicit by inventing Ziggy Stardust then killing him off in "Rock 'N Roll Suicide," while the Violent Femmes wrote "Death Drugs": "We be doing the death drugs / Long live the legend!" Generations of rock stars die and die again in their songs. It's a way of acting out the ultimate rock fantasy, and it's one of the main reasons why popular music often has trouble dealing with the reality of death as a serious issue, shorn of all the iconography, glamour, and posturing—the fake, shiny, pseudo-version of death is so deeply ingrained in its DNA.

All of which helps explain why the suicide song—and its variants, songs of drug- and drink-induced oblivion—is as authentically rock and roll as the Chelsea Hotel. It's not simply a fixation of mixed-up teenagers; suicide spans myriad musical forms. It has inveigled its way into huge pop hits such as "Suicide Is Painless" from M*A*S*H and Bowie's "Jump They Say." It rears its head in Dylan's bleak Appalachian blues "The Ballad of Hollis Brown" as well as gentle, polite folk like Simon & Garfunkel's "Richard Cory" and "A Most Peculiar Man." It's a staple in the work of theatrical singer-songwriters, popping up in Leonard Cohen's "Dress Rehearsal Rag," Nick Cave's "Shivers," Lou Reed's *Berlin,* and Tom Waits' hypnotic, spooky "The Ocean Doesn't Want Me Today."

Heavy metal tremblers like "Suicide" by Thin Lizzy, "Suicide" by Motörhead, "Suicide Note Pt. 1 & 2" by Pantera (say what you want about metal, but it gets to the point) and disco tearjerkers such as "Emma" by Hot Chocolate all indulge the impulse to auto-destruct. Suicide is there in the post-punk tears of Joy Division's "Exercise One" and the giggles of the Raincoats' "57 Ways to End It All." It's a part of both mainstream college rock—R.E.M.'s "Everybody Hurts"; Counting Crows' "Black and Blue"—and stadium rock staples such as the Red Hot Chilli Pepper's "Under the Bridge" and "Stuck in a Moment" by U2. It even turns up in rap, courtesy of Notorious B.I.G.'s "Suicidal Thoughts."

In common with many teen-oriented tracks, some of these songs explicitly flirt with the imaginary glamour of suicide; others clearly and sternly denounce it. The best ones detach themselves from the Velcro-grip of rock and roll orthodoxy and do neither, and simply leave a lasting impression of such genuine human turmoil that they become oddly life-affirming. Cohen's "Dress Rehearsal Rag" ("There's a funeral in the mirror and it's stopping at your face") is so bitterly, brutally funny it can only come from a true, honest place. Nick Drake's *Pink Moon*, meanwhile, plays like a final, thirty-minute curtain call that never fails to make me want to edge as far away from death as possible, and rejoice as I do so. How can anyone not want to hear this music of honest human frailty, struggle, and confusion and be uplifted by doing so? Far from being depressing, everything looks a little brighter by the end of *Pink Moon*, and the world seems a little less unforgiving. Drake's songs of struggle scour and cleanse, rather than sink.

Joy Division's *Closer*, the Manic Street Preachers' bleak *The Holy Bible*, and Nirvana's *In Utero* were, like *Pink Moon*, the last long-playing statements of the artists involved (in the case of the Manic Street Preachers, the lyricist Richey Edwards) before they took their own lives. This being the case, the records inevitably take on a retrospective weight, throwing up nuances and portents that may or may not simply be a trick of the light. In Cobain's case, certainly, the work and the final act are inextricably linked. He had been signalling his impending death in song for years. "I Hate Myself and I Want to Die" could just as easily be called "You Love Me and You Want Me to Die," so explicitly does it deliver the message that his audience are expecting to hear. And of course, he followed through. Cobain's referencing in his suicide note of Neil Young's lyric "it's better to burn out than fade away," from "Hey Hey, My My (Into the Black)," made his death an explicitly sacrificial rock and roll act, effectively his last song, his last gift to his audience. This, rather than sticking around for the reunion stadium tour and deluxe double-CD reissues, is how rock icons earn their status.

❧

Suicide is simply the most literal acting out of the self-destructive impulse that drives popular music. A recent study at the University of Pittsburgh School of Medicine discovered that one in three of the top 279 songs on the Billboard charts in 2005 mentioned alcohol or drug use. Only four of the total were deemed "anti-use," yet that kind of black-and-white judgment hardly seems helpful. The songs that truly evoke the reality of willful self-destruction are by necessity the ones that sail closest to the wind, the ones that possess a taut, tense, ambiguous quality that doesn't lend itself easily to such cut-and-dried concepts as "pro" and "anti." Just as a convincing suicide song must convey a sense of the sanctity of life, for music to capture the essence of drug or alcohol death convincingly it has to first acknowledge how seductive that life—and the drug—can be, and yet also understand the weary, mechanical compulsion that forces us to keep returning to the bottle, or the white line, or the needle, or the pipe, over and over again. It cannot be the banal finger-wagging of the Cranberries' "Salvation" ("To all the people doing lines / Don't do it, don't do it"), and it cannot be *quite* as simplistic as "I Like Drugs" by the Simpletones.

"It's no good to write a deliberate anti-drug song and hope that it will catch," said Eric Clapton, discussing J.J. Cale's

APPETITE FOR SELF-DESTRUCTION

"Cocaine." "Because the general thing is that people will be upset by that. It would disturb them to have someone else shoving something down their throat. So the best thing to do is offer something that seems ambiguous—that on study or on reflection actually can be seen to be 'anti'— which the song 'Cocaine' is. If you study it or look at it with a little bit of thought . . . from a distance . . . or as it goes by . . . it just sounds like a song about cocaine. But in actual fact, it is quite cleverly anti-cocaine."[1]

I'm not entirely sure about Clapton's reading of "Cocaine" —it sounds more than slightly revisionist to me—but his comments explain why most Just Say No songs fail to convince. There is usually some gross over-simplification or easily detected emotional hypocrisy going on. In the case of Melle Mel and the Furious Five's "White Lines (Don't Do It)," the explicit anti-cocaine message is rather undermined by their later admission that they were all blitzed on the drug at the time; certainly, they sound like they are having a blast, which is all well and good but hardly hammers home the point of the song.

Conversely, the same kind of sweeping simple minded-ness characterizes songs that glorify brushes with drug-death, like Mötley Crüe's "Kickstart My Heart," written after Nikki Sixx's clinical death from a heroin overdose in 1989 and his revival through two adrenaline shots. It's a gift of a subject for any decent songwriter, returning from the other side, bruised, battered but hopefully wiser, but all Sixx can come up with is "I got trouble / Trouble in my eyes / I'm just looking for another good time" before promising to keep "kickin' all that motherfuckin' ass." Look who bought the myth. He has cheated death and in doing so has proved that rock stars are indeed immortal. So let's party.

The best songs of self-obliteration are detached and slightly heightened, filled with a kind of terrible, haunting beauty. The Velvet Underground's "Heroin," the Rolling Stones' "Sister Morphine," Neil Young's "The Needle and the Damage Done" and "Tonight's the Night," U2's "Bad," and Talk Talk's "I Believe in You" all tackle heroin death up close by making very beautiful, descriptive, seductive music that, crucially, takes us through the experiences, both good and bad. They're animated by some odd mix of terror, ecstasy, grace, and sorrow, playing on the tension between pursuing the traditional rock and roll lifestyle of excess and a full awareness of the terrible darkness and loss it can bring. This knowledge is there, too, in "Hotel California," a great lumbering beast of paranoid disenchantment with the limitless means of oblivion that the rock and roll dream offers. The same interplay of fascination and revulsion runs through Ian Dury's "Sex and Drugs and Rock 'N' Roll" and Elvis Costello's "Pump It Up." Too much choice might just as well be no choice at all.

It's an approach that leaves a lot of gray areas, a lot of ambiguity. Listen to Sixto Rodriguez's mesmerizing "Sugar Man," in which he falls audibly in love with the death that the drug promises to deliver: "Sugar man you're the answer / That makes my questions disappear." Or the sweet, warm, narco dream country conjured up in the Stranglers' "Golden Brown." In the end, you have to make up your own mind whether you want to go there. Which is how it should be.

"Don't judge it, or put a spin on it or moralize, just place it there for all to see," argues Mike Scott, the lead singer and guiding spirit behind the Waterboys, and a child of the Beatles, Bowie, Velvets, and the Stones. "That's okay. But if you make it sexy or get off on it or glamorize it then I don't think that's okay. Or if you persuade kids that it's okay by osmosis and the power that performers have then I don't think it's okay. Music has an effect, just like books and films."

Certainly, anyone wanting to explore heroin after hearing the bodies mount up in "Tonight's the Night" must have a very deeply ingrained desire to take it in the first place. Johnny Cash's definitive version of Trent Reznor's "Hurt," which explicitly mines the psyche of the addict, the need to feel pain to feel at all, is another unflinchingly honest portrayal of what awaits right at the end of the line of the uncomplicated dream of sex and drugs and rock and roll —the struggles, regrets, and indignities of illness and old age. What if it's worse to survive than to expire?

Strip away at the surface and you find that these are

songs of ordinary, dreary dysfunction, unafraid to swill around in the spit and the sawdust to discover why humans push themselves to the edge of their own destruction. Richard Thompson's "God Loves a Drunk" refuses to either glamorize or condemn. He ennobles his dying dipso with many admirable qualities, casting him as the wise, unrepentant fool in a harsh world populated by pedants and pen pushers, but as he "wets in his pants" and looks forward to a heaven with "no more DTs, no shakes and no horrors," it is enough to steer you off the hard stuff for eternity.

American Music Club's wonderful "Gary's Song" is similarly humorous and yet unflinching. The two drinkers stumble idiotically and hilariously around the bar, before the writer pulls us all up short by articulating the sense of unsettling guilt many feel upon realizing they have become complicit—c'mon, just *one* more—in watching someone drink themselves into an early grave: "If you drink too much you drown," sings Mark Eitzel. "And the shame of my life is watching you drown." In Bill Withers' "Better Off Dead," he kills himself because he can't kick his habit.

The truth is complicated, and it's impossible to measure the precise impact made by this diverse collection of songs and dozens more of their ilk as they cascade into the great churning rapids of the big bad world; any attempt at identifying the source, force, and influence of one particular current as opposed to another can only result in an inconclusive, and ultimately rather thankless, game of chicken-and-egg. Lynyrd Skynrd's "The Smell" and "Poison Whisky"—"The only thing that was wrong with him / Was Johnny Walker's Red / He drank ole' poison whisky / 'til it killed him dead" —might inspire one man to reach for the bottle and another to throw it away. The difference between the mind-sets on display on Neil Diamond's mellow "Red Red Wine" and the Replacements' smash-up-the-bar rampage of the same name is immeasurable. The Kinks' "Alcohol," a great little cautionary tale of a high-flyer cut down by the demon booze, is both comedy and tragedy. Which will it sound like today?

As soon as a song hits the ears of someone other than its composer its influence can no longer be accurately measured and the way its intended message (if, indeed, it has such a thing; a vast number of songs do not, and a good thing too) is diffused can no longer be controlled. This is, by and large, a positive, allowing us to take what nourishment and inspiration we need from a song that we care about. When Mike Scott claims that "my life has been changed by music" he really means that he has *allowed* his life to be changed by music, letting it move him and act upon him in a positive and highly personal way. Most of us know the feeling well.

But at least one venerable songwriter thinks that pop music has badly let down its core audience by turning a blind eye to the effect their depictions of self-destruction has on their world view. "[Teenagers] are still much more innocent than we think," says Jeff Barry. "When I was writing I was always aware that I was creating music for kids—if I had to pick an age I was conscious of I'd say 9. Young, young minds. But we're living in a less innocent time. They are bombarded with today's stuff but when they are subjected to the opportunity to hear some old pop, they usually like it. It speaks to them on a very innocent level, because when they're in school it's still—'Oooh, there's Tommy!' or, 'There's Janey!' That's as it should be, because they're not really cynical and jaded. They're just accepting what they are given by nasty, greedy adults who don't care a damn about them."

This is not an argument that can be won or lost, but Barry sounds a little like King Canute trying to stem the flow of each successive new generation, addicted to controversy and boundary-pushing. It's worth recalling that there was a time when the music that Jeff Barry wrote attracted similar opprobrium from society's elders, dismissed as dangerously morbid, reckless, and unwholesome. Good and bad influence are not clear-cut values—nor do they remain fixed for each generation.

For Will Oldham, interestingly, the responsibility of an artist is less about the accuracy with which they portray the effects of whatever drug or drink they're taking, how it makes them feel, and how much closer it may bring them to death, and more about a wider duty not to send the world spinning into the pits of some monumental, self-hating comedown through your general attitude to being alive. Oldham's problem lies primarily with those who perpetuate the subtly pervasive "beautiful loser" philosophy—the writers who glamorize stumbling from one monumental fuck-up to another as they wait for death to put them out of their misery. This is the shabby-chic end of the self-destruction market, rather than the penthouse version of fast drugs, fast women, and fast cars often peddled in rock and rap, and which usually bears the brunt of the blame.

"Something like that Townes Van Zandt song 'Waiting Around to Die': What the fuck, dude? You're a prick!" says Oldham. "And he is. Well, he was. He hates himself and he wants everybody else to hate themselves and their lives. If I'm wondering about death and scared about life, if I'm questioning, then to find some song that addresses it like: 'Well, if you feel that way the best thing might be to either obliterate consciousness, or to obliterate consciousness through the destruction of yourself completely. . . .' That's not the kind of music that I like to listen to. But if someone deals with the end of conscious existence in such a way that they're not just trying to ruin your day with it, then it can be pretty great."

Of course, one man's prick is another man's genius, and one man's song of hope is another man's song of despair. The thorny question of popular music's responsibility to its audience is complicated by the fact that it wants it both ways. Rock music in particular invests rather a lot of its self-worth in the belief that it can assert a life-changingly positive influence on individuals, but on the other hand it is all too eager to keep its head down when it comes to taking responsibility for any of the potential negatives. When we are being lectured by rock stars on the necessity of reducing our global carbon footprint, helping Darfur, the importance of loving one another, and giving peace a chance, the singer and the song not only want their audience to soak up each and every word as though they represented long lost scraps of ancient scripture, they appear also to truly believe that we actually *will*. What else could explain events like Live Earth and Live 8, not to mention the seemingly incurable need to make public pronouncements through lyrics about a dizzying array of social issues? If rock stars don't think we are listening and taking it on board, why do they bother? It can't simply be explained away by liberal guilt, charity chic, and mild-to-severe megalomania. Somewhere deep down pop stars really do believe they can Make a Difference with their music.

And maybe they can. But only in a good way? It seems disingenuous that when music is painting less palatable —perhaps more realistic—worldviews concerning violence, drugs, death, despair, the same liberal voices that expect us to drink deeply of their positive exhortations are quick to play down the possibility of the medium as a whole having any negative effect. Clearly, there is a form of delusion going on here, centered around the misconception that teenagers in particular are more likely to heed good, wholesome advice from middle-aged rock stars than fall in thrall to a little naughtiness thrown over from the wrong side of the tracks.

Most reasonably well-adjusted teenagers—and adults, for that matter—pay much greater heed to their peer group than their pop stars, and most of them are smart enough to know when they are simply having fun flirting with a trend rather than letting it lead them by the nose into the abyss. The more cynical might even venture that it would be nice to think that people paid enough attention to song lyrics these days to leave themselves open to being influenced; if anything, it's likely to be the persona and the image that makes the biggest impact, rather than the message. Either way, making a choice remains a matter of free will, and to isolate music as a prime culprit in shaping society's ills seems just a little convenient.

That is not to say that musicians should not be aware of their power and think a little before they choose to exert it, for any ends, but there are many varying shades of influence, many ways and means of seeding a certain kind of worldview into the listener's consciousness. Most songs operate below radar—we can never quite see or feel the effect they are having. Yet it surely requires an enormous, almost unfathomable mental leap to move from assessing the minute cadences of influence a song has upon an impressionable mind to specifically blaming it for an act of horror and vio-

APPETITE FOR SELF-DESTRUCTION

lence. And yet the latter scenario has occurred enough times
to make it an issue.

Death is constantly used to fuel the molten engine of popular
music, but occasionally the feeding process is reversed, or at
least that's what a smart criminal defence lawyer might see
fit to tell you and your eleven fellow members of the jury.
It's worth stating right away that no song—not even Iron
Maiden's bold but ultimately misguided tilt at "The Rime
of the Ancient Mariner"—has ever actually killed anyone,
but that hasn't prevented many three-minute wonders
from being cited as willing accomplices to some genuinely
unspeakable acts.

During live performances of his song "Irresponsible Hate
Anthem" toward the end of 2007, Marilyn Manson back-pro-
jected press cuttings concerning Asa H. Coon, the 14-year-old
boy who mere weeks earlier had injured four pupils then
killed himself in a school shooting at SuccessTech in Cleveland, Ohio. One read: "He didn't believe in God and instead
worshipped Marilyn Manson." Reviews don't come any better
than that for the tiresome Manson. He'd been here before, of
course. Eric Harris and Dylan Klebold, responsible for the
deaths of thirteen people and injuring many more at Columbine High School, Colorado, in 1999, were also automatically
pigeon-holed as Manson disciples simply because of the way
they looked. Back then, any teenager wearing a black trench-
coat, black glasses, and an angry countenance was automatically labelled both a potential mass-murderer and a Manson
acolyte to boot. As he says in Michael Moore's documentary
Bowling for Columbine, "I'm a poster boy for fear because in
the end I represent what everyone's afraid of."

In fact, Manson is simply the media's most willingly
complicit hate figure, the number that always comes up on
speed dial whenever teens go off the rails. He relishes this
kind of attention, because the alternative is to be judged on
his music and then he would really be in trouble. Manson is
the dread warning ghost of Christmas future for every emo

band in the land: a 40-year-old forever doomed to play the part of the sulky teenager, perennially intent on shocking his parents.

No, what Harris and Klebold were listening to most avidly was European industrial dance music by KMFDM, whose music and lyrics they appropriated to endorse their fascination with Nazism and the notion of declaring war on humanity. Certainly the lyrics of KMFDM's "Son of a Gun" can be viewed as confrontational—"Shit for brains / Born to kill / All are equal / No discrimination / Son of a gun / A simple equation / Son of a gun / Master of fate"—but it was still faintly shocking when the band felt the need to put out a press release mere hours after the Columbine shooting, such was the public pressure to find some kind of explicit—preferably non-American—scapegoat for this tragedy:

"First and foremost, KMFDM would like to express their deep and heartfelt sympathy for the parents, families and friends of the murdered and injured children in Littleton. We are sick and appalled, as is the rest of the nation, by what took place in Colorado yesterday. KMFDM are an art form—not a political party. From the beginning, our music has been a statement against war, oppression, fascism and violence against others. While some of the former band members are German as reported in the media, none of us condone any Nazi beliefs whatsoever."

It's not always easy to feel sorrow in your heart for German industrial bands who write songs called "Urban Monkey Warfare," but this sad state of affairs elicited a real pang of sympathy.

How much credence can be given to the idea that popular music should shoulder even a tiny part of the blame for events like Columbine is largely a matter of individual choice. It requires a belief that music has such a profound and direct influence upon the behavior of some of those listening to it that it can essentially over-ride all other instincts, all other concepts of right and wrong. It's a notion that has its adherents. What follows are a few of the most high-profile examples of songs that have become embroiled in real-life court-room dramas through the years. We'll look briefly at the crime. We'll attempt to discern the true intent of the musician in the dock. Then we'll deliver a verdict.

The Eminem Killer: In May 2004, a 21-year-old British man named Christopher Duncan attended a karaoke night in a London pub. During an evening of heavy drinking he sang and danced along to several Eminem songs. At the end of the night 26-year-old law student Jagdip Najran willingly went back to Duncan's flat, where she was sexually assaulted, bludgeoned with a metal baseball bat, and stuffed into a suitcase. She took up to ninety minutes to die.

It was a singularly horrific incident, but it attracted a significant amount of additional media attention due to the extracurricular details. It's unlikely that anyone in the press would have called Duncan the "Eminem Killer," for example, or pointed out some general similarities between the way Najran died and a fantasy sequence in Eminem's video for "Stan," had Duncan not idolized the rapper to the extent that he dressed like him, styled his hair like him, and even sported identical tattoos. It was enough—much more than enough—to ignite a media frenzy, especially when rap, that most combustible and maligned form of modern music, was thrown onto the fire.

"Stan" is a breathtakingly skillful, thrilling, layered piece of writing and rapping. It is, ironically, a song concerning the dangers of obsessive fandom, written by a man in the first flush of global fame and notoriety warning his audience against taking the songs too literally and investing too much of themselves in the projected image of the person singing them.

The eponymous fan is obsessed with Eminem, addressed in the guise of his alter-ego Slim Shady, and writes his hero a letter. He has already sent several that have gone unreplied, but his latest letter is generally cordial and conversational, emphasizing what Stan believes are the similarities between the two men: "How's your daughter? / My girlfriend's pregnant, too / I'm 'bout to be a father." The second verse takes the form of another letter, veering between worship and violent anger that Eminem still hasn't replied. It is clear to anyone listening that Stan is unhinged: "Sometimes I even cut myself to see how much it bleeds / It's like adrenaline, the pain is such a sudden rush for me / See everything you say is real, and I respect you cause you tell it."

In the third verse, still without a reply from his idol, the rejected Stan tries to impress Eminem by driving his car off a bridge with his pregnant girlfriend locked in the trunk, before doing so making reference to another Eminem song, "Kim," in which the rapper fantasizes about slitting his wife's throat. "Hey Slim, that's my girlfriend screamin' in the trunk / But I didn't slit her throat, I just tied her up, see I ain't like you / Cause if she suffocates she'll suffer more, and then she'll die too." This is the part, it was claimed, that Duncan mimicked in the murder of Jagdip Najran. As Stan drives off the bridge, we hear tires screeching and a crashing sound, followed by a splash of water, a clear throwback to classic death songs like "Leader of the Pack" and "Dead Man's Curve" and, it could reasonably be argued, one that places the song in its true context of rather dark comedy, emphasizing the heightened, cartoon version of reality that we are hearing.

The fourth verse is Eminem finally responding to his obsessed fan, apologizing for not replying earlier, and expressing discomfort and disbelief at the way Stan is unable to distinguish between reality and fantasy: "What's this shit you said about you like to cut your wrists, too? / I say that shit just clownin', dogg / C'mon, how fucked up is you? / You got some issues, Stan / I think you need some counseling." At the last minute, Eminem realizes that he heard about Stan's death-plunge on the news a few weeks ago without realizing who it was, mutters "Damn!," a punchline of sorts, and the song ends.

This, then, is not a *gratuitously* violent song. Neither is it blind to the influence and responsibilities that come with being a musician. Instead, it directly addresses them, pointing out that the events a rapper writes about are not things he himself does or necessarily condones, and that there is a whole stretch of clear blue water between the life described in the song and the life lived in reality. It's a get-out clause, clear enough, a way of having your cake and beating it to death too, but it's also a statement of artistic freedom, making it very plain to any rational listener that these songs and the events they describe should be regarded as nothing more than part of the great spectrum of entertainment that runs from rap to Rollerblading, from *Lassie* to *Hellraiser*.

During his trial it emerged that Duncan was a desperately damaged man, his childhood scarred by abuse, drugs, and alcohol. He was high on ecstasy, LSD, and alcohol at the time of the murder. It's unlikely that watching videos and singing songs that depicted acts of extreme violence would have helped either his short- or long-term state of mind, but there were clearly other issues driving him to kill that took far greater precedence than a song. The prosecuting team didn't labor the Eminem connection, pointing out that there was "no sensible explanation for what he did." Duncan's defense lawyer said, "Things in his life were falling apart. He was a murderer waiting to happen." All of which suggests that Duncan's immersion in a twilit fantasy world that twisted the imagined life of a rap star together with his own was a symptom of an existing and profound disturbance, rather than the result of him being groomed by a song that had been heard by literally millions of other people without causing any direct dire consequences. Christopher Duncan was sentenced to life in 2005. The blunt question behind it all is this: if he had never heard Eminem, would he still have murdered? The only answer can be yes. Would he have killed Jagdip Najran in the same horrific way if he hadn't seen the video to "Stan"? Almost certainly. After all, ignoring the rather crucial fact that one is fictional and the other real, the two methods of murder aren't actually that similar at all. And if he paid such close attention to his idol, why didn't Duncan heed the song's final verse where Eminem suggests to his fan that this isn't a particularly smart way to be behaving? All the evidence suggests that "Stan"—a number-one record in the UK and an enormous hit single worldwide—isn't sufficiently poisonous to turn previously decent members of society into monsters.

What made this case more than a mere media feeding frenzy, however, was the fact that it opened up a debate about the more insidious, low-level impact of much modern music, particularly rap. The likelihood is that Duncan became fixated with certain elements of "Stan" and the music of Eminem in general because, as the judge said upon passing sentence, he had "an abnormal and unhealthy interest in violence and in particular, sexual violence toward women." In this regard, some saw Eminem as being guilty of a rather less specific complicity. A columnist in the free-thinking British newspaper the *Independent* used the incident to argue that "artists who glorify violence towards women contribute to a climate of ambivalence in which slapping a girlfriend, knocking a wife about, even a bit of sexual violence . . . are regarded with a staggering degree of indulgence."[2]

How that accounts for the countless cases of sexual violence that occurred in society long before the record player, TV, or internet had been invented isn't clear: was violence toward women any less "indulged" in the western frontier towns of the 1800s, or London in the eighteenth century? Possibly not, but it remains a valid point. The columnist went on to make a link between Eminem's eminent cultural position and the case of over 340 women and girls who have been murdered over a period of twelve years in the town of Ciudad Juarez, on the Texas-Mexican border, apparently to widespread local apathy. Nothing exists in a vacuum, was the gist.

Perhaps more significantly, Moby got involved, posting on his website around the same time: "Now we find out that a British man who is obsessed with Eminem killed a woman with a metal baseball bat and stuffed her body into a suitcase. Am I being 'too uptight' for not seeing the humor in this? Before this British man brutally killed this woman he was singing Eminem songs in a karaoke bar. Maybe there's no connection. Maybe there is. It's disgusting that we even have to ask that question. It's disgusting that people in the media and the press have celebrated and glamorized music and musicians who write lyrics that glorify misogyny and homophobia. Any employee of a record company or journalist or radio programmer or MTV employee who has promoted and celebrated misogynistic or homophobic music should be ashamed. You have blood on your hands, and you should be deeply, deeply troubled at the culture that you've helped to create."

Strong, emotive, unambiguous stuff. These are broadly the same sentiments as expressed earlier by Jeff Barry, but they can't be attributed to the vagaries of the generation gap, nor can they be dismissed as part of the usual chorus of reactionary commentators who love nothing more than jerking their knee in the general direction of popular culture's latest mutation. Partly, they *can* be attributed to a mutual loathing between Moby and Eminem that resulted in various instances of tit-for-tat name calling over the years. However, there is no question that Moby's comments represent a widely held viewpoint: one that's more complicated than simply claiming that a crime can be committed specifically because of the impact of a single song or an artist, and one that can't be so easily shrugged off. The net of complicity is cast far wider than just one song, one man, one art form, one country, or one easily digestible answer. We are all culpable in our varying degrees of complacency when it comes to tolerating songs of violence and aggression. And until we've ruled ourselves out of this enquiry, there's little to be gained by casting stones.

☙

Charles Manson:
"Before 'Helter Skelter' came along, all Charlie cared about was orgies."—Manson Family member Paul Watkins[3]

The Beatles' *White Album* seems forever fated to make cameo appearances in the footnotes to the lurid tale of Charles Manson and the Tate-LaBianca murders committed by his "family" of acolytes in Los Angeles in 1969. Manson, a habitual criminal since his pre-teens with a string of serious convictions and psychological problems, regarded the Beatles as the "four angels" of the apocalypse referred to in the Bible in Revelation 9 (a mere couple of stray vowels removed, of course, from "Revolution 9"), citing the image of "prophets with faces as the faces of men" but with "the hair of women" as further evidence that the mop-tops turned full-blown hippies were here to announce Armageddon.

When the *White Album* was released in December 1968, Manson picked it apart and found plenty of clues to add substance to his self-fulfilling prophesy. His belief in an impending race war, black rising up against white, was, he claimed to his followers, vindicated not only by the album's name— it is actually called *The Beatles*, of course, but its stark white cover gave it its common title—but also by messages hidden in many of its songs. Several tracks on the album, including more obvious confrontational candidates ("Revolution," "Revolution 9"), and far less likely ones ("I Will," "Blackbird"), were also obsessed upon and wildly (mis)interpreted by Manson as calls to violent revolution.

Manson named the coming race apocalypse Helter Skelter after the Beatles song, and began a murder spree in August 1969 "to show blackie how to do it." When members of his "family" of disciples murdered Gary Hinman they daubed "political piggy" on the wall in his own blood; when they slaughtered Sharon Tate, Jay Sebring, Abigail Folger, Voytek Frykowski, and Stephen Parent two nights later it was "pig"; when they stabbed Leno and Rosemary LaBianca to death the following evening the slogans left in the victims' blood were "rise," "death to piggies," and "healter skelter [sic]."

All the slogans were directly inspired by songs from the *White Album*; the clues were designed to lead people back to the source, where they would, apparently, be able to decipher a manifesto to murderous chaos, rise up and join in. What Manson may have overlooked is the fact that the *White Album* eventually led the police to him, and finally helped to bring him and his cohorts to justice. Almost a month after the crimes were committed the authorities were still no closer to finding the culprits, until a member of the LAPD team investigating the LaBianca murders noted a possible connection between the bloody writings left at the house and "the singing group the Beatles' most recent album." The *White Album* is, then, both accomplice to the crime and damning evidence against it—a situation that neatly illustrates the dangers of putting too much weight on the power of music; it can be bent to fit whatever purpose you so desire.

Unleashing slaughter on this scale is clearly the result of a profoundly diseased, though very powerful, mind, and even a cursory awareness of the kind of trouble Manson was in prior to 1968 makes it obvious that his insanity was ingrained somewhere a little further in his DNA than can be accounted for by a couple of spins of "Martha, My Dear."

Particularly when you consider the substance of the songs. Clearly, Manson heard something in the lyrics of "Helter Skelter" that the rest of us missed. The Helter Skelter is a British fairground attraction that involves sliding down a spiral chute on a mat—hence the opening line, "when I get to the bottom I go back to the top of the slide"—an experience used, loosely, in the song to suggest the exhilaration and out-of-control thrill of a highly sexual love affair. Manson, on the other hand, simply took the first syllable of the title and ran with it, believing it referred to an imminent descent into the bowels of Hell. He prepared an enormous hole called the Bottomless Pit—again, a reference to Revelation 9—in the grounds of the "family" ranch in Death Valley in the Californian desert, from which he and his tribe would emerge once the bloodshed was over to wrest control of the world.

Musically, "Helter Skelter" is what can only be described as Macca Metal, a terribly tame attempt to ape the growing trend for "maximum heaviosity," as Woody Allen once put it, that was thundering into popular music courtesy of bands like the Who, Cream, and the Jimi Hendrix Experience. It fails rather miserably. As Ian MacDonald points out in *Revolution in the Head*, the Beatles were "the quintessential sixties four-piece, their natural inclinations were for balance, form, and attention to detail, and in straining to transcend these obsolete values in 'Helter Skelter' they comically overreached themselves." It is a tendency that marred a few of their later songs. "Helter Skelter" wasn't so much dark and threatening as ersatz-heavy rock punching well above its weight.

"Piggies," meanwhile, is bad but not *quite* criminal. It is smug, sour, and pious, but on the surface—which is all jangling harpsichord and the bitter scratch of strings—it contains all the threat and menace of a wet sponge applied to the shins. In many ways the sentiments sum up all that went wrong with the hippie movement as it travelled from its original come-all-ye ethos to a holier-than-thou misanthropy that was rather spiteful. It's not an anti-police song, despite the popular counterculture coinage of "pigs" as a derogatory term for the police. The mention of piggies in "their starched white shirts" suggests Harrison's blunderbuss is aimed at the mythical Man, the besuited pillar of the British establishment, in which case such Beatle-friendly types as George Martin would presumably be among the number being sneered at.

"Piggies" has the sing-song, edge-of-violence tone of a dark old nursery rhyme, with very little evidence of any belief in the redeeming qualities of humanity, which makes it a far less palatable piece of music than the more rowdy "Helter Skelter." In the end, it is an example of the worst kind of anti-all-life song that Will Oldham talks about. But aside from the mildly interesting denouement that shows the piggies consuming themselves—"Clutching forks and knives / To eat their bacon"—this is hardly revolutionary satire. There is vitriol, but it's hard to really know or care who it is directed toward, so muffled and unlovable is the song, while there is only one couplet that could in any way be interpreted as a call to arms: "In their eyes there's something lacking / What they need's a damn good whacking." In the context of the song, only a madman, or perhaps a devout *Sopranos* watcher, would interpret "whacking"—part of a line written by Harrison's mother, Louise, a middle-aged housewife from Liverpool who occasionally taught ballroom dancing—as denoting anything other than a brisk slap on the back of the legs with a wooden spoon. But it is certainly a nasty little song.

Manson was a frustrated, wanna-be rock star who wrote songs and hung out with the Beach Boys. This has led some people to confuse his status as the orchestrator of mass murder with that of some kind of rock and roll martyr. Perhaps this explains why the most enduring link between popular music and the terrible events of August 1969 lie not in what came before, but what came after. Manson's murderous deeds swiftly engaged the popular imagination and spawned a subculture of sects, many of them with a musical bent, that are vaguely unsettling.

A rough estimate at the end of the Millennium counted around seventy rock groups playing his music and writing songs in support of Manson. Though his songs have been recorded by mainstream acts like the Beach Boys, Guns N' Roses, and Marilyn Manson, more representative of the level of his appeal are bands like Righteous Pigs and Edge of Sanity, who write lyrics like "A mastermind with intentions for chaos / Carnage / He murdered through will / Go now my children / There is work to be done / The pigs must be slaughtered / Our battle's begun" ("Helter Skelter," Edge of Sanity).

When you factor in the many other bands who have been inspired into existence by serial murderers—Macabre, the Ian Brady Bunch, Dahmer, Divine Pustulence—it says more about the relationship between music and murder than perhaps anything else. It's a perfectly legitimate subject, but it's hard not to come to the conclusion that the human condition is more than capable of plumbing deep, dark depths that no mere pop song will ever be able to fathom. It certainly requires little assistance from the Beatles as it does so.

☠

Last Exit: The penultimate track on U2's monumentally successful 1987 album *The Joshua Tree* was, according to Bono, a song about "a religious man who became a very dangerous man," which prompts the immediate—if uncharitable—thought that perhaps it's simply a work of straight autobiography. In one particular respect, however, the song is no laughing matter. In the trial of Robert John Bardo, an Arizona man accused and found guilty of murdering young actress Rebecca Schaeffer in Los Angeles in July 1989, one of the first high-profile cases outlining the dangers of celebrity stalking, Bardo's defense blamed "Exit" for driving him to commit the murder; he even danced in court when it was played at his trial.

"Exit" is clearly and unambiguously a song about murder, situated in the middle of the album's final three songs, which guitarist Edge once rather theatrically dubbed the Suite of Death (the others are "One Tree Hill," a requiem for Greg Carroll, a friend of the band who died in a motorcycle accident, and "Mothers of the Disappeared," about the vanished political prisoners in South America). It was perhaps the most musically intense and lyrically dark song U2 had released up to that point—during the album sessions it had the working title "The Executioner's Song"—and was apparently almost left off *The Joshua Tree* for those very reasons. Lyrically, it describes a fanatical, delusional interpretation of God's will taken to obsessive, deadly ends. The killer has something of Reverend Harry Powell about him, Robert Mitchum's crazed preacher man in the 1955 movie *The Night of the Hunter*, a man who, as the song puts it, got "the cure" but went "astray." Bono would introduce the song in concert as being about "a man who misunderstands the hands of love."

In Bardo's case, his corrupted obsession was not with executing the will of God but with impressing a minor celebrity, the 21-year-old star of the eighties TV soap *My Sister Sam*. However, he shares with "Exit" the sense of a dangerous devotion to an idealized object that has ceased to bear any relation to reality. There are some similarities, too, in the way the murder is described in the song and the way Bardo later described the moment that he killed Schaeffer. In the song: "Hand in the pocket / Finger on the steel / The pistol weighed heavy / His heart he could feel / Was beating, beating, beating, beating / Oh my love, oh my love, oh my love, oh my love." In Bardo's words: "I grabbed the door . . . gun's still in the bag . . . I grab it by the trigger . . . I come around, and kapow, and she's, like, screaming . . . aaahhh . . . screaming . . . why, aaahhh . . . and it's like, oh God."

In the end, of course, this kind of detail was all a mere adjunct to a cut-and-dried case of a man who had been seriously and demonstrably ill since his teens. Naturally, during the trial more credence was placed on the mass of evidence stacked against him, including the testimony of one of his former teachers who described him as "a time bomb on the verge of exploding," than on Bono's "hands of love." Bardo was sentenced to life without parole in December 1991. A year previously, the Los Angeles police department began the Threat Management Unit to deal with Stalking and Harassment cases, and by 1993 all fifty states had anti-stalking laws in place. U2 last played "Exit" in concert in 1989.

🎸

From the Sublime to the Ridiculous: The subliminal message is a long-serving and loyal accomplice of the dedicated conspiracist. If it's subliminal *and* Satanic, all the better. Usually, its existence is celebrated by people with a quite astonishing amount of time on their hands playing records backward—this is a game best played on vinyl or tape, but there are ways of doing it with modern technology if you so wish—and trying to decipher a hidden statement with some nefarious intent. There are those who hear "Oh, here's to my sweet Satan" as "Stairway to Heaven" spins drearily from Z to A, while others claim Queen's "Another One Bites the Dust" subliminally states that "It's fun to smoke marijuana." A line in Britney Spears' "Baby One More Time," played backward, apparently becomes "Sleep with me, I'm not too young," but I've got a feeling that's actually one of the original lyrics.

In particular, the music of the Beatles has been dredged from shore to shore in search of hidden messages, especially after the oddball conspiracy theory began doing the rounds in 1966 that Paul McCartney had died in a car crash and his place in the band had been filled by a look-a-like. It may sound a trifle improbable, but how else to explain the final

refrain of "Strawberry Fields Forever," where many will
swear they can hear John Lennon claim, "I buried Paul" in
a deep, slow voice? And at the end of "I'm So Tired," what
would seem to most untrained ears to be a chain of gobblede-
gook is actually, when played backward, the deeply poignant
lament "Paul is dead now, miss him, miss him."

If subliminists ever accidentally spun the records of the
Beatles in the *right* direction they would have heard Lennon chide, on "Glass Onion," "Here's another clue for you all:
the walrus was Paul," in exasperated mockery of such willful codifying. Whether that message ever really entirely hit
home is open to question. There's an old joke about the man
who used to sit up all night listening to Beatles songs, trying
to work out just what it was John Lennon actually meant in
his lyrics. One day the man sees Lennon being interviewed
on a TV show, where he is asked what his songs are about.
Lennon replied, "They're just words, really, just words that
rhyme." "God," says the man. "I spent hours trying to work
out what he meant by that. . . ."

Boom boom. Pink Floyd's swipe at over-analysis on their
1979 song "Empty Spaces"—"Congratulations, you've just
discovered the secret message. Please send your answer to
Old Pink, care of the Funny Farm, Chalfont"—should perhaps have been an end to it, but the spectre of the subliminal message and divining a band's true, hidden intent has
surfaced again and again, occasionally in less light-hearted
circumstances.

In 1990, a civil action was brought against the British
heavy metal band Judas Priest by the parents of 20-year-old
James Vance who, alongside his best friend, 19-year-old Ray
Belknap, had made a suicide attempt in 1985 after listening to Judas Priest songs, including "Better by You, Better
Than Me." Vance and Belknap—drunk and high—went to
the playground of a Lutheran church in their hometown of
Reno, Nevada. Belknap placed a shotgun under his chin and
pulled the trigger, dying instantly. Vance followed suit but
somehow survived, horribly disfigured. He killed himself
three years later by overdosing on painkillers, but before he
did so his testimony ("I feel like they murdered Ray"), backed

by his parents and Belknap's parents, dragged Judas Priest, and by implication heavy metal and popular music in its entirety, into the dock.

"Better by You, Better Than Me" was a cover of a song originally written in 1969 by Gary Wright of English progressive rock band Spooky Tooth. Judas Priest's version of the song, recorded in 1978, is an innocuous little hard rocker that would hardly incite you to switch radio stations, never mind commit suicide. It is rather vague lyrically. In light of being hijacked by future events, a few lines stand out—"Tell her the world's not much living for"; "They'll find my blood upon her windowsill"—but like so many weighty sounding rock songs, you would be hard pushed to argue that it was *about* anything. In any case, it had been making its way in the world for nearly two decades without incident before the incidents of late 1985.

It wasn't really the lyrical content that was under scrutiny, however, as much as the assertion that a repeated subliminal message—"Do it!"—had been included in Judas Priest's version of the song, and that this had acted as a command to the boys to commit suicide. As Halford pointed out during the trial, even if the existence of such a "message" was proven to exist—which it never was—the meaning of the phrase is entirely dependent on the listener's interpretation. Of all the phrases with which to drag a band into court on the accusation of inciting suicide, it would be hard to think of one that had less intrinsic meaning than "Do it." It signifies nothing. It contains no message of its own. If it could inspire one person to take their own life, could it not also help another become a doctor or an Olympic athlete? Or to wash their car? The fact that such an empty phrase could be regarded as making the difference between living and dying is a damning illustration of the general ignorance regarding the reasons behind the emotional isolation that plagues many teenagers. Do it? Uh, okay! If only life, in many ways, were that simple.

During the trial, covered in the excellent but thoroughly depressing documentary *Dream Deceivers: The Story Behind James Vance vs. Judas Priest,* the defense team successfully illustrated the extent to which an accidental combination or collision of sounds could lead to the creation of what could be interpreted as dangerous, outrageous, or simply silly messages; it was particularly easy to "hear" things once the idea of what you were *supposed* to be hearing had been seeded in your mind. Halford later dryly commented that if Judas Priest had wanted to insert subliminal messages into their music, instructing their fans to kill themselves could be regarded as somewhat counterproductive to their long-term career prospects. They would prefer to insert the command "Buy more of our records."

Humor proved by far the most effective weapon in puncturing the absurdity of the case. Bill Hicks memorably referred to it throughout 1991 in his stand-up routine: "What performer wants his audience dead?" he pondered. "What are these guys in the band doing: 'I'm sick of the free drugs, the free booze and the groupies. . . . I'm in a rut and I want out. . . . What if we kill the fucking audience? Could I go back to my day job? I could sell shoes again.' It doesn't make a lot of sense."[4] Hicks' contemporary, Denis Leary, went a little further: heavy metal bands should put *more* subliminal messages in their records: "Kill the band, kill your parents, *then* kill yourself."

The suit was eventually dismissed as the extent of both boys' long-standing unhappiness and the highly dysfunctional nature of their respective domestic environments became abundantly clear; they each had issues with drugs and alcohol that were symptomatic of problems that could be laid at a door much closer to home than that of a Brummie metal band. And yet even as the case unraveled, the central irony—that a group playing heavy metal, a genre that often attempts to articulate the desperation felt by many teenagers, cut adrift in the modern world and unable to communicate or reach out to those closest to them, was being blamed for *creating* that isolation and desperation—was one that still appeared to escape many of the participants.

The case was not without precedent. "Suicide Solution," a song about the perils of alcohol, written by Ozzy Osbourne's bass player Bob Daisley as a warning to the former Black

Sabbath hellraiser about his own drinking—"solution" in this context meaning "liquid" rather than the Answer—was dragged through the courts following the death of 19-year-old John McCollum in October 1984. Having spent the night listening to several Ozzy Osbourne albums, McCollum took a handgun and—with his headphones still on and Osbourne's music still playing—shot and killed himself. "Suicide Solution" was not playing at the time, but he had been listening to it earlier in the evening. At the time of his death, McCollum was suffering from alcoholism, depression, and emotional instability.

His parents filed a lawsuit against Osbourne and his record company, Columbia, which came to court in 1986. The basic thrust of the case was that the lyrics, music, and overall "aggression" of Osbourne's music encouraged self-destruction. Furthermore, the suit claimed that Osbourne and his record company knowingly targeted adolescents, a vulnerable group struggling with myriad emotional difficulties during a time of enormous transition, and that therefore they should have been aware of the effect this music would have on those listening. Namely, that there was a real possibility that it would drive them to suicide.

There was more. A testimony by the McCollum family lawyer argued that "Suicide Solution" contains a "Hemi-Sync," an audio process often used in sleep induction and relaxation aids designed to create a "frequency following response" in the listener through the use of sound. In other words, it had a hidden hypnotic undertow. Not only that, but there were apparently extra subliminal lyrics in the song that weren't included on the lyric sheet that said "Why try, why try? Get the gun and try it! Shoot, Shoot, Shoot," followed by a peal of Ozzy's trademark Satanic laughter. Listening to the song today, it is genuinely impossible to decipher anything other than an extemporized, screeching mish-mash of syllables toward the end of the song. But the combination of all these techniques, claimed the prosecution, left Osbourne with blood on his hands. And this time it wasn't the blood of a dead bat.

Of course, the case was thrown out. We haven't lost our collective minds quite yet. It was dismissed not on the basis that anybody looking beyond the song's punning title would be able to tell that it did not advocate suicide, but on the rather simpler and more graceful grounds that Osbourne had the right under the First Amendment to write and sing about whatever he liked.

☠

Which brings us back to where we came in: the distance between the expression and the deed, the fact that to understand an essential part of the appeal of rock and roll you need to first understand the dual levels that it works on. Popular music constantly evokes death and destruction because they are concepts that signify real dedication to the cause and give fans an illusion of the kind of total emotional commitment they crave: I would die for you. But songs of suicide and self-destruction are not written as a set of literal instructions or a manifesto. Pete Townshend chose not to die before he got old. Leonard Cohen didn't after all put on the final show after his jittery dress rehearsal in front of the mirror. David Bowie didn't die alongside Ziggy Stardust.

On dismissing an appeal against the initial Osbourne ruling, the Californian Court of Appeal concluded: "Lyrics and poetry cannot be construed to contain the requisite 'call to action' for the elementary reason they simply are not intended to be and should not be read literally. . . . Reasonable persons understand musical lyrics and poetic conventions as the figurative expressions which they are."

The only sane and fair conclusion. But both the trials of Osbourne and Judas Priest were cautionary tales that reflected badly upon a culture that had become accustomed to looking for scapegoats for the ruined lives it saw scattered all around rather than taking responsibility for its own role in their downfall. Watching *Dream Deceivers: The Story Behind James Vance vs. Judas Priest*, the willing abdication of responsibility and power—by society, parents, and teenagers, in very different ways—is both achingly sad and enraging. In the age of Columbine and Virginia Tech, it remains a relevant story twenty years on. The voices that whisper "murder" at pop music rather than face often deeply unpleasant home truths are the only subliminal messages we really have to worry about. In the end, it has nothing to do with music at all.

6
SWEETNESS FOLLOWS?
Into the Great Beyond

In a handsome old stone house in the north of Scotland, a pebble's throw from the seashore and even closer to the spiritual retreat that dragged him here, as though magnetised, from New York a decade or so ago, a pale, thin man goes cheerfully into battle once again against a formidable foe. "I have a disagreement with the common concept of death," says chief Waterboy Mike Scott, positioning himself somewhere between mystic and mischief maker. "I've always felt, since I was a little boy, that death is not the end. And so all my songs that deal with death or the songs I cover all focus on this idea. That's what it's about for me. It's a battle of ideas. I disagree that death is the final curtain and all that bollocks. I don't believe it, and so I sing songs that contest that idea. And I enjoy doing it, putting those songs into people's minds and knowing that they have to think about it. I'm presenting an idea that may be counter to the one that they hold."

Scott has certainly put his money where his mouth is over the years. A flick through the Waterboys' back catalog confirms that he writes his own version of gospel music. Sometimes his beliefs are articulated solely through the joyous yelp of his voice and the vitality of his music; at other times, it is more explicitly expressed: "Love That Kills," "I've Lived Here Before," "Spirit," and "I'll Meet You in Heaven Again" ("Like the meeting of two rivers / All will be delivered / When I meet you in heaven again / Some say it's over / As if there is no more / But death is not an ending / Death is but a door") could hardly be clearer statements of the belief that the soul continues to live on after the body is cold in the ground.

If songs written by other people convey Scott's beliefs even more clearly, then all the better. The Waterboys have covered George Harrison's "All Things Must Pass" and Bob Dylan's "Death Is Not the End," as well as reinterpreting old gospel blues such as "The Gospel Train Is Coming" by the Guitar Evangelist, "Meet Me at the Station" by Brother Williams' Memphis Sanctified Singers, and Minister Thomas Whitfield Company's stunning version of Roscoe Corner's "Soon as I Get Home," which concludes with the declaration, rolled out over and over again on a rising tide of uplifted voices, that "I'm gonna put on my robe, and tell the story / Of how I made it over." It could, I suspect, make even the most entrenched atheist ask for directions to the nearest house of worship.

For Scott, a man who follows no strict religious doctrine but harbors a deep spiritual belief, the sound simply tells him that he has been right all along. Music may or may not have the ability to make us change our minds about the big issues, but it can certainly help explain what has previously lain unexpressed within our own hearts. "I remember when I first heard 'Soon as I Get Home' it had a profound effect on me," he says. "It touched me in a very deep place, the eternal part. These songs are like confirmation. Like a sword in the war of ideas. It's almost a crusading thing—I'm going to fight this lie with the songs. They touch the part of me that knows there is continuation after death. It's not a question any more."

It's an almost enviable certainty, but it's worth bearing in mind that, though they speak clearly and directly to Scott, some of these songs are open to differing interpretations by other artists. Just as the strangest, silliest little song can sometimes touch us in an unexpectedly deep place—carrying all kinds of personal messages, memories, hopes, and dreams within a seemingly banal code—even the most affirming song can be turned upon its head: Nick Cave's version of "Death Is Not the End," for instance, holds little truck with the notion that there is a better life waiting beyond. As it lurches on and on, gathering momentum like a hearse with faulty brakes, Cave and his hell choir, including Polly Harvey and Shane MacGowan, instead take an increasingly wicked delight in suggesting that all our earthly suffering will simply go on and on for eternity. "It seemed a good punch line," he later cackled.[1] Same words, whole different attitude.

Scott is a genuinely fearless writer, refusing to bow to any external notions of what is expected of him, and who furthermore displays a consistent willingness to upset the accepted rock conventions by engaging so earnestly with matters that stretch far beyond the immediate here and now. It means that, spellbinding though the Waterboys can be, he doesn't always hit the bullseye. The listener can occasionally feel a little excluded from such cast-iron notions, especially considering we are living in far from certain times. But his songs certainly force you to think. And feel. Of all the songwriters I interviewed on the subject, only Richard Thompson shares a similarly clear consciousness of what he is doing when he approaches death and its ultimate meaning. Perhaps it's because he also has a firm spiritual foundation. Thompson has believed in reincarnation from a young age, which filters directly into songs like "Meet on the Ledge." And as he gets older, he is attempting more and more to write songs that "embrace" the idea of dying, such as "Sunset Song," the closing track on his *Sweet Warrior* record, where Thompson drags his suitcase into the hallway and makes to leave for the final time.

"I wrote it [as] a valediction," he says. "It's saying the big goodbye. As I get older I start to think about those kind of things and I start to write those kinds of songs. It preoccupies you more; hopefully it becomes a friend rather than an enemy. Society sees death as an enemy but I think you have to try to embrace death and to 'die before you die,' is the expression. It's something that is always there, you have to deal with it in any belief system. It's important to understand how to live and it's important to understand how to die."

But it's not only a firm spiritual footing that can give a writer confidence in dealing with death. Across the Atlantic, in Kentucky, another pale skinny fellow faces the same dread foe as Scott and Thompson with a similar thoughtfulness. Will Oldham approaches mortality from a very different perspective, both as a songwriter and a man. Instead of writing songs that attempt to fathom the unfathomable, to in effect reopen the channels between earthly existence and an afterlife to prepare for the journey, he embraces the notion that death is simply inevitable. Rather than invest our faith in a contemplation of what may or may not happen beyond that, he makes music that celebrates death's omnipresence in order to give added meaning and piquancy to the fact that we are alive: the more we emphasize the certainty of our deaths, the greater the imperative to celebrate life. "Death to Everyone," one of his most compelling songs, is a musically muted but lyrically ebullient clarion call to drink, fuck, and make merry "since we know an end will come / It makes our living fun."

"'Death to Everyone' came from a religious fanzine that was handed out called *Death to the World*," says Oldham. "It was pretty intense. It seemed to be kind of bearded young men with monkish uniforms, with a faraway glassy look in their eyes, who were turning away from dissolute lives towards lives of greater purpose. *Death to the World* meaning, for them, death to having any tangible goals or passions.

"And every time I saw this fanzine it gave me such glee, seeing this phrase, knowing that behind it was a striving for a greater grasp of consciousness and direction and pretty much a greater grasp of life. And so I started imagining someone abandoning purpose for trust. Because whatever death is, it's coming. You can trust in that. It doesn't matter what you believe, it's coming. Nothing you can do about it, there's no way to prepare more and no way to know more about it. Not even the most brilliant artistic and scientific minds have come to a conclusion about death that helped any great sector of the population. So that's a *relief*. It's like, well, *they* couldn't do it, so I'm not going to be able to do it. Let death itself do it. And in the meantime, *carpe temporem*."

But we're already ahead of ourselves, which is ironic. Because what happens *next* is not a subject often discussed in popular music. As a medium it instinctively craves the thrill of the chase and the drama of the event itself, but doesn't willingly face up to the consequences. In rushing to capture the excitement of the eternal now that it instinctively swims in, it shows no compunction about leaving the messy aftermath out of frame as it pans away in search of the next emotional—or actual; don't let's forget Tommy and Laura—car crash. Pop music homes in on adrenalin like a heat-seeking missile, but what happens when the moment cools?

Bruce Springsteen once said that he wrote "The River" to depict the way life tends to unfold after the hot, fleeting clinch in the back of a car ends and reality comes crashing back in. It's not a terribly popular approach, even less so when it comes to contemplating death. The "wham bam!" of the moment of impact holds a much stronger visceral appeal than the complications that it ushers in, the endless, fathomless depths that stretch out afterward. Popular music adores clean breaks and absolutes: so what am I supposed to do, it asks, with all this *nothingness*?

All of which explains why records that focus on what happens after we die without resorting to schmaltz, macho clichés, or vague platitudes are relatively thin on the ground. A study of all the US top forty songs between 1958 and 1993 that specifically talked about death—songs as diverse as Sam Cooke's "Frankie and Johnny," Gilbert O'Sullivan's "Alone Again (Naturally)," Elvis Presley's "In the Ghetto," Curtis Mayfield's "Freddie's Dead," "The Killing of Georgie" by Rod Stewart, Gordon Lightfoot's "The Wreck of the Edmund Fitzgerald," Barry Manilow's "Copacabana," and Aerosmith's "Janie's Got a Gun"—discovered that their collective responses were enormously limited and overwhelmingly favoured avoiding the specifics.

The study went on to observe that "the primary focus in rock and roll death songs is on the act (how the person died) and not upon the less exciting effects of death. The deceased, both figuratively and literally, is seldom laid to rest. In fact, [these songs] support the illusion that the deceased is not gone, so the memory of the deceased is allowed to live on. Unpleasant thoughts and images are avoided, with ceremonies and rituals occurring at some later time."[2]

In other words, pop is a recidivist hit-and-run offender. Again and again it struggles to provide a response to the aftermath of death that is anything other than trite and simplistic. Cowardly, even. There has never been a shortage of songs where the hero shoots, kills, turns on his heel, and heads for the border: this is the outlaw-cowboy view of death that is sold in everything from gangsta rap to "Hey Joe" and, while fun, it is an emotional and moral cop-out to anyone seeking something with a little more substance. Neither does pop music have an aversion to filling the vast, gaping holes of grief with angels, long sleeps, and benevolent spirits: this, while comforting, is essentially the same view of death as that described to a young child when its pet hamster dies.

Neither approach can make much claim to face the facts. There is comfort here but neither approach is much *help*. Both feel like diversions. Pop music isn't proud. It's more than happy to leave bullet-riddled stiffs strewn in alleyways, or back away from corpses entangled in the wreckage of their souped-up Chevrolets, or spirit the soul to Elysium on the wings of naked cherubim for celestial deliverance, or gaze back fondly and remember the good times—but it rarely ever troubles itself with the messy business of burying its dead. It almost never picks up a shovel and actually digs. Or sticks around for the funeral and the ensuing long dark nights of the soul. Whether it's "The Baby" by Blake Shelton or "Demolition Lovers" by My Chemical Romance, "How Can I Help You Say Goodbye" by Patty Loveless or Johnny Cash's "Give My Love to Rose," typically the curtain falls at the deathbed scene.

But what then?

Back in the real world, most of us have little choice but to face the consequences when death comes calling close to home. We can't all head for Mexico on horseback. Aside from all the grief, guilt, anger, and regret, there are endless tasks, duties, and questions. We may be seeking some guidance on practical matters of what do to, and how, and when. It's very possible we'll be confronting, renewing, or rearranging our spiritual beliefs at a time of pressure and confusion. It's a big ask, but where can we go to hear something that is talking this kind of language?

"Unfortunately, strangely, it's so rare that a song that deals with death actually parallels somebody's real experience with death," says Will Oldham, absolutely correctly. "Usually it's [presented] as a dramatic event like suicide or self-destruction, or something that deals with ghosts." The reality is rather more prosaic. The world doesn't stop and, usually, we also choose to go on.

Amid all this spiritual torment and very real physical pain, there are practicalities to be negotiated. One aspect almost never covered in pop music is the struggle with day-to-day drudgery. That numb period between the death-bed and the burial or cremation is a torturous one, a sad little series of days that almost everyone experiences at least once in a lifetime but is almost never discussed in music.

The practicalities of burying a loved one can be disorienting. Does the cost of the funeral, the scale and magnitude of the send-off, somehow indicate the extent to which the departed was loved? Is it possible to reconcile the wishes of the dead with the wishes of their remaining family? Lucinda Williams' "Fancy Funeral" lays down a few home truths: spend your money on groceries and bills instead of long black limousines and ostentatious bouquets—goodbyes can still be beautiful. Describing the song as "a literal portrayal of what I'd gone through planning my mother's funeral,"[3] Williams recalls how her immediate family's plan for a simple cremation service in Arkansas were scuppered when her mother's Louisiana relatives insisted she be given a traditional burial in the family plot back home.

"It really turned into a Flannery O'Connor/Eudora Welty/ Carson McCullers short story," she says. "I found myself in a funeral parlor for the first time in my life shopping for caskets. It was the most surreal and disturbing experience I ever had. Funeral parlors should all be shut down. They just suck you in. As soon as you walk into that door you might as well forget it, you lose control over your senses. In my case, my mother just died and I was the one paying for everything and handling it all. And somehow I got talked into buying all this stuff I knew my mother didn't want. It was a nightmare. I had to write that song."[4]

This is real nitty-gritty death music. Eels' "Going to Your Funeral" describes driving to his sister's funeral after her suicide, and "feeling I could scream," while Luke Haines' "What Happens When You Die?" takes us even deeper down into the murky, awkward realities of death: smoke-filled rooms, long drawn faces and even longer silences, the struggle to find the right words. Guilt. The overwhelming desire to be somewhere else. "A doctor from the north, a friend of the family / Is comforting your mother drinking in the front room / I couldn't make the funeral I know it really hurt you / Right now it just seems to me everybody's dying." This, truly, is a world without angels.

There again, death would not be death if it wasn't accompanied by some mildly hysterical laughter. Funerals in particular are often punctuated by odd flashes of black humor. Worried that you might start giggling at the service? "That Day Is Done," written by Paul McCartney and Elvis Costello, and performed by both, definitively by the latter in the company of the Fairfield Four, is a wry song that illustrates that humor, sadness, and love aren't mutually exclusive emotions. Whenever Will Oldham has to attend a funeral he finds practical guidance in the quiet, comradely dignity of Cindy Walker's "Jim, I Wore a Tie Today," particularly the version on the first Highwaymen record.

"It's about a guy attending the funeral of a friend of his, who he knew would be stuck in the casket with a suit and tie on, so he wore a tie himself, 'even though I look like a dummy.' When you go to funeral after funeral, a tie can become some kind of issue: who do I dress for? Do I dress for the bereaved, or the person who died? It's nice to have that song. It has a lot of silly lines, but it stuck with me and it helped me find levity in that situation, that I wasn't completely on my own in my own strange predicament." Comfort and guidance, it can be soothing to remember, sometimes appear in the oddest places.

The really tough bit for a songwriter is approaching the subject of what happens after the body disappears from view. "I've always had spiritual songs on my albums: 'There's a Rhythm,' 'Tell Me Again,' and songs like 'God Loves Everyone' and 'Golden Hills,'" says Ron Sexsmith. "At that time in my life things were really falling apart: I'd been dropped and my family fell apart and I was trying to look for something a bit deeper and more reassuring, just for myself. And I guess I'm still there. Since I was a kid everyone has always told me there is a better place waiting for us. There's gotta be something better than this! It's amazing to be alive but you look around at all the horrors all over the world . . . "

Most musicians strive to be hopeful. They try to retain a sense of optimism in their music, but many have only an inkling of what they actually *believe in* once the body has negotiated the ashes to ashes, dust to dust part. Uncertainty and confusion are interesting emotions but tough to capture; it's not easy to convey these thoughts and articulate them for a wider audience in any kind of literally meaningful way.

"I don't think the view of heaven and hell that I grew up with is particularly meaningful for me anymore," says Neil Finn, the songwriter and lead singer of Crowded House, who was raised in New Zealand as a Catholic. "I can't say that I've got something else in place, but lately I've been trying to concentrate on the idea that if this is all there is it's not that bad. I'm not a Buddhist and I don't follow the disciplines of it, but I do love the idea that the Dalai Lama speaks of that happiness is attainable [on earth]. If that's as close as we're going to get to heaven I don't think there is anything wrong with that. It doesn't make you a less deep or even a less spiritual person not to believe in heaven and hell."

What artists like Sexsmith and Finn do well is transmit a kind of humanity and warmth through their uncertainty; they emit a sense of reassurance and communality that can give comfort in virtually any situation. Hence, probably, why a song like "Don't Dream It's Over" is listed on a website for grief songs. This is also the default setting of many of rock's bigger, less abrasive groups: R.E.M., U2, Counting Crows, Coldplay, all bands who trade in a vague, nondenominational spirituality that rarely wades into the muddy waters of specifics, but rather conveys a sense of life-is-tough-but-we're-all-in-it together.

R.E.M.'s "Sweetness Follows" and "Find the River" represent the closest many of us get to a forming a rounded belief system these days, ping-ponging between mortal torment and vague hope and spirituality. The former track approaches death tumultuously, "readying to bury your father and your mother." It's all reaction and reflection after the event, but this is not a song of memorial. Instead, it offers a bumpy, hellishly hard-won feeling of solidarity to those left living: "It's these little things, they can pull you under / Live your life filled with joy and wonder . . . sweetness follows." The music is suitably turbulent, rumbling, and rolling, but by the end of it there is a sense of having come through something fiery and fearsome, emerging on the other side scorched but cleansed and somehow stronger. "Find the River," the last song on the *Automatic for the People* album, by contrast offers a more peaceful ride, a sense of the natural and spiritual world intertwined, the dead flowing into some great eternal ocean. Something not to be feared but embraced: "All of this is coming your way."

This kind of song doesn't operate on a particularly literal level. It relies on the full combination of the words, the music, and the voice to make the emotion resonate. Remove one part and it loses most of its potency. Its considered vagueness displays a fluent mastery of the language of our times, but anyone seeking a more concrete and tangible depiction of what happens when we die needs to look elsewhere.

The *really* strong-hearted might have a listen to "Worms," a wriggly little traditional song rendered with tongue-in-cheek relish by the Pogues in 1988, which spells it all out in terms that have more to do with biology than theology. "The worms crawl in and the worms crawl out / The ones that crawl in are lean and thin / The ones that crawl out are fat and stout / Your eyes fall in and your teeth fall out / Your brains come tumbling down your snout / Be merry my friends / Be merry."

This kind of blunt certainty has a cheerful, solid quality that can be rather comforting. More typically, however, in the immediate aftermath of dealing with death nothing seems to make sense, even if—perhaps especially if—you do believe in the existence of some specific spiritual entity. The vain search for some over-arching plan in God's actions lends Depeche Mode's "Blasphemous Rumours" its dolorous bitterness and anger. This isn't a Godless universe; instead, the argument lies with a God who views life as a joke, death being the ultimate didn't-see-it-coming punchline. Based on the true story of a teenage girl who survived a suicide attempt, recovered, and subsequently "put her faith in Jesus Christ," only to be hit and killed by a car at age 18, it reiterates the aspect that many people find hardest to deal with about death: the sheer randomness. You can't choose when it comes; it isn't fair and its meaning isn't usually easily decipherable.

"Anytime," one of Neil Finn's finest solo songs, makes this fragile hold on existence explicit but chooses to be more affirming: "I was thinking of the chain of events: 'I see a dog upon a road / Running hard to catch a cat . . . ,' and it being interesting to suggest the idea that your life is hanging in the balance at any given moment," says Finn. "And actually, it's not gloomy or morbid to think so. It's useful and life affirming to remember that." It's the same sentiment as "Death to Everyone" and Flaming Lips' "Do You Realize?," turning the terror and absurdity of existence and the certainty of death into a compulsion to instill every moment and relationship with meaning, beauty, and purpose. Martin Gore, the man who wrote "Blasphemous Rumours," may not agree. If there is a loving God, why would He do this? Because, according to Gore, He has a "sick sense of humor / And when I die I expect to see Him laughing." Rest assured, it's a point of view that has its fair share of takers.

♠

It's often impossible to contemplate the death of those close to us without it impacting—often rather drastically—upon our own fears and beliefs. Which is why John Donne's famous "Send not to know for whom the bell tolls / It tolls for thee" is as resonant today as when it was written nearly four hundred years ago. Lou Reed, the smart-ass English student gone heroically bad, will be familiar with Donne's dictum, and he's not above giving it a modern twist. Any song by Reed called "Cremation: Ashes to Ashes" is unlikely to invoke memories of a day spent chasing fireflies at the fairground and, indeed, this transpires to be a very forthright song about the day "they burnt you up, collected you in a cup."

Part of the mortality-fixated *Magic and Loss* record, it finds Reed standing on the shore, ruminating on death after watching the ashes of his departed friend being tossed into the sea. It doesn't take him long to see images of his own final resting place reflected back at him in the wild Atlantic waters. "The coal-black sea waits forever / When I leave this joint at some further point / The same coal-black sea will it be waiting." (Only Reed, incidentally, could refer to the great miracle of planet earth as a "joint" and get away with it.) Particularly in recent times, death so close at one's elbow calls into question not the solidity of our spiritual faith, but the very absence of it. The lack of any concrete certainty comes under interrogation. Not, can I still believe? But why, why, why *can't* I believe?

The music of atheism, agnosticism, and fear of the void is rather interesting. Writing about the absence of faith and the absence of knowledge puts some modern writers in a vulnerable position, an uncomfortable stance that often creates compelling music. Like the Streets' "Never Went to

Church," in which the death of Mike Skinner's father leaves him admitting that he "never cared about God when life was sailin' in the calm." Now he's hit a bit of rough water, he's "gonna see a priest, a Rabbi and a Protestant clergyman." Luke Haines, in "What Happens When We Die," opts for "talking to a stone, wailing at a grave / Maybe when a year has past, go and see a medium / I'd really like to know what happens when we die."

This is a very twenty-first-century noise—the low hum of existential panic in times of hardship. "Thoughts of a Dying Atheist" by Muse looks at death "through a faithless eye / And the end is all I can see." Well, what else can you reasonably expect? The finality of the End is the whole deal with atheism, but this sounds suspiciously like someone who doesn't quite have the full courage of his (non)convictions. Anthony and the Johnson's "Hope There's Someone" displays a similar dread of the unknown, a beautifully conveyed mixture of curiosity and terror that many of us will recognize: "I'm scared of the middle place / Between light and nowhere / I don't want to be the one / Left in there."

It's left to Tom Waits, who has been around the block a few times, to knock their heads together and dish out a large helping of Home Truth pie: "The wind through your bones / Is all that remains / And we're all gonna be / Just dirt in the ground." It sounds marginally preferable to Rap Heaven, which, if Notorious B.I.G.'s "Suicidal Thoughts" is any indication, isn't going to be much fun: "God will probably have me on some real strict shit / No sleepin' all day, no gettin' my dick licked."

Never mind the dick for once, Biggie. What about the soul? The cast-iron certainty displayed by Mike Scott that our physical existence is but a staging post on the soul's eternal voyage, with death a mere "trysting point," might be less compelling—and perhaps less personally resonant to many of us—in a purely dramatic sense than listening to all these existential wobbles, but he is far from alone in his belief in the continuation of the soul after death. He makes the connection between the power of his belief and the power of his music more explicit than most, but in fact his views on death are broadly shared by many mainstream songs, particularly in commercial country and modern R&B, genres that still maintain their links with their spiritual roots in the Methodist and Baptist churches.

A song like "One Sweet Day" by Mariah Carey and Boyz II Men is really just the sentiment of a hundred gospel testimonies filtered through the medium of a disappointingly anaemic song, the depth of feeling measured out in melisma. It's clearly a popular song, but this transcendence-by-numbers is a real problem for me, because words and sentiment alone cannot show me a glimpse of heaven. I need to be transported there by the will of the performer and the sheer force of the music so that, even if I don't share the belief, I am at least alive to the feeling that it truly exists in someone else's head and heart, which is the only place it matters, after all.

On this basis, "One Sweet Day" fails to deliver. And so do the likes of "When I Get Where I'm Going" by Brad Paisley, a premonition of heaven as a happy hunting ground where we will meet all those we have once loved, or "I Believe" by Brooks and Dunn; these are in effect pale retreads of scores of old-time hillbilly songs, such as Hank Williams' "When God Comes and Gathers His Jewels."

There are hundreds of these kinds of songs, from Celine Dion's "Fly" to Hilary Duff's "Someone's Watching over Me." Entire websites are dedicated to them. Browsing through just one, the Memorial Music Library, is an odd experience. Several of the near-six-hundred listed songs "about grief and loss" are actually about no such thing. Of course, grief changes your perspective on everything; people reach out for whatever is at hand. The most unlikely song might prove capable of bringing comfort and relief, just as the lightest, sunniest song can become a Trojan Horse, sneaking sorrow in under cover of darkness to shatter your heart into splinters. That is the great miracle of music.

Even so, in the Memorial Music Library the connection between song and subject sometimes seems to extend only as far as the title. Listing Bob Dylan's "Don't Think Twice, It's Alright"—that bitter, deluded little put-down of a departing lover that contains the line "you just kinda wasted all my precious time"—as a song designed to bring peace and comfort to those grieving seems a little odd. Similarly, "I Have a Dream" by ABBA or Belinda Carlisle's "Heaven Is a Place on Earth" just seem a little tangential. Again and again, it's clear that certain words and phrases in the title act as emotional triggers: Dream. Angel. Heaven. All right. Home. Fly. Very often, the message conveyed in the lyric will be one of sadness coached in terms of vaguely expressed consolation. Typically, the verse might outline the trials of the life lived, the occasional highs and inevitable regrets, while the chorus will offer resolution and comfort, portraying the afterlife as a safe, warm retreat.

Sarah McLachlan's "Angel"—"You're in the arms of the angel / May you find some comfort there"—is one of the most popular songs in this mould, one that typifies the soothing, uncomplicated view of the great beyond that an enormous amount of people reach out for in times of loss. I should confess straight away that it does very little for me, but there are plenty of others for whom it brings deep solace. Darryl McDaniels of Run DMC, no less, claims that hearing the song on the radio saved his life when he was struggling with acute depression in 2003.

But the wider impact of a song like this, the means by which it takes on a kind of hymnlike status, is essentially viral. It gets picked up by films and TV shows—*City of Angels, Dawson's Creek, Cold Case*—as an easily accessible piece of music that unambiguously (and unchallengingly) signposts loss, grief, and the afterlife through its slow piano melody and clear words. Later, it becomes unofficially linked to a communal catastrophe such as 9/11 and, suddenly, the emotional reaction to it is less about the depth of meaning contained within the song and more about the song's ability to create the context for a shared outpouring of emotion. Nowadays, we find comfort in the fact that we know others are finding comfort in exactly the same place. That's how popular sad songs work: they surrender themselves to the will of the masses. Robbie Williams' "Angels" is exactly the same. When you hear "Angel" or "Angels" it packs a punch containing an accumulated weight of emotion and a shared history that far exceeds its literal meaning.

This is not for one second to denigrate or deny the very real and vital comfort these Angel songs bring. If the Memorial Music Library proves one thing, it's that these songs do touch people, over and over again, and that their writers are —often consciously, sometimes calculatedly—performing a kind of public service. Though they often deal with death and dying by using the kind of platitudes found inside Hallmark cards, platitudes can do the job. Hallmark won't, after all, be going bust anytime soon. Sometimes—most of the time, perhaps, especially in the darkest hours—a dose of harsh reality is plainly not what is required. Sentiment is a powerful means of connection, and one that most of us are grateful to lean on at certain points, particularly as we grow older. Expressing it is certainly nothing to feel guilty about: who wants to exist solely on a diet of Slipknot and G.G. Allin?

The problem lies not in the message but the medium. To my ears these songs too often lack the conviction to convey their message; they are comfort blankets rather than stout, sturdy staffs with which to soldier on, and I can't help thinking that at some point, stranded somewhere out in the vast moonlands of grief, their words will simply not be enough. Not for me, anyway. Furthermore, invoking beneficent angels isn't necessarily more constructive, or more intrinsically positive or spiritual a response to death, than the hit-and-run songs that leave the bodies lying where they drop.

The popularity of the Angel genre ties in with an increasing vogue for songs that level the varying gradients of loss into one long, flat road, songs that can be used to grieve the end of a relationship or mourn the death of a loved one: "It's So Hard to Say Goodbye to Yesterday" by Boyz II Men, "Nobody Knows" by the Tony Rich Project, "The Dance" by Garth Brooks, even "Good Riddance (Time of Your Life)" by Green Day. Are these handy, altruistic multipurpose songs? Overly vague, rather cynical attempts to cover as much of the market place as possible? Or simply poorly written, the thought process loose and flabby?

The answer will vary wildly depending on the individual tuning in, but it's fair to say that the end of a relationship —however painful—and the end of a life are not the same things, and that any song that can be freely interpreted as being about either is perhaps in danger of being just a little too wishy-washy. For bespoke solace about the end of a relationship, I'd recommend "It's All in the Game," preferably Van Morrison's towering reinterpretation, for the optimist, and, well, "Don't Think Twice, It's Alright" for the rest of us.

And for beautiful, melodic depictions of the great beyond? There's no harm in moving a little further away from the modern commercial conveyor belt. Prefab Sprout's "Doo Wop in Harlem," with its promise of a "reunion in the air," is hard to beat for sheer beauty, but it doesn't have to be all hushed reverence. Norman Greenbaum's "Spirit in the Sky," by contrast, is a blues-gospel-garage stomp that pulls off the trick of making the afterlife sound like an after-show party. It's a gloriously incongruous track: a Jewish man declares he has a friend in Jesus in a song written in fifteen minutes flat as a cynical exercise in making a commercial hit. Intriguingly, the very act of composing the song (which has enjoyed its own afterlife: it was a huge UK hit for Doctor and the Medics in 1985 and still buzzes out of radios all over the world) gave Greenbaum a fresh perspective on his own spiritual beliefs, releasing something from deep within him that he wasn't aware of at the time he wrote the song. He now proudly displays testimonies on his website from people who have played the song at funerals and found a sense peace in its message.

Sometimes, it's the songs least burdened by their own self-importance that mean the most. Other times, the opposite applies. At the other end of the scale is "They Won't Go When I Go," written after Stevie Wonder's near-fatal car accident in 1973 when mortality was clearly uppermost in his mind. Even so, it was his sister-in-law Yvonne Wright who wrote the text, a dizzying meditation on the afterlife, a world to be aspired to and *earned*, where all the human detritus of the conscious world, the liars, the greedy, the sinners, those with unclean minds, would be shaken off like fleas from a sick dog's pelt.

It's maddeningly self-righteous in its moral superiority, its flaunted piety, but there is a solemn stateliness to the song and an almost terrifying conviction that combines to make me believe that, whatever awaits for the rest of us, *this* "destiny" and none other is what awaits Stevie Wonder. He poured as much care and consideration into the music as Wright did to the words, garnishing the decorous piano melody with a series of mesmerizing, cascading vocal arrangements. It contains a depth that you can measure; a weight that you can practically feel. This is way above and beyond the constraints of most pop or soul music, and I can hardly think of another song that so fervently presents the next world not just as an active, existing entity, but as something that is so clearly superior to the one we are experiencing right now. It's a lot to strive for. But are we worthy?

In the end, perhaps we should all listen to the late Laura Nyro: "I'll never know by livin' / Only my dyin' will tell." Wise words, and true. And by now she'll know. But for many the stakes are too high to wait until the final end before we form some kind of crude hypothesis, whether it's the enviable sureness of Mike Scott; the focused preparation of Richard Thompson, writing his songs with the care and precision of an old captain guiding his vessel into harbor for the last time; the affirming *carpe temporem* philosophy of Will Oldham; or the rather more extemporized patchwork quilt that many of the rest of us, including Neil Finn and Ron Sexsmith, use to keep the chill wind at bay.

If we're going to resort to pointless speculation—and we must—I'd prefer to build my rickety foundations upon the words of Tom Waits. Not the ones about us becoming dirt in the ground; I already know all about that. I find something a little more hopeful, and solid, and simple to which to nod a quiet assent in "Take It with Me," the one that says that "all that you've loved / Is all you own." The one that tells us "In a land there's a town / And in that

town there's a house / And in that house there's a woman /
And in that woman there's a heart I love / I'm gonna take
it with me when I go."

That would be enough, surely, for any one of us. Just
hearing it is enough for me.

Come here you sweet bitch, give me that pussy let me
   get in your drawers
I'm gonna make you think you fuckin' with Santa Claus
I'm not playing, I'm trying to fuck tonight, ya heard me?
Clothes off, face down, ass up, C'mon.

You possibly won't be surprised to learn that the lines printed above were written, no doubt with a thesaurus in one hand and a bitch/Uzi/Hennessey cradled in the other, by the most obediently clichéd of the current crop of gangsta rappers, 50 Cent, taken from his track "U Heard Me." Except—forgive me—I'm cheating a little: only half of those choice words come from "U Heard Me." The first two lines are from "Make Me a Pallet on the Floor," an epic and highly explicit blues recorded by Ferdinand "Jelly Roll" Morton in 1938. It's hard to see the join, isn't it? And Mr. Morton has plenty more where that came from: plenty of cunts, bitches, and guns, not to mention a belt full of knives that will "cut your fuckin' throat." His tastes also extended beyond the violent braggadocio of "I'll drink your blood like wine" to encompass a fondness for bling: he had diamonds embedded in his teeth and reportedly owned some two hundred tailor-made suits.

The point is this: appearances can be deceptive and our memories are often conveniently short. There is a tendency to talk about rap, especially gangsta rap, as though it were an entirely new species, a virulent new strain of music that could only have thrived in the peculiar social conditions of the late twentieth century. In particular this applies to the aggression of the delivery, the highly violent stance of the lyrics, the bludgeoning sexism, and the vast, faceless body count. But in reality, although the specifics and the details are thoroughly modern, gangsta rap's glossily updated death music did not spring into life from a vacuum. As "Make Me a Pallet on the Floor" and many more recordings by bluesmen (and women) like Two-Time Slim confirm, crudely expressed tales of sex, violence, and exaggerated acts of derring-do told in the first person are hardly new to music. One thing, however, is certainly true. Rap is the only major musical form of current times that would be significantly diminished—both in terms of its content as well as the sheer quantity of releases—if it was somehow prevented from writing about murder. It has become the big bad daddy of the death song.

❧

Gangsta rap announced its existence and agenda with a flourish: the cops are at the door and our hero makes his dawn escape out through the bathroom window—"gold on my neck, my pistols close at hand"—before embarking upon an adventure that takes him out onto the streets, rolling dice, admiring and admonishing women, getting caught by the police with an Uzi, a .44, and a hand grenade in the back of the car, heading into jail for a seven-year stretch, then out again and straight back into the arms of gang life. The adventure ends with a shoot-out: "Six punks hit, two punks died / All casualties applied to their side." It's a film—gangsta rap has always been the most cinematically savvy of musical forms—in under four minutes.

Ice T's "Six in the Mornin'," released in 1986, certainly had precedents, most notably Schooly D's "PSK (Park Side Killers)" and Toddy Tee's "Batterram," an effectively literal account of the interaction between LA drug dealers and the police, who had started using armored cars to ram-raid crack houses: its opening declaration neatly sums up the shifting rap tides from east to west in 1985: "In New York (it's comin') / In Detroit (it's comin') / In LA (it's comin'—No, it's here!)." No song, however, had previously articulated the life of a "player" so clearly and in such detail as "Six in the Mornin'."

"It wasn't truly the first gangsta rap, but it was just the most blatant," Ice T tells me over twenty years later. "It was inspired by 'PSK.' The only difference was the 'PSK' is a very vague record, the lyrics aren't as blatant as 'Six.' Gangsta rap was . . . written from the perspective of the street hustler, so we took that and ran with it. When you are actually in the game, the game is glorious to you, so you are kind of bragging on it because that's your perspective at the time."

The song's recurring refrain—"didn't have time to ask"— perfectly captured the jumpy, quick-fire nature of these lives, where "just livin' in the city is a serious task" and life-changing decisions are made on a whim. It has humor, sass and style but it's not without self-knowledge either: as he slips out onto the city streets, Ice T describes himself, with some pride, as a "self-made monster." In reality he was a 28-year-old ex-Marine named Tracy Marrow, originally from New Jersey, but this was not the time to let reality get in the way of legend building.

In any case, "Six in the Mornin'" was a long way from the South Bronx and the break dancing and block-party ethos of the east coast hip hop pioneers of the early-to-mid-seventies, the scene that grew up around the groundbreaking cuts of Kool Herc, the Sugarhill Gang, Kurtis Blow, Afrika Bambaataa, Run DMC, and Grandmaster Flash and the Furious Five. The latter's "The Message"—released in 1982—was early evidence that rap was not merely party music but also had a sharp eye for social commentary when it felt so inclined.

Something tougher, darker, and harder, however, was starting to brew on the west coast. An inescapable confluence of social factors created the febrile habitat for gangsta rap to flourish. Under Reagan, unemployment and disaffection were at a nationwide high in the early eighties. With the blight of crack cocaine arriving in the inner city, the gang scene in Los Angeles and the other major US cities suddenly combusted.

"I've read articles by sociologists expounding on the roots of gangsta rap, but to me it is very simple: crack cocaine hits Compton with a vengeance," wrote Jerry Heller, cofounder of Ruthless Records. "In the mid-1980s, crack screamed down on . . . South Central like the fucking Four Horsemen of the Apocalypse. Imagine your own streets, your own city, your own neighbors under assault by a drug that basically makes people lose their minds. What if your homies ran outside and began jacking everyone in sight? What if fathers left their families, mothers neglected their children, friends attacked friends like rabid dogs? It happened in Compton. Murder, assault, burglary, and street violence rolled over the place like a tsunami."[1]

The language is typically immoderate but the impact of crack was indeed colossal. Nothing was ever quite the same again. N.W.A.'s "The Dayz of Wayback" took a nostalgic look at street crime in the days before the rock came, when apparently all that was on the criminal agenda was a little light mugging after breakfast: "Now let me tell you a little something about Compton / When I was a kid and puttin' my bid in / Yo, Compton was like still water—just strictly calm / Now it's like muthafuckin' Vietnam."

It's a classic piece of rap over-statement, but it succinctly captures the changing mood of the times. With the arrival of crack and its faithful sidekick, the Uzi, LA suburbs like Compton, Watts, Carson, and North Long Beach quickly became, as Toddy Tee's "Batterram" verbalized, almost militarized zones of conflict. They were certainly among the most extreme and hostile urban environments the modern western world had known. Is it any wonder that they spawned the most extreme and hostile music? "New York was based off of the party scene which was happening in New York at the time," recalls Ice T. "When west coast started there was no hip hop scene there—there was a gang scene. So in order for the rappers to play to the same crowd, to our crowd, we had to make music that catered to the type of people we were playing to, which was more of a gangster audience."

Soon, the gangsta ethos crystallized. Every form of music bends a little to the desires of its core audience—if gangs were in your crowd, then you'd better make sure that you were talking their language. Almost immediately, the violence that was all around was being explicitly rendered: Eazy-E's "Boyz N the Hood" and N.W.A.'s ferocious opening trio of songs on their 1988 album *Straight Outta Compton*— the title track, "Fuck tha Police" and "Gangsta Gangsta" ("Do I look like a motherfucking role model? . . . / Life ain't nothin' but bitches and money")—remain perhaps the defining statements of the genre.

Visceral, exploding with tension, anger, braggadocio, misogyny, and, yes, life, the lyrics to all four were written by teenager O'Shea Jackson, to be known ever after as Ice Cube. The two Ices were at the forefront of pioneering, popularizing and defining gangsta rap. T with his confrontational, powerhouse albums *Rhyme Pays, Power*, and *O.G. Original Gangster*; Cube with the more politically conscious but no less nightmarishly bloody *AmeriKKKa's Most Wanted*. Gangsta didn't have a monopoly on aggression—Public Enemy were equally furious without being so murder-minded—but when it worked it often made for the genre's most extraordinarily thrilling moments.

Almost every rap album in the late eighties and early nineties contained a murder; many recounted dozens and dozens. Most still do. Then and now, you don't have to travel far to find vicious cuts where the death toll becomes almost incidental. In keeping with the cinematic style, punk niggas are killed in the manner of extras in action movies: nameless, faceless shadows, irrelevant accessories to the main story.

A significant proportion of these songs are worthless, thudding works of little consequence: it was no fun to hear groups like 2-Live Crew placing all their faith in profanity and misogyny without the wit to back it up, their only mission to push the boundaries of the First Amendment as far as possible. And there was no escaping the extreme, gleeful

blood-lust in songs like "Mind of a Lunatic" by Houston's
Geto Boys, whose eponymous breakthrough album pictured
them in classic criminal mug-shot poses. The song is a long,
deeply unpleasant tirade of escalating violence ("The sight of
blood excites me, shoot you in the head / Sit down, and watch
you bleed to death"), but at some point you begin to realize
that this is murder, rape, and mutilation taken to the realms
of the absurd, and taken there for a reason. It makes a funny,
awful kind of sense. There is a slasher-flick relish in these
depictions, certainly, but the sheer scale of it also means that
it becomes about something more than simply revelling in
the violence and gore.

Even in the badlands of Los Angeles, the body count represented a far greater bloodbath than could be accounted for
by the claim that gangsta rap was merely reflecting reality.
Though it began partly as a howl of rage at the social iniquities that allowed this mess to happen, that purpose didn't
reveal its true depth. N.W.A. might have preferred to call
it reality rap, but this was always about more than that. It
swaggered. It glamorized. It *poeticized*. Even at its most visceral, gangsta rap drew on cultural and musical influences
that hailed from a lot further afield than the hyper-real
streets of Compton and Queens.

Musically, it called upon the Last Poets, James Brown,
Curtis Mayfield, Booker T and the MGs, Gil Scott-Heron,
Jamaican dub, ska, and reggae, Parliament, Funkadelic,
and later more mainstream pop acts like Sting and Phil
Collins for inspiration. It approximated the modern, mytho-
logical gangster-heroes seen in the films of Melvin Van
Peebles, Martin Scorsese, John Woo, and Brian De Palma
for its swaggering sense of style. It echoed the monologues
of Lord Buckley and Richard Pryor in its joyous irreverence. Where it had a political agenda (which, with the
highly notable exception of Public Enemy and Ice Cube,
wasn't actually all that often: "Gangsta rap was supposed to
always be apolitical and written from the perspective of the
street hustler," according to Ice T) it somehow contrived to
mix the ultra-radical ethos of the Black Panther movement
and Nation of Islam figureheads Malcolm X and Louis Far-

rakhan with the rampant pursuit of a capitalist agenda. But although Ice T also cites the cold-eyed cowboy ruthlessness of songs like "Folsom Prison Blues" as early influences on his outlook, lyrically and in its over-arching demeanor gangsta rap owes it greatest debt of honor to the blues, one of the cornerstones not only of black music, but of black experience and identity. As well as the ribald Jelly Roll Morton, rap carries within it the spirit of Lloyd Price, Howlin' Wolf, Muddy Waters, Screamin' Jay Hawkins, Sonny Boy Williamson, and John Lee Hooker, singers who blurred the line between fact and fiction in recounting their exploits, who sang songs of heightened masculinity, boasting explicitly of sexual conquests, simmering with the threat—and often more—of violence, then blindsiding the listener with flashes of humor, tenderness, and verbal dexterity. Morton might be one of the more extreme examples, but the more literate, self-aware hip-hoppers have always protested that their posture and language—including the scattergun use of obscenities for which they have so often been vilified—are an important and significant part of African American culture. You don't have to look far to find ample evidence.

"We need to go back to the blues, to the baaadman tales of the late nineteenth century, and the age-old tradition of 'signifying' if we want to discover the roots of the 'gangsta' aesthetic," writes Robin Kelley in his essay "OGs in Post-Industrial Los Angeles: Evolution of a Style." "Irreverence has been a central, component part of black expressive vernacular culture, which is why violence and sex have been as important to toasting and signifying as playfulness with language. Many of the narratives are about power. Both the baaadman and the trickster embody a challenge to virtually all authority (which makes sense to people for whom justice is a rare thing), [it] creates an imaginary upside-down world where the oppressed are the powerful, and it reveals to the listeners the pleasures and price of reckless abandon."[2]

The black writer Julius Lester, in his *Black Folktales*, describes the infamous, eponymous hero of the murder ballad "Stagger Lee" (or "Stagolee") as "undoubtedly and without question, the baddest nigger that ever lived. Stagolee was so bad that the flies wouldn't even fly around his head in the summertime, and snow wouldn't fall on his house in the winter." You can practically touch the sense of pride exhibited in Lester's knowing exaggeration: "You think your gangsters are bad? Look at *ours*! But don't look too long or they'll rip your eyes out!"

The head of the Black Panthers, Bobby Seale, used the song as a recruitment drive for young black men, for the sole reason that Stagolee was "a bad nigger off the block and didn't take shit from nobody."[3] A St. Louis pimp, his status defined by his women, his guns, his money, he became a "young god of virility, as impulsive, as vulgar, as daring and as adventurous as the young black [men] wanted him to be."[4] His legendary cultural position legitimized transgression as an act of underdog empowerment.

Stagolee continues to show up at many of the significant points of black cultural expression, like some depraved, ice-cool Zelig. As Greil Marcus has pointed out, Stagolee was "Muddy Waters's cool and elemental Rollin' Stone; Chuck Berry's Brown-Eyed Handsome Man; Bo Diddley with a tombstone hand and a graveyard mind; Wilson Pickett's Midnight Mover, Mick Jagger's Midnight Rambler. . . . When the civil rights movement got tough, [Staggerlee] took over. And Staggerlee would come roaring back to the screen in the 1970s, as Slaughter, Sweet Sweetback, Superfly."[5]

When Nick Cave covered "Stagger Lee" in 1995 he brought the archetype right up to date by drenching the song with the kind of expletives that would make the Geto Boys glow with pride. Here was "the bad muthafucker Stagger Lee" who "put four holes" in the barman's "motherfucking head," while a "bitch" called Nellie Brown "struts across the bar, hitching up her skirt." Cave said he always regarded it as a "comic song" but also a "truly violent song."[6] In other words, it's a gangsta rap song. For where else does gangsta rap make its home if not wedged right between those two seemingly contradictory notions: humor and death?

Like the blues, then, gangsta rap was part social reality and part self-aggrandizing fantasy. Hence its ability to move within a wide spectrum, from the gritty, lowering realism of

Mobb Deep's *The Infamous* to the overblown, cinematic black comedy of "Natural Born Killaz," which played on the notion that Ice Cube and Dr. Dre had perpetrated the murders in the high-profile Menendez and O.J. Simpson murder cases. As well as broadly recounting the truth it has at the same time always reserved the right to create heroic caricatures out of its main players, as a means of transforming the mundane into the powerful and glamorous. In the words of Kelley again, it began as "a magical response to political, economic and social degradation: a fantasy of gun-blazing, dick-swinging omnipotence."[7]

Critics who argue that rap's portrayal of death is dubious or gratuitous because it perpetually swerves like a squealing getaway car across the line separating authenticity and glorification/glamorization are essentially missing the point. Cultural authenticity and realism are not the same thing; the notion that rap's only intrinsic worth, the entire justification for it existing as an art form, hinges almost wholly on its ability to communicate a form of ultra-truthfulness that other musical genres simply can't deliver is a misreading. Because it lends itself to the first-person narrative, the tendency is to take rap at face value as reportage, but the "I" is almost always ambiguous. As with every other form of music, notions such as "authenticity" and "sincerity" are essentially red herrings. In rap, the extreme gestures, the bragging, the two-dimensional characterizations and exaggeration are all culturally important. The puffed-up cartoon element is as authentic a part of its heritage as its early roots in tell-it-like-it-is social realism.

That's not to underestimate the extent to which gangsta rap is rooted in reflecting a dramatized version of reality. The murder rate of young black men in US cities was—and remains—truly horrifying; the LA riots in 1992, foreshadowed by eerily prescient songs like Ice Cube's "Black Korea," illustrated that random acts of violence, racial tensions, and the virtual breakdown of law and order in LA and elsewhere were hardly imaginary. The savage beating of black petty criminal Rodney King by four white policemen in 1991, and the six days of rioting that ensued the following year when the policemen were acquitted, inspired some hard-hitting responses from the gangsta rap community, including Dr. Dre's "The Day the Niggaz Took Over," Ice Cube's *Predator* album, and "Cop Killer" ("Fuck police brutality / Better you than me") written by Ice T and performed by his off-shoot metal band Body Count in 1991.

"Cop Killer" was withdrawn from release following the LA riots after an outcry of moral indignation from police associations; Vice-President Dan Quayle and President George Bush obediently joined the chorus of condemnation. Despite the obvious similarities between "Cop Killer" and established anti-authority songs from other musical genres, such as "Pretty Boy Floyd" and "I Shot the Sheriff," the strength of the association between what rap stars represented and what they were singing about was too much for conservative America. Ice T bowed to the pressure and removed the song from the first Body Count album, but stands by the sentiments of the song. "I've no regrets, because 'Cop Killer' was a political record that was written at the moment," he says. "It was the time to write that record. Would I write that record today? I don't know, because mostly I'm not feeling the same. But I don't regret doing it. It's a landmark part of my life."

Gangsta rap put murder at the heart of the musical agenda in a way that is unprecedented in popular music. Rap began as a hopeful story, and to some extent it still is, but it also connected mainstream music to those on the fringes, and often much closer to the center, of serious criminal behavior. Popular music has never exactly been squeaky clean, particularly behind the scenes, but this was new territory. Looking in from the outside, Richard Thompson, a Tupac fan, speaks for many when he observes that "it's strange to have a musical style that is performed and promoted by gangsters."

Inevitably, it wasn't long before art and reality became intertwined. Quite quickly, rap discovered that fame and notoriety don't make you bullet-proof. Scott La Rock, who alongside KRS-1 and D-Nice made up New York's Boogie Down Productions, was shot and murdered in the Bronx in August 1987, only months after the release of BDS's influential debut album, *Criminal Minded*, the cover of which portrayed the rappers surrounded by an arsenal of firearms. Inside were songs like "9mm Goes Bang," a graphic first-person narrative about the killing of a crack dealer and his vengeful posse.

The list of rappers who have subsequently died violent deaths in the past twenty years is a depressingly long one, and includes Paul C, Charizma, Randy "Stretch" Walker, Tupac Shakur, Yaki Kadafi, Biggie Smalls, Fat Pat, Freaky Tah, Big L, E-Moneybags, DJ Uncle Al, Jam Master Jay, Camouflage, Half-A-Mill, Soulja Slim, Mac Dre, Bugz, Blade Icewood, Proof, Big Hawk, and Stack Bundles. That's before you factor in the numerous foot-soldiers, hangers-on, and bodyguards who have also been gunned down—such as Israel Ramirez, who lost his life in 2006 while working as security for Busta Rhymes. It's a shocking roll call, all the more so when you consider that only a fraction of those murders have ever resulted in convictions. Only black metal, that dark, Satanic, Scandinavian subgenre of heavy metal whose participants list church burning, blood drinking, and animal cruelty among their hobbies, makes such an explicit link between the life portrayed in the songs and the violent and very occasionally murderous activities played out in the real world.

But no form of music has ever taken its association with murder and carried it quite so explicitly into the heart of teenage pop culture, which is where rap music now lives. The connection many rappers and their labels cultivate with organized criminal gangs, corrupt policemen, drug racketeers, and a host of generic low-level thugs is no invention. Shootouts are frequent, stretches in prison commonplace. Snoop Doggy Dogg was a member of the Crips who had served time for dealing cocaine before he got a record deal. He later faced trial for murder in 1995, at which he was acquitted. Death Row boss Suge Knight was imprisoned for racketeering and again later for associating with gang members. The list could and does go on. These are the waters rap swims in, and they don't so much trickle as flood into the music.

The stark reality is that true-life murder does rap's profile no harm at all. As its death wish grew more explicit in the early to midnineties gangsta rap became, commercially speaking, the only show in town. With Dr. Dre's G-funk masterpiece *The Chronic* and Snoop Dogg's *Doggystyle*, the cult of gangsterism slowed its beats down and crossed over in an astonishingly pervasive way, infiltrating movies, literature, fashion, and television. As it became an overtly commercial commodity and found a happy hunting ground within millions of white suburban middle-class homes, it had more and more to live up—or, perhaps down—to.

In 1995, Raekwon's *Only Built for Cuban Linx* exemplified this exhilarating upping of the stakes; where once the gangsta rapper was content to be regarded as a tough, mid-level street thug, now he was happy with nothing less than kingpin or drug lord status. Mafiosi-style aliases abounded. The lines between fact and fiction became even more blurred. This was rap scratching its cinematic itch. Raekwon appropriated samples and imagery from classic mob films like *Carlito's Way*, John Woo's *The Killer*, and *Scarface*: Tony Montana, as portrayed unforgettably by Al Pacino in the latter, became gangsta's number one role model. The poor, put-upon immigrant criminal made omnipotent crime lord. The girls. The drugs. The money. The clothes. The entourage. The status. The sheer power. Biggie Smalls, trading as Notorious B.I.G., and Nas followed suit. As gangsta rap walked in Montana's footsteps from the 'hood to the penthouse, the boasts got more and more outrageous, the insults nastier, the feuds more violent and more widespread.

This was the "baaadman" finally taking his rightful place on the global stage and loving every spotlight-drenched second; the "upside-down world" had righted itself. Rap equalled pop. Unlike the blues singers in the earlier part of the century, who in many ways belonged to another world, the people articulating black urban consciousness at the end of the twentieth century had gained power, wealth, credibility, and cultural visibility. But instead of turning away from the ghetto life, the stakes simply got higher. Rap began believing its own hype and acting upon it, and in the process arguably lost a portion of its soul.

The way the shiny cinematic myth bled into real life is still best personified by Tupac Shakur, the young, intelligent, politically engaged, widely read, college-educated kid with a Black Panther mother who, like the actor he was, "gangsterized" his image—and eventually his life—not just to slake his fascination with the dark side of life, but also to gain greater credibility among his peers and his audience. Moving to LA from Baltimore at the age of 17, he watched his mother become addicted to crack and began immersing himself in the thug life. By his fourth album, 1994's *All Eyez on Me*, his natural instinct for uplifting poetry, positive female representations—notably on "Keep Ya Head Up"—and dark introspection had largely been smothered, replaced by a fascination with the gangsta lifestyle and a deeply ingrained death wish.

Tupac was already half in love with the idea of death, predicting, writing, and rapping his own demise long before it arrived in songs such as "How Long Will They Mourn Me," "Only God Can Judge Me," and "Life Goes On," in which he imagines his own funeral ("Nobody cries when we die / We outlaws"). It became, of course, a self-fulfilling prophesy; in that sense, the oft-made comparisons with Kurt Cobain have some foundation. Tupac was first shot and badly injured in New York in 1994, sparking a feud with east coast rival Biggie Smalls—who had just released his own debut album, titled with prescience and commercial nous *Ready to Die*— and between their respective labels, Bad Boy and Death Row. Both men were heavily involved in criminality and violence, and when Tupac's assassins came calling again in a drive-by shooting in Las Vegas in 1996, this time they finished the job. Shakur died of gunshot wounds on September 13, 1996, aged 25. Smalls was murdered in Queens the following year, aged 24. Nobody has been convicted of either crime.

Three things happened subsequent to the two murders that have had a significant bearing on rap's ongoing relationship with and attitude to death. First, the industry quickly realized what the rock industry had known for decades: that not only did *songs* about death sell, but dead artists sold too, to the point where death now threatens to completely overshadow the work. That is certainly now true of Tupac and Smalls, who reached a whole new stratosphere of fame through their deaths to the extent that they are now best known not for living but for dying.

Posthumously, Tupac has become the most iconic and biggest selling rapper of all time, shifting at least thirty million albums compared to the ten million he sold in his lifetime. He has also rather cleverly managed to release twice as many albums dead as the five he made while alive, and has even posthumously published a book of poetry. Perhaps, like Elvis, he will one day start touring again. Biggie Smalls' *Life After Death* album, meanwhile, was released fifteen days after his murder and has sold over ten million copies.

In such a boldly commercial fashion does death rub out the line separating art and reality. It becomes not only the ultimate subject matter but the ultimate career move—everyone wins: it's the final piece of the marketing jigsaw for the record label; and it's the final, essential step in the great lunge at mythologized immortality for the artist. The mortality of a gangsta rapper is now open to perpetual speculation in the same manner as the self-destructive rock stars of the late sixties and early seventies. It's no coincidence that this decade's most commercially successful gangsta rapper, 50 Cent, called his debut album *Get Rich or Die Tryin'* and consistently plays upon the fact that he is a former crack dealer who was shot nine times in 2000. The ever-present implication of imminent death is a significant part of his appeal.

Second, after the deaths of Tupac and Biggie, rap mined its sentimental streak to ruthless effect. Like many hard-boiled hard men, it often turns to mush once the dust and cordite has cleared and the eulogizing of the fallen "soldiers" gets under way. Every self-respecting gangsta now must have at least one teary eulogy to the heroic dead in his or her canon. "I'll Be Missing You," Puff Daddy and Faith Evans' 1997 memorial to Biggie Smalls, heavily sampling the Police's "Every Breath You Take," was a colossal worldwide hit in 1997 and is the bedrock of a subgenre that started with Ice Cube's genuinely moving "Dead Homiez" and also includes Bone Thugs-N-Harmony's "Crossroads" and Dre's "The Message." The phenomenon has now dripped down to street level. Like every other form of music, rap has been revolutionized by technological advances and the reach of the internet. There is a relatively recent and burgeoning trend for young men who have lost friends in America's—and increasingly also in Britain's—appallingly routine incidents of gun violence to post hastily recorded and heartfelt R.I.P. songs on their MySpace sites or elsewhere on the web.

Finally, the murder of both Shakur and Smalls re-enforced the legitimacy and strength of gangsta rap's connection with the more violent, some might say glamorous, parts of society. The subsequent mystery that surrounded their deaths, a labyrinthine plot featuring appearances by the Crips and the Bloods, scheming rap bosses, corrupt LAPD cops, and the persistent belief that Smalls was implicated in Shakur's murder, has been well documented elsewhere and need not trouble us here. The bottom line, as Tupac's sales figures showed, was that gangsterism sold. And sold and sold.

In the process Tupac has become the Black Elvis. Every form of music has its martyrs, but part of the problem with the manner of Tupac's death and its subsequent surrounding soap opera is that it presents no great imperative for rap to widen its horizons. Quite the opposite. The vibrant countercurrents of the Daisy Age movement pioneered by De La Soul; the politically correct, jazz-influenced progressive hip hop of Arrested Development, Disposable Heroes of Hiphoprisy, A Tribe Called Quest and Common, among others; and the current crop of "conscious" rappers like Mos Def and Lupe Fiasco have, according to hip hop author Stephen Rodrick, "drawn little more than barely concealed yawns from other rappers and urban audiences."[8]

Rap badly needs a new song to sing, but like the drunk who fears that sobriety will make him boring, the millionaire rapper seeks an association with danger as a spur not just to creativity but to maintaining status. Writing, speaking, and maintaining eye contact with death is still widely regarded as somehow hipper than tackling less abrasive, more moderate subjects. As long as an association with death bestows a kind of honor, this will continue. Rap holds great store in credibility. Having traded on explicit representations of death and violence for so long, as a genre it has grown suspicious of any artist who appears not to have—or at least who refuses to pretend to have—a connection with the violent world from which it first emerged.

DMX embodies the mind-set of the successful modern rapper. The sixth best-selling rap artist of all time, he continues to live his life like he's just jumped bail: carjacking, numerous assault charges, scrapes with hard drugs and firearms. Rap was initially a gut-level response to living with circumstances that were not of its own choosing or making; now that the initial context no longer applies to many of its success stories, the most high-profile gangsta rappers find themselves beholden to the language and rule book of a war whose origins they have largely forgotten and need not be fighting. Is this a problem?

"I'm not dealing with LAPD in 1992, I'm not dealing with the same issues I was," argues Ice T. "Although I may not be out on the street living that life, personally I'm [still] surrounded by that life. It would be the equivalent of saying that somebody like [*American Gangster* author] Frank Lucas, who lived the life, can't write about it. It's something that is always there, it always surrounds me. I try to insulate myself from it, [but] the lyrics aren't that far from the truth."

Once a gangsta always a gangsta. But at some point in a gangsta rapper's career, dull repetition, death, or self-parody become the most likely career moves. It becomes harder and harder to move the story forward. Admittedly, Eminem took ultra-violence in a different direction in the late nineties by reclaiming it from gang/street culture and relocating it to his living room. This was rap that tackled highly dysfunctional domesticity: working through the issues of paternal abandonment, a dreadfully abusive mother/son relationship, a marriage to Kim Mathers for which the word "tempestuous" barely does justice, and the responsibilities of trying to be a father to a young daughter amid the chaos of violence, drug abuse and mental anguish.

This staked out new emotional territory for rap, at least at the harder end of the genre, and it was recounted with thrilling dexterity and enormous linguistic skill. But it remained *unbelievably* violent, particularly in its attitudes toward women. It attracted publicity, the bad-good kind that never harms sales, but it also suggested that all that splatter and gore had become a commercial crutch; there was an element of giving people what they wanted. Eminem partly got around the inevitable media outcry that greeted his *Slim Shady LP*, notably "'97 Bonnie and Clyde" and "Guilty Conscience," by pointing out that he was clearly performing in an exaggerated dramatic persona. The follow-up, the *Marshall Mathers LP*, displayed no such obvious dramatic distance. On its most notorious tracks, "Kim" and "Kill You," we hear him describing slitting his wife's throat and raping and murdering his mother. The closing get-out clause on "Kill You" ("I'm just playing ladies, you know I love you") was hardly persuasive.

Eminem may have simply been venting a lifetime's worth of unexpressed rage without utilizing his internal censor—and he has always been savvy enough to mimic the critiques of his liberal naysayers in song, thus beating them to the punch and covering all the angles in the process—but his stratospheric success proved that rap and graphic murder remained a winning combination. It wasn't just reactionary right-wingers who felt a little uneasy. These songs of sodomy and throat cutting, it must be recalled, found their way into over thirty million homes all over the world. They were written by one of music's biggest stars. Setting aside any debate about the quality and integrity of the material, am I alone in finding remarkable the sheer enormity of cultural assimilation achieved by music this howlingly aggressive and blood-thirsty?

Eminem may be white, but his success—alongside a new generation of rappers like 50 Cent, Jay-Z, Nas, and Kanye West—is conclusive and final proof that black culture has become mainstream business. They have become hugely successful moguls, their fingers buried in a wide variety of pies, from clothing and jewelry to TV and sports. Music is only a part of what they do. Socially, this can't be seen as anything other than a sign of positive progress. Musically, in terms of rap's journey it might be argued that it marks the point where the lifestyle trappings and the caricatures have become much bigger and more important than the music will ever be able to convincingly convey. It has succeeded like no other from of music before or since in building its own world, but it has become rather trapped within its confines.

Old-school pop songwriters like Jeff Barry will happily— furiously, actually—write off all rap music as worthless, violent rubbish, filled with a hate and fury and a glorification of drug-dealing that contaminates young minds. He calls it "misogynistic, promoting cop killing, glorifying illiteracy and gangsterism." He is far from alone in this view. But for a musical idiom that has attracted more venom and downright blame than perhaps any other—even the incipient rock and roll—for the negative impact it has had on society in general and young people's attitudes in particular, it's worth noting the extent to which rap is now at the mercy of its audience. As the lingua franca of the young all over the world, it no longer has much control over how it projects itself. Gangsta rappers, for all their brawn and bluster, bow to the expectations of their audience and the industry just as obediently as any other group of pop musicians, be they boy bands, heavy metallists or indie groups. And what the audience wants, apparently, is bang, bling and bitches.

In "OGs in Post-Industrial Los Angeles: Evolution of a Style," Robin Kelley notes that "the message of poor, urban black rage is bought and sold by multinational corporations and eagerly consumed by, among others, white middle-class suburban teenagers. Given gangsta rap's popular and commercial appeal . . . is this culture of resistance reporting and reflecting upon the rough justice of the ghetto or merely perpetuating and profiting by it?"[9]

Both, clearly. The two aren't mutually exclusive. Rap has only been able to so frequently and recklessly use death as its badge of authenticity because it so successfully and convincingly projected it in the first place. That, however, leaves it in an increasingly difficult place, and not just because its flirtation with death looks more and more complacent and dubious as the death rate among black males becomes more and more catastrophic and nobody seems to care too much. Buried under bluster, bravado, sentimental eulogies, and reaching for the nearest platitude—"untimely," "premature," "cut short" seem to fit all sizes—when it matters rap and its immediate community are too often content to look the other way: the murder of Busta Rhymes' bodyguard Israel Ramirez occurred on a closed video set of only five hundred people. Nobody saw anything. And when Hurricane Katrina came sweeping in, killing an estimated unofficial total of four thousand people and displacing tens of thousands more, the majority of them members of the black community, nobody saw anything either.

If death doesn't pick a rapper off in a hail of bullets, then increasingly he is left with only two options: admit that gangsterism was always a bit of a game and relax into something approximating fluffy respectability and knowing caricature: see Ice T and Snoop Doggy Dogg; or keep playing the death and violence card until it topples into parody or numbing tedium: see 50 Cent's 2007 album *Curtis*, limp with a lack of ideas, endlessly retreading old rhymes, ancient threats, idle boasts. The bodies fall all around him but it means nothing anymore.

Like any other form of music, the key lies in the ability to communicate. Ice T compares it to the work of novelist Stephen King, someone "who is not writing about their life [but] can continually come up with more and more weird events—book after book on death. If you listen to a Mobb Deep album about a thousand people get killed, which we know isn't true. So it's kinda like who writes about it in the most real way and makes you feel it and sends the chills through your body, you know? I believe that today's rap music is watered down to almost a disco level."

Most contemporary gangsta depictions have become that most unforgivable of all artistic crimes: boring. The desperate circumstances of black urban reality are hardly less pressing than in 1985, but mainstream rap has all but exhausted the lexicon of death and violence, while most of us have become inured to what is actually being said. Keeping it real isn't enough, which is why 50 Cent, for all his bullet holes and his truly unenviably tough upbringing, might as well be played by an actor from RADA or NYFA. Whether or not his tales of teenage crack dealing and shoot-outs are one hundred percent genuine or not, he doesn't communicate on any serious artistic level. He plays to the lowest common denominator bitches-and-guns demographic and his primarily teenage audience lap it up.

He is proof positive that in rap, the biography now counts for more than the creative act. You start with the life and work backward through all the back-story bullshit, the long-as-your-arm list of felonies, the highly stylized image, the petty, highly publicized feuds, the stock heroic movie depiction, until you eventually, reluctantly, face the music. It's character driven but now we're in on the joke: when Snoop Doggy Dogg was first due to arrive in the UK in 1994 to tour *Doggystyle* he was greeted with a front-page tabloid headline that screamed: "KICK THIS EVIL BASTARD OUT!" Now that kind of sensationalist hysteria is reserved for Islamic fundamentalists and, occasionally, homophobic Jamaican dancehall stars. Gangsta rappers and their various criminal exploits are usually regarded with the kind of light-hearted affection with which a mother regards a cute but wayward toddler.

"The shock value is absolutely over with," agrees Ice T. "When you heard N.W.A. and Too Short and Geto Boys and Ice T it had never been heard before, so therefore it was like, 'What the fuck is this?' At the end of the day . . . I think people realized that the true fear behind the music isn't real. In other words, you heard Snoop Dogg and you really thought Snoop Dogg was a mean person, or somebody who would really hurt you. Once people finally got to know us and realized we had kids and played video games and stuff like that, I think the fear left. That's the part that is gone, it's like anything: once people get used to it and acclimatized to it, it doesn't have the same impact."

So where does that leave us? Looking at rap with a hollow, cheated feeling because not every word is true and not every rapper is a psychopathic killer? Or left merely to enjoy the entertainment in the same way we enjoy *The Sopranos*, pulpy crime thrillers, and Sam Peckinpah films? As a white middle-class male living in a white middle-class neighborhood in a white middle-class British city, it's instructive to ask: what do I get out of gangsta rap? Well, if I want an in-depth sociological account of what is happening in the poorer parts of Los Angeles, Detroit, New York, Baltimore, Houston, or Philadelphia, I'm likely to read a book, or a newspaper, or perhaps watch television. But the best of rap can also provide a vital part of the jigsaw, the part not filtered through academic or secondhand sources, not edited to meet a preordained conclusion or to minimize offense. It may not be the unvarnished truth, it may often return again and again to core clichés, it may adopt views and use words that jar, but in its representation of how young black men *want* to be portrayed and their struggle to earn money, status, respect, power, and success it has been highly significant. And death has been absolutely central to that portrayal, as central as it is in songs like "Stagger Lee."

The extent to which you take it seriously is a personal choice, but to deny the thrill of those murderous beats and the visceral appeal of secondhand violence is to deny the strange and sometimes dark mysteries of our own hearts.

"Looking back on it," concludes Ice T, "I still see it as entertainment. I see it as no different than watching *Goodfellas* or *Casino* on television. It's what I call Gangsta Tales; it's like watching a western. I totally understand [why white middle-class kids like] it. What did I get out of watching John Wayne? What do people get out of watching *Black Hawk Down*? Any time there is action and adventure, people are going to be intrigued by it. I'm not a Cuban, but I was intrigued by *Scarface*. You don't really have to be from somewhere or something to be entertained by the adventure of that world. It's always going to be entertaining, especially to men. Come on! Men like that type of shit!"

And he cackles like the pantomime villain he is. It's a familiar sound, the leisurely, cocksure motif that threads its way through the songs of Jelly Roll Morton and Muddy Waters, Gil Scott Heron and Snoop Dogg, Lloyd Price and 50 Cent. It sounds like the punctuation point to a fine old joke. But you just can't be sure.

8
SOMETIMES IT SNOWS IN APRIL
The Music of Loss

"A songwriter's existence depends on his or her ability to trivialize experience." Mark Eitzel, the lead singer with American Music Club, has often struggled through the years with how to write about those he has loved and lost. He is under no illusions. "It's broad strokes. The songs I've written about people who've passed away have been so fumbling, so self serving, because that's how I was using them: 'Oh, look at me. Look at the loss, look at my genius.' I almost can't bear to think about what a prat I've been. I'm like the American Dream: proof that all kinds of crap can be sold given the right context."[1]

Songwriters have always been opportunists by nature and instinct, in the same way that authors, poets, and playwrights are opportunists. Nothing is off limits. Even as they are lamenting the passing of a relationship, a lover, a friend, or family member—any event that strikes at the very heart of their existence, and none strikes deeper than death—at least some tiny part of their subconscious is already snapping to attention, making mental notes for a song, then spooling forward to preview how that song and its sentiments will come over on record, on stage, in interviews, on the internet and, ultimately, how the whole thing will reflect back upon them as a performing artist. This is why Eitzel's appraisal of his own work in this area—though harsh and mocking—is so thoroughly and extraordinarily frank and on the money. Give a songwriter a piece of bad news and the first thing he or she will do—if they're any good at all—is reach for his guitar.

Neil Finn recalls that he wrote the song "Hole in the River" "directly after getting some very bad news from my father about my aunt [who had just committed suicide]. I kind of just wrote down what he told me. I guess that was a conscious decision to write about death." This is simply what modern songwriters *do*. They turn their own reality into art, partly as a means of emotional release through self-expression, and partly because they know that if they do it well they can touch us profoundly. The connection between the song and the audience relies on the writer having a degree of emotional detachment that enables the song to be written in the first place, without it toppling over under the weight of its own grief or self-importance into a huge, self-regarding hole. We can hardly turn around afterward and complain about their methods, or suggest that they put the song in the bottom drawer and leave it there, pulsating with unshared sadness.

But it wasn't always this way. As the parameters of pop have stretched to the extent that almost anything is now permissible, those working within them have become, depending on your perspective, either more shameless and brazen in their expression of grief, or braver and more fearless. It's not so much a question of *what* they will use to make a song, but rather the *way* that they are prepared to use it. Eitzel is one of our finest working songwriters, with an Honors degree in wry self-deprecation and a PhD in applied melodrama, and his comments do himself—and by extension, many other writers—a disservice of sorts: AMC songs such as "Blue and Gray Shirt," "Another Morning," and "The Hula Maiden" are genuinely affecting, reassuringly complex reactions to the deaths of lovers, family, and friends. There is no sense of them ringing hollow, but they make for uncomfortable, sometimes voyeuristic listening, so near the emotional knuckle you can practically taste the bone marrow.

Neil Finn's music, too, has of late carried the somber hum of death. He wrote the songs for Crowded House's *Time on Earth* record in the shadow of the suicide of the band's former drummer Paul Hester in March 2005. Although he recognizes that there are conflicting motives in writing about the dead, he also points out that songwriting in general, and writing about grief in particular, is not something over which a composer can always exercise full content approval. Things creep in without express permission. Finn gives the listener a gentler ride than Eitzel, but while he is never mentioned by name or the events of his death specifically alluded to, Hester's suicide is etched deep into the grooves of the record in a way that could hardly be achieved entirely consciously and is, perhaps, all the more moving for it.

"It's very hard for me to be objective about the weight of that event on the record, because it had a huge resonance on my life. The songs that I was writing around that time are probably all influenced by that—they're not all *about* that, some clearly not at all, but if it's in the songs then that's the way it is. I certainly understand the idea of it being an opportunistic thing. In periods of dark humor you say, 'Well at least you got a good album out of it!' We joke about those things all the time, and it's true: there's ego and selfishness wrapped up in it. But underneath it all there's a certain universality, a desire to create empathy and comfort for somebody that is at the heart of it as well."

☠

Bereavement is the great boom area of modern music. Songs of loss can be mawkish, intrusive, or plain discomfiting, but at their best they are perhaps music's most noble, useful undertaking. These are also the very hardest songs to write. And to write about. Grief is a notoriously exclusive emotion—it is perhaps the most private and personal process humans ever go through. How do you write about your loss? Where do you start? Do you spell it out plain and pained for all to see? Do you find some lingua franca of grief that connects on a universal level? Do you wrap it all up in metaphor and symbolism? All are perfectly legitimate approaches, but none are easy.

Music has always remembered the dead, of course, but only recently has it started to wear its loss so extravagantly, so publicly, so *specifically*. For centuries, antiquated songs of sorrow, Gaelic laments, old traditional English folk songs, classical pieces, American blues have all provided forms of comfort to those who have lost loved ones, but their function was primarily to create something utilitarian and practical: to convey death's purpose, its necessity, rather than simply provide a vessel for a deep, explicit outpouring of private grief.

Indeed, there were rules about this kind of thing. Take the traditional ballad "The Cruel Grave," in which a woman prays every night for "seven long years" for the safe return of her beloved sailor, not knowing that he has already drowned and is buried in a distant land. In time, the ghost of the lady's young sailor love returns to her and pleads, "I'm gone, love, please pray no longer / For never more can I come home to you."

On a recording of the song by Duncan Williamson, the great Scottish traveling singer takes a few moments before he starts singing to explain why this story remains relevant to us all. "Death touches everybody at some part of their lives, no matter who they are," says Williamson. "It's a sad thing, but the thing is . . . you should never love anyone after they've gone. Love must never be carried to the grave because, if you do, according to the old traditions down through time, if you keep trying to make life the way it was with your loved one . . . then their soul never can rest at peace. You must never forget a loved one, but you must never love them the way you did when they were alive."

"The Cruel Grave" is a melodious warning: do not dwell on the dead; not for your own sake, nor for theirs. Let them go. You will see them again. The Gaelic lament "An Cronan Bais" returns to this central refrain: "Sleep, O sleep without any sorrow." This wasn't merely a random, breakaway strand of pre-twentieth-century thinking, but a very real and important part of the way many societies dealt with grief. From Native American Indian to Inca and Aboriginal cultures, it has long been thought seriously unwise to disturb the dead, either physically or spiritually. If you believe in an afterlife and the channels of communication that existed between the living and the dead, it was important to maintain the relationship properly, in a manner that would bring no additional sorrow to either party.

A song like "Molly Bawn," a ballad of Irish derivation (also known as "Polly Vaughan"), which has travelled the world in at least eighty-eight known variants, and has been in printed form since 1799 and in oral form since long before then, speaks of the Celtic-British belief in transformation, shape-shifting, and the correct procedure of remembering the dead. The pale young protagonist is mistaken for a swan—or perhaps she really *is* a swan at this point—in the half-light of dusk and is shot dead by her lover, out hunting. Molly later returns as a ghost to visit her distraught lover.

As with most revenants who pop up in the old ballads, she returns with a specific purpose rather than as the kind of Scooby Doo–style spook so popular in the enjoyably trashy horror songs that pop music loves and does so well: "Cool Gool" by Sharky Todd and His Monsters, Bobby "Boris" Pickett's "Monster Mash," even Michael Jackson's "Thriller." "It was a widespread belief that excessive weeping for the dead will disturb them in their graves," writes Jennifer O'Connor in the *Canadian Journal for Traditional Music*. "Since most variants [of 'Molly Bawn'] indicate the hunter's terrible remorse following the shooting, including his crying fountains of tears, we may assume Molly returns as a result of his tremendous grief."[2] Molly speaks up for her lover to spare him from execution, but also to free herself from an eternity of unrest.

The seventeenth-century Irish poem "I Am Stretched on Your Grave," translated into English by Philip King and recorded by, among others, Kate Rusby and Sinead O'Connor, tells a story of an obsessional love that death cannot kill. It offers no redemption, no hope for the bereaved, simply the desire to die and join the deceased. It's all very bruised and romantic, and hauntingly beautiful, but within the words there is an acknowledgment that this transgresses the healthy, natural process of grief: "The priests and the friars / They approach me in dread / Because I still love you / My love and you're dead."

Traditional bereavement songs rarely get this personal or despairing. They are designed as universal touchstones, songs to help not only the writer through a crisis, but a multitude of listeners too, wherever and whenever they may need it. The original event that inspired them isn't deemed to be more important than death itself—the names and places didn't necessarily matter, because it's coming to us all. In the best of these songs there's no self pity and no emotional fat, simply a clear and utterly convincing expression of loss, and a glimmer of hope shining somewhere amid all the rubble.

Hundreds more conform to type. Sturdy. Built to last. Adaptable. Eminently useful in troubled times. Richard Thompson wrote "Meet on the Ledge" for Fairport Convention in 1969 while still a teenager, shaken by the loss of a close friend. It carries the same sense of hope buried in bereavement as many great traditional songs, and has long since slipped the moorings of the circumstances of its composition. It now enjoys all the universality of an ancient lament. "The way is up along the road, the air is growing thin / Too many friends who tried, blown off this mountain with the wind / Meet on the ledge, we're going to meet on the ledge / When my time is up, I'm going to see all my friends."

Already well schooled in the sparse art of the folk ballad, the teenage Thompson was aware—consciously or not—that sparing the detail would make the song sing out all the louder as the years passed by. It is at once a memorial and a song of comfort. "I've always believed in an afterlife," says Thompson. "Even at the age I wrote that I had that belief and that is reflected in the song in a subtle way. It can be taken in many ways, as fans continually remind me! It's a song that I feel I outgrew, actually fairly quickly, in about five years or so. I felt that song didn't really speak for me —not because I thought it was an adolescent song, but I thought it was a slightly clumsy song in its delivery. It's only because it became kind of anthemic for some people that I revisited the song. I had to drag it out and look at it and think, 'Are there things I can extract from this song so that I can continue to enjoy it?' And there are. I can find things in it that still speak for me."

And for many, many others. It's little surprise that "Meet on the Ledge" was voted number seventeen in BBC Radio Two's top one hundred songs in 2004. It speaks to people about love and loss without treading all over their toes with its own concerns. It's often sound practice to leave some space in a song for the listener's own story to crawl inside and find a place to live.

Thompson's "Never Again," a much sadder song, a song speaking of the sheer desolation that loss brings, does the same thing. Compare it to something like Puff Daddy's "I'll Be Missing You," so soddenly, specifically sentimental in the face of Biggie Small's 1997 murder you seriously begin to suspect its motives—it's nothing to do with any limitations of the rap genre, it's simply down to the skill of the writer. Ice Cube's "Dead Homiez" is a brilliant bereavement song that weaves personal loss into a social narrative: "Remember we painted our names on the wall for fun / Now it's 'Rest in Peace' after every one."

Death Cab for Cutie's "What Sarah Said" is all piss, tubes, ICUs, LCDs, and enormously intimate detail; alt.country artist Dale Watson, meanwhile, wrote and recorded an entire album of songs—*Every Song I Write Is for You*—for his dead fiancée. It's difficult to know what we as listeners are supposed to do with something quite so relentlessly personal. Then again, it's surely better than being fobbed off with dross like Bobby Goldsboro's 1968 hit "Honey," a ripe slice of sentiment in which the husband muses upon the death of his wife using the tree in the garden as a measuring stick for his grief. Judging by the lyric it must be a mighty small tree: "And honey, I miss you / And I'm bein' good / And I'd love to be with you / If only I could." Is she dead or just spending the weekend at her parents? Is this the eternal void or a trip to the shops?

This almost offensively neutered version of loss clearly won't do, but communicating real emotion rather than the ersatz variety has become harder than ever for songwriters in modern times. Between the ho-hum clichés of "Honey" and the autopsical approach of "What Sarah Said" times changed. Ideas changed. The media changed. Disease changed (AIDS is a particularly intimate, invasive illness). The world changed. As Jackson Browne observed in "Looking East," "These times are a famine for the soul, while for the senses it's a feast." One need only look back at the outpouring of grief when Princess Diana died in 1997 to comprehend that the emotional temperature of Britain, at least, is now very much higher than it was fifty, even twenty years ago.

This is an immeasurably more forward—some might say incontinent—age. People have "journeys" rather than mere experiences; they seek "closure" rather than understanding. At a time when it has become routine to post intimate details on web blogs and social networking sites for complete strangers to browse through, there is little stigma attached to laying our feelings out bare for all to see or hear. A problem aired is not really a problem anymore—it becomes something quite different. It becomes yet another form of entertainment. We demonstrably care less about one another but have an almost inextinguishable supply of sentiment to dispense and an apparently inexhaustible thirst for discovering personal information about people we will never meet. It has to find a home somewhere. In a culture that has set about dismantling the extended family unit and its belief systems and instead worshipping solipsism and the idealized version of fame, we increasingly want to make a great big galloping show out of death, for it to be morbidly glamorous and gossipy.

This has seeped into music. Lyrically, there is a tendency for songs touching upon bereavement to confuse graphic detail with emotional truth: the more you say, the more you reveal on a purely surface level, the more you are connecting. Disclosure is all. The best songs of loss know this to be false. That is not to say that sharing the raw and acutely personal can't be profoundly affecting. It would have been impossible for Mark "E" Everett to create an album as brave and moving as Eels' *Electro-Shock Blues*, for example, while preserving a stiff upper lip or worrying whether it was all a bit too much for us to bear.

But there again, a song like "Sometimes It Snows in April," a lament for the death of a fictional character played by Prince in the not-good-*at-all* film *Under the Cherry Moon* is, to my ears, equally moving, though the entire emotional premise of the song is based on an essentially bogus construct and is at the service of a very lightweight film. Still, Prince finds something in it that is quietly haunting and very powerful. Bereavement songs are not always simply dependent upon strip-mining an autobiographical seam—they are about investing a song with real emotional truth, no matter what its origin.

There's no hard and fast rule, but there is a whole vale of tears between the old days of dignified suffering and this brave new dawn of music-as-psychotherapy. Perhaps songs like "I'll Be Missing You" and Elton John's "Goodbye England's Rose," written for Princess Diana, are simply reinventing the *memento mori* to suit the mood of our times. Or perhaps, in an age defined by confessional realism, we have forgotten what a fitting memorial is.

━━▭━

The arrival on the British music scene of the middle-class art school boys in the early sixties changed everything; in the US, it was Dylan, although Buddy Holly and Chuck Berry must stake a claim as pioneers of the idea of a musical career as a creatively self-sufficient cottage industry. Here were men—and it *was* mostly men for a long time—who played their own instruments, who began to take control over the way the finished record would sound, and on top of that wrote their own songs and were articulate and confident enough to express themselves in a lexicon that went beyond pop's emotional ABC of "happy" and "sad," "love you" and "lost you," or simply "isn't this funny?" Artistic careers seem to attract a disproportionately high ratio of people with dysfunctional backgrounds, odd upbringings, multiple hang-ups, and exotic emotional deficiencies. In other words, they have plenty to get off their chests, and ever since they were given/took the opportunity to do so they certainly haven't shirked from the task.

The shift is there for all to hear in the Beatles' "Help!," its jaunty exclamation mark and perky folk-rock shape failing to mask John Lennon's cry of real, personal anguish. Dylan's monochrome diary songs, "Boots of Spanish Leather" and "Ballad in Plain D," were doing similar things in folk music. This is the beginning of literate, mass-market, autobiographical revelatory pop music as we know it today.

Before then few, if any, pop singers—if we trace that lineage from Louis Armstrong to Elvis Presley, taking in the likes of Al Bowlly, Bing Crosby, Frank Sinatra, Pat Boone, and Connie Francis along the way—were granted the indulgence of expressing their innermost feelings through the words of a song. Fewer still, you suspect, would have wanted to. They were part of the entertainment industry, not poets. Being a popular musician still had something of the whiff of the circus about it. It was not an altogether respectable trade; a craft, a living, rather than an art form.

Crucially, the singer and the songwriter were almost always two completely distinct entities: the unifying singer-songwriter with a message to proclaim or some deep emotion to unburden was not a concept that had penetrated the pop charts or the music industry as a whole, while the notion of musicians being "spokespeople for a generation" was a ludicrous one. The best interpreters would imbue their songs with a convincing draught of personal experience, but they were messengers and mediums, not cultural shapeshifters. Like modern celebrities they became rich fodder for the gossip sheets, they may have been lusted after and screamed and swooned over, but few listeners were looking for them to sing about their lives or their innermost feelings.

When Elvis Presley's beloved mother, Gladys, died in 1958, he didn't retreat into himself and write a song about it. Even if he'd possessed the songwriting ability, he would still have been severely restricted by the mores of the times. His mother's death was perhaps the defining moment of his life, and he was in a sense doomed from that moment on into increasingly desperate attempts at finding a way of expressing his incalculable sense of loss—hence the slow, sad descent into overblown, maudlin balladry. This is the flip side of all the stoicism and economy wound tight in the old-time death songs: the repression of individualism and self-expression hardly encourages an artist to grow or satisfy their own deeper needs. Even Sinatra, who instinctively understood the appeal of wallowing in sadness and who had the voice and the songwriting talent at his beck and call, and the knack of choosing the right song to convey—indeed, completely *inhabit*—an utterly convincing sense of male aloneness, eventually ran aground on a sea of schmaltz, secondhand over-emoting, and show-boating.

The next generation of musicians, slipped loose from the shackles of songwriting teams and the all-encompassing power of the record labels, were to be so much more free in so many different ways. The legacy of that freedom hasn't always made for great music, but it opened the floodgates to a far more personal type of songwriting. John Lennon's mother, Julia Stanley, died in a road accident just a month before Gladys Presley, in July 1958. Where Presley was stymied, ten years later Lennon, his emotions shaken up and stirred by acid and the liberating influence of Yoko Ono, but primarily by the intellectual and emotional permissiveness that the sixties bequeathed pop music, could hardly shut up about it.

"Julia," written in the Himalayan foothills in 1968, is not merely an attempt to commemorate and communicate with his dead mother—"Half of what I say is meaningless / But I say it just to reach you"—it is also a way of finally facing up to the enormous psychological scar her death left upon him, and of working out how to get on with the rest of his life without her. As Ian MacDonald points out in *Revolution in the Head*, Lennon's new lover Yoko Ono is the "ocean child" of the song who "calls me." The Beatle is bringing his soulmate home to meet his mother through the medium of song. He is also, finally, saying goodbye to a woman he never quite knew well enough, transferring his emotional allegiance from the dead mother to the living lover, and in the process freeing himself.

It is a staggeringly beautiful song and transcendent art. We get the whole package: the glistening, shimmering sound evokes the clear, calm waters of eternity, taking precedence over the lyrics, many of which are lifted—with only minor alterations—from Kahlil Gibran's lengthy poem "Sand and Foam," which includes the line "Half of what I say is meaningless; but I say it so that the other half may reach you." But "Julia" works on levels other than the merely literal, hovering between the conscious and the unconscious, just as the world it inhabits, indeed creates, seems to hang somewhere between the earth and the sky. It states very little in clear terms, but I think we all understand. The vulnerability and emotional freedom required to write a song so generous and far-reaching is something new for pop music: Lennon is using his position as an artist (yes, we can use that word now) to extricate himself from his own emotional maze, and as a result we all feel the benefits.

"Julia" suggested that the peace and security that deserted Lennon when his mother died had been regained. Or so it seemed. Under the auspices of Dr. Arthur Janov's primal scream therapy, the ex-Beatle would go on to mine this confessional maternal seam to the point where it yielded less successful, more directly expressive songs that painted a considerably less contented picture: "My Mummy's Dead" and "Mother"—both from his 1970 solo album *John Lennon/Plastic Ono Band*—publicly work through the same issues, but where "Julia" is universal, as wide open as the ocean, these two songs are almost intrusively personal, and the listener is made to feel more like an eavesdropper than a guest or confidante. They worry away at a single preoccupation in a manner that suggests that Lennon was still in many ways trapped in the feelings of the 17-year-old he had been when Julia died.

Whether or not Lennon's creative catharsis was ever truly successful or not, it is clear that, between the death of Gladys Presley and the birth of "Julia," pop music had come a long way in a very short space of time. It was now entering the world that Mark Eitzel described, a place where the lines between indulgence, sincerity, cynicism, exploitation, honesty, sentiment, pain, and beauty are often indistinct and in a state of frequent intersection. Forty years on from "Julia," when this wild creative alchemy works it is intensely powerful and affirming, operating on a very different level from that of a traditional song of loss and addressing a need that isn't tended by the glossy morbidity of most aspects of popular culture.

According to the 1993 study "Death as Portrayed to Adolescents Through Top 40 Rock and Roll Music," modern music offers "few models . . . to emulate in terms of appropriate behavioral responses to death, and how survivors are supposed to think and feel about death. . . . In terms of behavioral responses, the models provided in rock and roll death songs indicate that escape and avoidance are most appropriate. Leaving town, joining the deceased in death, or engaging in some other diversionary behavior are the most frequently cited acts. Emotionally, mourning is portrayed as an abbreviated process, with little sustained attention given to grief and grieving. Sadness . . . often is ignored or at best implied. . . . On a cognitive level, little conscious attention is given to the meaning of death or trying to understand it. . . . The tangible realities of death, the visible reminders, are markedly absent."[3]

Certainly, the English-speaking western world that—still—dominates popular music has some of the least expressive and inclusive mechanisms on the planet when it comes to responding to death. Real up-close-and-personal death, that is, rather than the death at a distance of a celebrity or an icon. "When you look at how other cultures and classes around the world deal with grief, they do it so much better," says Will Oldham. "Think of an Italian-American wake, where the body is lying in state for a couple of days. It's much more expressive."

Iris DeMent's stiff-upper-lip country song "No Time to Cry" acts as a finely drawn warning about the hazards of not allowing yourself to surrender to grief now and then, but it also underlines the fact that our society tends toward a kind of guilt-ridden stoicism. "And there's just so many people trying to get me on the phone / And there's bills to pay, and songs to play / And a house to make a home / I guess I'm older now and I've got no time to cry."

You have to shop around, but popular music is capable of talking about bereavement in an adult, realistic manner, regardless of genre: Loudon Wainwright III's "Sometimes I Forget," Pet Shop Boys' "Your Funny Uncle," Steve Earle's "Fort Worth Blues," Pete Rock & CL Smooth's "They Reminisce Over You (T.R.O.Y)," U2's "Tomorrow," Gram Parsons' "Brass Buttons," Emmylou Harris' "Boulder to Birmingham," and, perhaps the greatest of them all, the Carter Family's "Will the Circle Be Unbroken?"

Eels' *Electro-Shock Blues* deals head on with death over the course of an entire album, in the face of Mark "E" Everett's sister's suicide and his mother's death from lung cancer; his father had died of a heart attack when Everett was 17. "Suicide, cancer, heart attacks," said Everett. "Death is the greatest American taboo since sex. [This album] is the phone call in the middle of the night that the world doesn't want to answer." He's right, but it's a call worth taking. What finally comes through is Everett's resilience of spirit, but he pulls no punches in getting there: the album opens with "Elizabeth on the Bathroom Floor," taken from his sister's final diary entries ("My life is shit and piss") and moves through funerals, radiation treatment, and psychiatric hospitals, before finally arriving at an exhausted, low-key, utterly plausible affirmation of life and love on the closing "P.S. You Rock My World": "Maybe it's time to live . . . / Cause I know I've only got / This moment / And it's good."

Likewise, when Lucinda Williams' mother, Lucy Morgan, died in March 2004, the album that followed, *West*, was written from within the chill and gloom of the shadow of the event. "Mama You Sweet" is as visceral a portrayal of grief as I've ever heard; no sooner does a fond maternal memory slip innocuously into view than it is hijacked by a wall of pain and anger that "courses through / Every vein, every limb / Trying to find a way out / Between the secrets in my skin."

"The Living Years" by Mike & the Mechanics doesn't so

much offer a solution to closing the gap between the things we feel when someone dies and the things we feel able to express, as simply acknowledge that it exists. Which is a start. The fact that it became such a hugely successful song, reaching number one in the US and Australia and number two in the UK in 1988, would suggest that the message behind "The Living Years" struck a collective nerve, although it's often unwise to place too much faith in the commercial evidence—it's impossible to measure the myriad reasons why a song plugs into the public consciousness; a million people might just like the bass line. The mass of anecdotal and web evidence, however, suggests that its central theme of deep regret over words left unspoken was a major part of the reason it resonated with so many people. Its recurring refrain—"I just wish that I had told him / In the living years"—was born from true experience: the song's cowriters Mike Rutherford and B.A. Robertson had each recently lost their fathers, the former in particular lamenting the lack of meaningful communication between father and son.

There is resolution and consolation in the song's final verses. Though the singer "wasn't there that morning / When my father passed away" he is able to reach a kind of spiritual reconciliation with the traditional idea of life and death being an integral part of the eternal cycle. "I think I caught his spirit / Later that same year / I'm sure I heard his echo / In my baby's new born tears." This may be a convenient way out of all that grief and guilt, but it plugs into ideas of seasonal growth, death, and rebirth that go right back to ancient Indian and Egyptian civilizations. Not to mention Dylan's "Ballad of Hollis Brown" ("There's seven people dead on a South Dakota farm / Somewhere in the distance there's seven new people born") and Laura Nyro's "And When I Die": "And when I die / And when I'm gone / There'll be one child born / And a world to carry on."

Though musically staid—it is, truth be told, as downright stiff and buttoned up as the relationship it describes, and probably not intentionally—"The Living Years" still stands as an uncommonly thorough, adult, and unflinchingly honest rummage through the big bag of conflicting emotions one is often left clutching when a close family member passes away. Written by Whitfield and Strong, the Temptations' bone-hard "Papa Was a Rollin' Stone" is another; death does not always bring reconciliation and peace. You shouldn't speak ill of the dead, but here is an acknowledgment that you can tell the truth about them, and it isn't always pleasant. Lou Reed and John Cale's album-length tribute to the dead Andy Warhol, *Songs for Drella*, also refuses to flinch from the awkward stuff. "A Dream" writes from the perspective of a bitchy Warhol—"I hate Lou, I really do. I saw him at the MTV show and he was one row away and he didn't even say hello"—while a "hurt" Reed responds in the closing "Hello, It's Me." These are tough songs to write, and often to hear, but they fulfill a vital purpose for those wrestling with feelings of unreconciled anger and rejection, the kind of emotions often deemed to be socially unacceptable in the aftermath of a bereavement.

Similarly, it takes an extraordinary song to truly convey the sheer disorientation of loss, that sense many people describe of being little more than an automaton stepping through a waking dream. The world around remains the same, but everything has changed forever. "Life's like bacon and ice cream," Lou Reed sang on "What's Good." "That's what life's like without you." Willie Nelson's remarkable "I Still Can't Believe That You're Gone" was written after the wife of his drummer and compadre Paul English killed herself, and captures that sense of someone groping through life as though in a trance, mindless of the traffic when they cross the road, indifferent to the consequences: "I'm alone and I'm still living / I don't like it but I'll take it 'til I'm strong."

In response to the almost incalculable shock of 9/11, Bruce Springsteen panned in, scaled the horror down to the finest hair's breadth of physical and emotional detail, and in doing so captured that same jarring, shocked sense of emptiness. Springsteen doesn't do death in particularly realistic or explicit terms—his fondness for the cinematic and heroic is too deeply ingrained (although he may be learning: "Terry's Song," the final track on *Magic*, is a moving lament for a dead friend, low-key, honest, and relatively reined in). But he certainly understands what makes the human heart tick. James Joyce memorably wrote that absence is the highest form of presence; in "You're Missing," Springsteen captures the recent loss of a loved one by reciting a litany of normality with one crushing void at its center: "Coffee cup's on the counter, jacket's on the chair / Papers on the doorstep, you're not there / Everything is everything / Everything is everything / But you're missing."

That's the kind of pole-axing reality many of us will recognize, even if we haven't ever suffered a significant bereavement. ABBA captured this acute pain of absence in "The Day Before You Came," but the story runs in reverse: the life before the lover arrived on the scene is characterized as a kind of living death, a life fossilized by a relentless routine with no emotional center. "You're Missing" inhabits the same bleached world, as one death echoes down the corridors of many more lives, diminished and drained of purpose to the point where death seems almost like the preferable option. Almost unfathomable, the difference another human being makes to a life: "Your house is waiting / For you to walk in, for you to walk in / But you're missing."

It's a merciless line. A killer. How on earth do you get past *that*? Well, just hearing it helps; feeling the hard, cool words of empathy. It's clear that the greatest songs of loss, the ones that are really serious about their intent, share one common thread: they are tough as old leather. Not mawkish, or hysterical, or maudlin, or easy; there is very little talk of angels, very little false hope. They are firmly in control of their use of language and their emotions. They know that nothing is ever going to be the same again and they don't shirk from stating it. These songs succeed in perfecting that tricky balancing act between personal experience and professional distance that can make many songwriters, as Eitzel and Finn acknowledge, a little uncomfortable in their own skins. But their composure, their steady aim, their determination to get to the heart of the matter doesn't in the end make the writer self-serving, or cold, or manipulative, or dismissive. It simply means he or she is doing their job properly.

My favorite bereavement song shares this distaste for

pussy-footing around. It's a sinewy, deceptively clever, wonderfully practical slice of life and death, so skillful it's not immediately clear that it's even about loss at all. New York City. 1964. It feels like it should be spring time. A young girl has lost her lover to the grave and is naturally grief-stricken, turning away from the world and instead trying to hold on to the past, to live among the dead. A concerned young man urges her to return to the light. Somewhere between the opening cry of her name and the closing line of vulnerable empathy, he shows her that there is a route out of this gloom.

Bob Dylan's "To Ramona" starts after the crucial event. In classical pop terms, the sexy part of the action—the lead up to the death, the act itself, the teary farewells—are long gone. The story has moved on to a less emotionally dramatic place: that awkward life moment when the time to absorb your loss, allow it the live on privately within you, and to move on appears to have arrived. This unusually beautiful, sensitive song boldly negotiates this rocky terrain. It is one of the clearest expressions the young Dylan made about his beliefs concerning the dead and the spirit world, and how crucial it is not to linger on the departed; he really *had* been listening hard to the words of those spooky, ancient songs like "The Cruel Grave" (as well as Rex Griffin's country standard "The Last Letter," which inspired the melody for "To Ramona").

This being Dylan, his ideas would not stay fixed for all that long, but "To Ramona" is a forthright, gentle, earthbound consideration of another's bereavement and how best to help her with it. Ramona is in pain but stretching upon her lover's grave will no longer help. Dylan puts his arm around her and spells out the truth. He is firm and grounded: "There's no use in tryin' to deal with the dyin'," he says, "Though I cannot explain that in lines." Today it would be called something silly like tough love. It just sounds like love to me. And later: "But it grieves my heart, love / To see you tryin' to be a part of / A world that just don't exist."

He reiterates these sentiments in another song written shortly afterward, "It's All Over Now, Baby Blue": "Forget the dead you've left / They will not follow you." It seems that Dylan is a life-is-for-living kind of guy after all. Who knew? But there is also—not unusually for Dylan—the sly scent of seduction on the wind in "To Ramona." His ulterior motive in soaking up all those grief-stricken tears is to steer Ramona away from thoughts of her deceased lover and very firmly toward thoughts about him. Don't forget, babe, but move on. And move on with me. It should sound cold, manipulative, and sleazy, but instead it comes over as a lovely little nudge back into the land of the living. It's time, in the words of teen R&B queens Blaque on "When the Last Teardrop Falls," to find your happiness again. Or as Elvis Costello instructs his lover from beyond the grave in "The Birds Will Still Be Singing": "Don't waste your precious time pretending you're heartbroken." It's perhaps the hardest thing a song can ever say: "You can't go on. But go on." Maybe that's why we don't hear it more often.

Good bereavement songs are not possessive of their emotions. At some point they hand over the reins to the listener, allowing us to give vent to our own feelings. This transference of emotion is easier when the deceased person being written about is a blank canvas to the listener, a cipher. The dynamic of the bereavement song changes, however, if the song is written about somebody famous. They inhabit and personify the song in a way that is quite radically removed from something like "Meet on the Ledge" or "You're Missing," no matter how exact or precise the inspiration for writing those songs may have been.

What might be called the celebrity death song has a long tradition in music, stretching right back to Egypt's wailing women singing "The Lament of Isis on the Death of Osiris" and going up to and beyond the Fugs' "Rameses II Is Dead, My Love." The important figures of any age have always been memorialized and posthumously glorified in song. Woody Guthrie doffed his coon-skin cap to the life of FDR in "Dear Mrs. Roosevelt," written after the President's death in 1945.

In pop terms, we could—stretching a point, perhaps—look back to "The Ballad of Davy Crockett" in 1954. Certainly "I Dreamed of a Hillbilly Heaven" qualifies, a stately Stetson raised to the late heroes of country music that became a top five hit for Tex Ritter in 1961.

From the midsixties onward, however, songs like "Abraham, Martin and John" marked a pronounced gear change. Just as the individual had become bolder in staking out his or her emotional territory, there was also a deeper sense of loss creeping into the communal consciousness and seeking an expressive outlet. The end of the sixties was in many ways a time of mass bereavement, a mourning of deaths both real and figurative: the assassination of John F. Kennedy lingered, brought back into sharp relief by the murder of his brother Robert and Martin Luther King; the slow death of the idealistic dreams of the decade; the lingering, deepening scar of Vietnam; the Cuban missile crisis and the onset of the Cold War; the increasingly violent student and civil rights protests; and an end of the cosy certainties and picket fence innocence of the fifties. This accounts for a proliferation of songs of social despair: from Barry McGuire's "Eve of Destruction" to Crosby Stills Nash & Young's "Ohio" to the Temptations' "Ball of Confusion" up to Marvin Gaye's "What's Goin' On." All—in their own way—songs articulating a shared sense of profound loss.

The rapidity of change in the sixties left many feeling a little travel sick when the exhilaration wore off. In this sense, "Help!" and "Abraham, Martin and John" are simply different sides of the same coin. Both are stark admissions of crumbling confidence, a goodbye to all the old guarantees of the past. One speaks for the fears of a man alone as he feels his life spiralling out of his control, holding on rather desperately to the fictional idylls of childhood; the other speaks for the fears of a country, even a world. Both approaches struck a chord with audiences.

As pop music took on a far more confessional, autobiographical hue, the deaths of prominent public figures became the source of increasingly agitated soul searching and, not unrelatedly, rich creative pickings. From its biblical-sounding title onward, "Abraham, Martin and John" was an attempt to deify America's holy trinity of modern crusaders—Dr. King and the two Kennedys—placing them in a lineage that stretches back to the nation's great historical liberal icon, Abraham Lincoln. There is a clear Messianic subtext: all were cut down in their prime before their good work on earth was done. In the case of King and Bobby Kennedy, their deaths had occurred only months prior to composition, making the song a work of real topicality and genuine sincerity.

Written by Dick Holler, "Abraham, Martin and John" was first recorded in a stately folk-rock style by Dion in 1968, then both Moms Mabley and the Miracles the following year, and later in its most enduring version by Marvin Gaye. Oversimplistic but grounded in a common consensus of feeling, it struck a chord as much for its simple, hymnlike melody as its aching sadness at all that waste and its underlying concern at a society drifting off into stormy waters without a figure of sufficient moral authority at the tiller. The recurring refrain of "it seems the good die young"—a phrase that crops up again and again in songs of bereavement, to the point of cliché—makes the Christ analogy specific, as though these men, too, were somehow too pure for this world and had to be sacrificed for the greater good. "Pride (In the Name of Love)" by U2 trod a similar path almost twenty years later, linking the assassination of Dr. King to the betrayal and crucifixion of Jesus.

In "Abraham, Martin and John" each of the dead men is described as a "good friend"; the country's loss is played out at a personal level. Whereas previously, celebrity death songs were respectful but hardly bereft, performed with a sense of social duty and even fun, now an emotional bond between the distant figurehead and the man on the street was being established. A few years earlier, in 1965, the Byrds took the traditional folk song "He Was a Friend of Mine" and tweaked it considerably—with its mention of "gunners" and "Dallas Town"—to make it explicitly about the death of JFK in November 1963: "Though I never met him, I knew him just the same / Oh, he was a friend of mine / The leader of a

nation for such a precious time / Oh, he was a friend of mine."
It's a succinct encapsulation of the message at the heart of
many subsequent celebrity death songs: "I didn't know you,
but I believed we were friends. Now you are gone, I am grieving your death."

And so it begins. A combination of the changing times and
the profusion of television, radio, newspapers, magazines,
and ultimately computers, bringing the whole wide world
into our living rooms, eventually persuades us to make a
serious emotional investment in those we will never really
know. JFK was arguably the Princess Di of his day, except
his death symbolized the demise of something far more profound than simple flesh and blood, but over the ensuing forty
years the net of bereavement has been cast far wider than
our most beloved friends and family, or even society's most
prominent figureheads. Now its reach encompasses dead
film stars, dead rappers, dead artists, dead princesses. Dead
singers, in particular, have always attracted the attentions
of the living of the same vocation.

They make an odd bunch, these songs. Not all of them are
somber and tear-stained—some of them throw a good wake
and seek nothing more complicated than to tip their hat in
praise. Stevie Wonder's "Sir Duke" was a rambunctious celebration of Duke Ellington, who had died two years earlier,
in 1974. The Righteous Brothers' "Rock and Roll Heaven"
was essentially a rock update of "I Dreamed of a Hillbilly
Heaven," which gave us the enduring image, much loved by
rock sentimentalists, of our beloved heroes, united by a fondness for class-A drugs, alcohol abuse, and flying in very small
planes, forming a "helluva band" and jamming their hearts
out in heaven: "Jimi gave us rainbows / And Janis took a
piece of our hearts / And Otis brought us all to the dock of a
bay / Sing a song to light my fire / Remember Jim that way /
They've all found another place / Another place to play."

Sounds horrible, doesn't it? Nowadays, of course, our rock
stars don't even bother to die—they just reform and book a
stadium tour; for £110, the Police will bring heaven to you
on a silver platter. A more poetic evocation of Pink Floyd's
"Great Gig in the Sky" is the Commodores' "Nightshift,"

written in memory of Marvin Gaye and Jackie Wilson, both of whom died in 1984 but were, apparently, still creating some "sweet sounds" up there. The "nightshift" remains one of the more ingenious and oddly moving euphemisms for the other side—any direct mention of expiration is discouraged in these kind of songs. Heaven and angels, yes. The cold, merciless clamp of death, no. The emphasis is on being taken before one's time, on tragedy and heroism.

These are songs that simply use a famous death as a timely excuse to pay tribute to their talents. Bereavement is too strong a word, although a song like Don McLean's "American Pie," a worldwide hit in the summer of 1971, comes close. McLean remembers the death of Buddy Holly and "the day the music died," but really he is waving s'long to his own childhood and a time of perceived hope and innocence.. He followed it in 1972 with "Vincent," his pensive, wordy musing upon the death of Vincent Van Gogh, and another song as much about the singer as the subject, a rather precious rumination upon the fragile temperament of all creative types, whether they be Van Gogh or, well, Don McLean.

It all becomes rather more complex, however, when genuine, personal grief is invested into a song about a publicly revered celebrity. When a personal relationship is played out in a public arena, often the expectations and perceptions of the audience have to be acknowledged, which is why most songs where a living celebrity pays tribute to a dead one aren't terribly interesting—they almost inevitably pander to the public image of the deceased rather than addressing the individual that they knew.

Paul McCartney was almost contractually obliged to write and release a song about John Lennon following his murder in 1980. That he did so in 1982 with the simplicity and grace displayed on "Here Today" was a relief; here he is talking to an old friend, not Beatle John, and there are vague hints at the rocky road their relationship took. But wouldn't it have been interesting to have heard an early draft, or perhaps the other songs McCartney tried to write for Lennon, rather than the one expertly polished up for public consumption? Still, it beats Elton John and Bernie Taupin's "Empty Garden (Hey

Hey Johnny)," which labored a metaphor of Lennon as a gardener—"It's funny how one insect can damage so much grain"—to the point of perversity. The symbolism practically perspires with all the effort not to be too straight or artless, which is not really the point at all.

Only occasionally is the emotion allowed to flow through loud and clear, travelling beyond respectful tribute to summon up a really resonant, forceful display of personal grief. The death of Kurt Cobain was a Princess Di moment for many teenagers. Legendary British DJ John Peel recalled meeting his children as they came off the school bus to break the news to them, as though there had been a death in the family. They probably felt that there had. It was marked by the rock community with two songs of greater emotional clout than the standard heroic goodbye. R.E.M.'s "Let Me In" is a raw howl, Michael Stipe exasperated at his inability to get close enough to his friend to save him from himself. There is little sense of a rock star addressing another rock star; it's just one man trying to connect with a fellow human being. Stipe sent Cobain plane tickets in an effort to get him to come and work with the band, but it was too late: "I had a mind to try to stop you / Let me in / Let me in," he sings through a blizzard of guitar. "Say goodbye / Nice try." The guitar used on the track is one of Cobain's own, and you can feel it.

Neil Young's "Sleeps with Angels" also tackles his sense of bereavement from a very personal perspective. In his suicide note, Cobain quoted from Young's 1979 song "Hey Hey, My My (Into the Black)": "It's better to burn out than to fade away." Young was profoundly shaken by this extreme interpretation, the fact that his words were used as some kind of artistic justification for Cobain's suicide. He was even more spooked because, although the two men had never met, Young, like Stipe, had been trying to get in touch with Cobain in the days leading up to his death.

"I read something and someone told me a few things that made me think he was in trouble that week," he later explained. "I even had my office look for him. It's just too bad I didn't get a shot. I had an impulse to connect. Only when he used my song in that suicide note was the connection made. I felt it was really unfortunate that I didn't get through to him. I might've been able to make things a little lighter for him, that's all. Just lighten it up a little bit."[4]

Maybe so, but *Sleeps with Angels* certainly isn't a light album. Named in Cobain's honor, the title track, though not a specific lament for the dead singer, features a recurring refrain—"too late, too soon"—that cuts right to the heart of the matter. It's likely Young was also shaken by the similarities between Cobain and Crazy Horse guitarist Danny Whitten, who died of a heroin overdose in 1973 and whose death—alongside that of roadie Bruce Berry—inspired the album *Tonight's the Night*. The title track is another great requiem for the dead, capturing the sense of needless waste, the fear and paranoia, the jittery mood of a time when heroin was even more of a blight on the musical community than it became even in nineties Seattle. Both songs eschew specifics and easy sentiment for the real core emotions of bereavement—guilt, anger, rage, and more than a hint of shit-scared panic: "Dear God, when is this curse coming to get *me*?" Songs of loss—whether about rock stars or road sweepers—only really work if we get to see a little of this mortal dread and discomfort, if we are permitted to hear an echo of the tolling bell. It's a two-way street.

The most remarkable song raking over the uneasy, undefined relationship between a dead musician and a living one keeps every emotion in check but speaks volumes about both the singer and the subject. A couple of years after her death, Leonard Cohen remembered his fleeting lover Janis Joplin in "Chelsea Hotel #2" with an honest touch and a lack of pity—for either party—that chimed perfectly with the subject of the song, who never cared much for all of that "jiving around." It also boasts one of the all-time great closing stanzas: "I don't mean to suggest that I loved you the best / I can't keep track of each fallen robin / I remember you well in the Chelsea Hotel / That's all, I don't think of you that often."

It's touchingly honest and slyly nostalgic without ever over-playing the importance of either person in the other's life. There is no attempt to shanghai the grief of those who *did* love her the best, precious few that there were. And so we see Cohen's stab of grief for what it is for so many of us; no great dramatic torrent, but rather pared down to a few pangs in memory of a handful of shared, private moments. No more, no less. Most of those we lose had other lives, other lovers, other memories. We only hold a little bit of them for ourselves.

It's useful to compare Cohen's sure, steady touch with perhaps the most famous song of celebrity bereavement, Elton John's "Candle in the Wind," a song so enduring and mutable it was able to change funeral horses midstream and yet continue wringing tears from its audience. The original lyric, written by John's long-time collaborator Bernie Taupin, is a contemplation of the personally corrosive yet publicly enduring nature of fame, set against the backdrop of the death of Marilyn Monroe in 1962. The song was later co-opted, perhaps appropriately, as an anthem for Princess Diana after her untimely death in August 1997. Taupin and John hastily rewrote the lyrics and equally hastily entitled it "Goodbye England's Rose" (forgetting, perhaps, that Diana had been the Princess of Wales) whereupon it provided the official soundtrack to the UK's remarkably extravagant festival of grief.

The rewritten version is distinctly at odds with Stipe and Young's straight-from-the-hip emotional outpourings and McCartney's measured restraint; its glutinous grief is the absolute antithesis of Cohen's self-denying economy. Here the famous dead lady is not allowed her other lives, her contradictions, but instead is instantly deified according to the most simplistic version of her highly complex life story. The lexicon is textbook grief-lite: roses, heaven, stars, sunsets, golden, wings. It sold over 3.5 million copies in a week.

"Candle in the Wind"/"Goodbye England's Rose" comes closest to exemplifying the notion that certain types of bereavement songs have become our modern-day hymns, and that shared sorrow over the deaths of people we never really knew are where we now express grief most openly and comfortably as a society. When the actor Heath Ledger died in New York early in 2008, Nicole Vaughan, a 24-year-old law student, walked to his apartment when she heard the news, "because of the way our generation is, we sort of feel we're a part of each other's lives."[5] Hundreds did, and presumably felt, the same.

No disrespect to Ledger, who was shaping up to be a fine actor, but this wasn't someone who helped to define his generation in the manner of a Lennon or a JFK. No matter. It seems these days we'll grasp any opportunity to dip our toes in the cool, dark waters of tragedy.

These events become a point of communion. In a time of increasing spiritual and familial absence, the crutch that is closest to hand is celebrity. We feel we know these people because we do know them, or at least a version of them. The currency of celebrity has been devalued—or if you prefer, democratized—to such an extent that each one of us is now only one break away from being famous: one phone call, one tragedy, one blurred photo, one drunken night. Perhaps the fact that we increasingly see ourselves reflected back in the mirror image of today's celebrities explains why we invest so much time, energy, and emotion in following their lives. We're *that* close to having what they have. Little wonder that when they go they leave a big, ragged hole in our day—their deaths are a jarring reminder of our own mortality.

And so we mourn, openly and almost greedily, and turn to "Goodbye England's Rose," to "I'll Be Missing You," to "Angels" and "My Heart Will Go On," to help us unload all that emotion, uncertainty, fear, and confusion; songs written by men and women who not only display an astonishingly accurate understanding of the perilously hollow mood of the times, but who are arguably instrumental in helping shape it. Whatever gets you through the night is just fine by me, but there is another path. Lend an ear to "Meet on the Ledge" or "To Ramona": "It's all just a dream, babe / A vacuum, a scheme, babe / That sucks you into feelin' like this." These songs aren't designed merely for this transient age, but for all time.

9
WHO WANTS TO LIVE FOREVER?
The Fat Lady's Songbook

When I asked Ice T if he'd ever thought about the music he might like to have played at his funeral, he laughed mirthlessly before nominating his own song—how gangsta is *that?*—"Some of You Niggas Is Bitches Too." He was joking. I think. If, as seems likely, he hadn't given the matter any serious thought, then Ice may well be among the minority. Nowadays, more and more death carries us off to the accompaniment of a hand-picked soundtrack, often comprised of popular music. According to a poll of 45,000 people conducted in February 2005 by the digital TV station Music Choice, the most popular funeral songs in Europe are:

1. Queen, "The Show Must Go On"
2. Led Zeppelin, "Stairway to Heaven"
3. AC/DC, "Highway to Hell"
4. Frank Sinatra, "My Way"
5. Mozart, "Requiem"
6. Robbie Williams, "Angels"
7. Queen, "Who Wants to Live Forever?"
8. The Beatles, "Let It Be"
9. Metallica, "Nothing Else Matters"
10. U2, "With or Without You"

A diverse selection. Heaven and hell and everything in between. What does it say? What message do these songs convey? What does the fact that we even compile such a list mean? First, let's spare Mozart this interrogation. He is not a pop man and, besides, "Requiem" is simply doing its job by being in the top ten. I suspect very few of the writers of the remaining nine pop songs on the list, however, could have foreseen their songs fulfilling such a purpose during the writing process.

One obvious point. It is an *astonishingly* masculine list, positively simmering with testosterone. That's not for a minute to suggest that women don't like rock music, and it must also be taken into account that mainstream tastes on mainland Europe tend to be slightly heavier than in the UK, which may sway the findings, but still it seems clearly weighted toward a male sensibility.

The inferences that might be taken from this are that many women don't want to play popular songs at their own funeral, or that they have rather more eclectic tastes than their male counterparts. Perhaps. But it's more tempting to surmise that women would simply rather not contemplate their own demise in such vainglorious terms. Because what strikes you immediately is the sheer sense of drama in these songs. These are big, powerful, explosive pieces of music, clearly designed to wreak maximum emotional havoc upon those filling the pews. No one sliding through the pearly gates with this playlist ringing in their ears is intent on going gently into that good night.

"Let It Be" is, perhaps, the exception. Of all the songs here it sounds the most muted emotional fanfare. Hardly rousing, perhaps a little sanctimonious, but suffused with a sense of respect, decorum, and ersatz spirituality that might be deemed appropriate for such a somber occasion. It's unlikely to turn the insides of a church to dust, at any rate. Performed by the world's biggest, still-most-beloved band, it employs a simple, circular, gospel-style chord structure, which pads around easily and predictably and exudes an air of comfort and resolution. Lyrically, there is a quiet certainty that the hurt will mend, and a Zen-like acceptance of fate, while the mention of "mother Mary" (a reference to McCartney's mother, clearly, rather than Jesus') has an obvious religious ring. Personally, I find that McCartney's other hymnal piano ballad from the Beatles' dying days, "The Long and Winding Road," communicates a more touching sense of loss and a far greater depth of feeling, while at the same time being more open to individual interpretation, but maybe all those attributes are a drawback in these circumstances. "Let It Be" is uncomplicated enough—both linguistically and intellectually—to be almost universally understood.

The rest of the songs are rather less restrained. The popularity of Queen at funerals may have something to do with the fact that Freddie Mercury died relatively young and wrote the song at the top of the list, "The Show Must Go On," with the explicit knowledge that his remaining time was short. That kind of contextual poignancy puts a lot of wind in the sails. The sentiments of the song itself are personal but wide-ranging. A reflection upon social ills; a look back at old love affairs; the pondering of the meaning of existence; and a liberal dose of good old British strength-in-adversity—"I'll face it with a grin"—that instructs those left behind: "Be strong." Musically, it's vintage Queen, madly over-the-top, a mock-operatic power ballad that bangs rather than whimpers. It is hugely self-regarding, unashamedly self-important, and yet contains a pantomime element that ensures it is almost impossible to take completely seriously. It's lyrically appropriate, sentimental but not self-pitying. You can see why it's so popular. It could have been written specifically for such a purpose and probably was.

"Who Wants to Live Forever" is a different beast altogether, an atmospheric, ethereal orchestral ballad that forwards the idea that all life is contained within each fleeting moment and, as such, we all live on eternally: "We can have forever / We can love forever / Forever is our today." Written for the soundtrack of the film *Highlander*, it was composed by Brian May but still links to Mercury's death. Seal performed it at the singer's memorial concert in 1992 and it makes for a rather appropriate final farewell, refusing to shirk issues of bereavement and the inevitability of death, but at the same time offering hope and consolation.

It's the roaring defiance of "The Show Must Go On," however, that echoes through many of the other songs: "Nothing Else Matters" is about a love so powerful it excludes and eventually destroys the rest of the world, and sits uncomfortably at odds with the rather more inclusive aims of a funeral service. "Highway to Hell," meanwhile, is clearly the choice *du jour* of the unrepentant metal monster (or wannabe monster). Letting it ring out around the funeral parlor says, "I had a very good time, thank you, and I want you to know it. Now I'm more than happy to burn for my sins." Choosing it perfectly encapsulates heavy metal's most enduring and endearing streak: its wonderful mock bravado, the way it screams down at death with a tongue planted firmly in its cheek.

There's no such redeeming qualities in the case of the unspeakable "My Way," in which the defiance arrives in the form of one last rant from beyond the grave. No quiet valediction this, but instead a great, spittle-flecked, red-faced, vein-popping fuck-you to the world, the last will and testament of some deranged despot. "A deathbed ego rant," according to Richard Thompson. "Refusing to go quietly. Horrible song, full of bluster: 'I showed 'em and I'll keep showing 'em.'"

Though it was perhaps his least accomplished recording, a world away from the emotionally pitch-perfect performances of his Capitol years, Frank Sinatra had at least lived long, hard, and dramatically enough to embody the song's litany of boasts with a certain authority and plausibility when he recorded it in 1969. When it comes, however, to Terry or Bill or George or Sam (and I'd bet good money that it's almost always men who choose this song to escort them over to the great beyond, borne aloft on a carpet of self-importance and cigar smoke), the middle managers, local government employees, the shop-keepers, lawyers, and teachers—mere mortals just like the rest of us, in other words—its absurd puffery simply sounds hollow and ridiculously inflated. On top of all that, the lyric jars: by this stage the end isn't "near," it has clearly arrived. That's why we're all here.

"Stairway to Heaven" is another risky one. Too long-winded. You don't really want people getting *bored* at your own funeral, their eyes drifting out through the stained-glass window, their minds turning to the weather or the football scores. Filled to the brim with mystical nonsense, it's one of these supposed death songs where the title alone seems to suffice. U2's "With or Without You," meanwhile, is as musically straightforward as "Let It Be," the same, four-chord pattern on an endless loop, but substantially more tortured than McCartney's contemplation of fate, building in momentum until it comes crashing in a climactic wave of emotion. It's a dark song, a song about the lengths and depths love can push us to, but "I can't live / with or without you" seems an odd sentiment to express at your own funeral. The rather unpleasant suspicion remains that it is designed to put words into the mouths of those left behind.

This is the dispassionate, detached view of these songs. I have never heard any of them played at a funeral service and so can't make any claims on their transportative effect in that context. But without wanting to review the occasion as though it were no different from a night spent watching Coldplay at Wembley—strong opening number, muddy sound, they lost the audience somewhere near the end—the inclusion of pop music turns a funeral into something else: a celebration of the life lived, rather than a solemn gathering in preparation for the soul's departure. It doesn't require a genius to point out that it mirrors the increasing secularization of society: clearly, these aren't songs that you would pick to reaffirm your relationship with your God of choice, or to prepare for or confront what lies ahead. They are instead one last attempt to communicate the essence of what it was that made you *you* while you were alive.

In a sense, this brings us back to where we came in. Very few people choose pop songs that confront the reality of death and dying, while traditional religious or spiritual songs don't provide blanket comfort anymore, or else people aren't sufficiently aware of them to be able to make an informed choice. Instead, many individuals prefer popular songs that say to those left behind, "Remember me this way."

The fact that in most cases these songs reflect delusional, exaggerated, aspirational, heroic, or humorous images of self should not detract from any comfort they provide, but they do underline that our modern relationship with death has changed fundamentally: a UK poll conducted in 2000 found that almost sixty percent of us would choose pop songs rather than hymns, while nine out of ten of us would prefer family and friends to wear bright colors instead of the traditional black.

The debate continues to rumble about the use of pop music at funeral ceremonies. Is it a dumbed down response, the jocularity and myth-making reflecting our increasing inability to handle death or even properly acknowledge it? Does it emphasize the fact that we view death as a joke right up to the point where we leave this world, as well as underscoring our self-obsessive natures: all we want to do is slide one more coin into the jukebox from beyond the grave instead of preparing in an appropriate fashion.

On the other hand, shouldn't the fact that we want to play Metallica and Robbie Williams at a funeral be celebrated as a break from the constraints of religious piety, a joyous reclaiming of the right to say goodbye to our loved ones in the manner that those involved would regard as fitting and appropriate? It's important to remember that this isn't happening under anyone's jurisdiction or instruction. It is happening because people want an alternative from convention and what many feel are the emotional straight-jacketed responses to grief that have existed, in Britain at least, since Victorian times. And if you can't play to the gallery at your funeral, then when can you?

I canvassed for opinion among friends and family and the responses ranged from: "There's no way that I would have this nonsense at one of my family member's funerals. I believe in having a eulogy, a short sermon, and maybe a song or two. But in the end we are there to bury the body and move on—just as their spirit has." From another: "The point of a funeral is to remember someone. When I have a funeral I want people to remember how I lived not died." And another: "It's distasteful, tacky, and self-indulgent. It's all about them rather than the people who are left behind to grieve." And finally: "Do you think you could book Willie Nelson?"

The importance of remembrance is a significant one. Nothing evokes time, place, people, and events like a pop song. Pop music has only become culturally omnipresent in the past forty years, but in that time it has become shorthand; it can connect the listener instantly to emotions far beyond what it literally describes, which is why playing songs that speak clearly about the manner in which an individual has lived their life, about their personal experience on earth, about what was important to them, in the circumstances can be hugely powerful.

If he was a prankster, a trickster, a practical joker, then something in jest like "Another One Bites the Dust" might well be more fitting than "Amazing Grace." If she was a sensitive, sentimental sort, easy to tears, then "My Heart Will Go On" might do the job better than "Eternal Father, Strong to Save." And so on. Some of these songs have become modern hymns. "Let It Be" and Robbie Williams' "Angels" belong to the entire world now; it's just a shame, perhaps, that so many of the sentiments of the most popular songs have been scoured away through overuse. They convey hardly any unique sense of the individual, which—seeing as that is the point of having pop music at a funeral—seems to rather defeat the purpose of playing them.

Another recent poll of songs most frequently requested for funerals in Britain, conducted by the Research for the Bereavement Register, found some overlap with the Music Choice poll, but there were some variances that revealed a few cultural idiosyncrasies. In Britain, the closing song from Monty Python's film *The Life of Brian* came in at number three: "Always Look on the Bright Side of Life" captures that wry, could-be-worse quality that makes it a perfect death song for those who despise great shows of emotion but want to convey a convincing sense of who they were and the manner in which they regarded the world.

The list also included songs such as "Goodbye, My Lover" by James Blunt, "I've Had the Time of My Life" by Jennifer Warnes and Bill Medley, "Wind Beneath My Wings" by Bette

Midler, and—rather eerily—"Every Breath You Take" by the Police, a song written from the perspective of an obsessive ex-lover. These—like "Nothing Else Matters," a gruff, heartfelt tribute to a relationship that is all-consuming—fall within the spectrum of love songs, pure and simple, and they throw up an interesting problem when they are heard at a funeral service.

Each of these songs will, almost certainly, have been chosen by the deceased with the intention of conveying a message to one person only. In common with "With or Without You," I'm not sure what any of these songs say to the aunts, uncles, cousins, grandparents, and even mothers and fathers in attendance; would they feel just a little excluded, perhaps, by "Goodbye, My Lover" assaulting their ears? Or perhaps they'd feel that they're being asked to sit through an in-joke/ private message that they aren't invited to share.

The pay-off for the personal touch, the bespoke musical menu, is this narrowing of the focus of grief. One respondent in a recent online debate about funeral songs on the BBC6 website recalled his brother's funeral, where he elected to play "You're History" by Shakespears Sister and Queen's "Another One Bites the Dust." "My brother Dave and I used to joke about this when we were younger," he wrote. "We were always changing our minds and, looking back, I suppose we treated it quite lightly. Dave was killed in a car accident seven years ago and I along with the rest of the family had to make choices about his funeral and what songs to play. One song we used to laugh at was 'You're History' by Shakespears Sister, so I chose that and [Queen's] 'Another One Bites the Dust.' I know Dave would have seen the funny side, but sadly some of my relatives didn't and were quite upset by my choices."

In the 2003 film *Love, Actually*, one character chooses the Bay City Rollers' "Bye Bye Baby" as her funeral song. As it plays in the church, it is accompanied by some damp, indulgent smiles, as well as some stiff, disapproving shakes of the head. It is probably the only vaguely plausible scene in the whole movie. Given the broad social and generational spectrum of those attending funerals, it's likely there will always be someone who will take offence at the inclusion of a popular song. For some, hearing "life's a piece of shit / When you look at it" as they say goodbye to a loved one will be an appropriately wry comment on the vicissitudes of existence; to others—those for whom Monty Python is off the cultural radar, or whose sensibilities are a little more delicate—it could prove to be offensive, inappropriate, and could genuinely sour one of the most significant events of a family's life.

The appearance of pop music at a funeral elbows not just God out of the picture but also many of the mourners, in a way that "Amazing Grace" or "Abide with Me" do not. But what, after all, could be a more appropriate signifier of the mood of the times? This is about me, me, me—and possibly one or two of you. Nothing else, as Metallica might be roaring as the curtains slide open, matters.

It's ultimately a rhetorical debate. There is no right or wrong. There is no end to the lists of songs that may or may not work. The online debate on BBC6 revealed some other interesting choices: "In My Life" by the Beatles; "Fly" by Celine Dion; Bob Dylan's "Knocking on Heaven's Door" and "Shooting Star"; Kirsty MacColl's version of "Days"; "Enjoy Yourself" by Prince Buster; "Turn, Turn, Turn" by the Byrds; "So Long, It's Been Good to Know You" by the Spinners; "Goin' Back" by Dusty Springfield; "The Long and Winding Road" by the Beatles; "Fields of Gold" performed by Eva Cassidy; "Softly, as I Leave You" by Matt Monroe; "November Rain" by Guns 'N Roses; "Wish You Were Here" by Pink Floyd; "Sloop John B" by the Beach Boys; "I Still Haven't Found What I'm Looking For" by U2; "Freebird" by Lynyrd Skynrd and "Bright Side of the Road" by Van Morrison.

In the end, if a song fits, if it makes you think fondly of the person being sent onward, if it brings them back into your thoughts, then it's hard to argue than it's not an appropriate, fitting choice. But be warned: it's a tough crowd to please, and few songs are written to order. Neil Finn wrote the Crowded House song "She Goes On" for a friend whose mother had died and whom he had been quite close to. "I made a little song for them and played it at the funeral," he recalls. "It wasn't a song that I was intending necessarily to record, but we tried it one day and it felt universal enough to earn a spot. If you can be useful as a songwriter—at weddings, funerals, whatever—then great. I couldn't be happier when people tell me they played songs at key family occasions. You just feel really useful."

More often, as these top ten lists illustrate, it's an awkward fit. Although I'm as susceptible to cheap sentiment as the next man, and I wouldn't be averse to hearing Jimmy Cliff's "Many Rivers to Cross" ringing out at someone *else*'s funeral, on balance I think I'd rather hear something traditional like "Over Yonder" or "Meet Me at the Station." More importantly, the music obsessive within me knows that when it comes to my own Goodnight Vienna moment, I'd still be scribbling alterations to the set list even as the plugs were being pulled, which might not go down too well. It's probably best, therefore, to leave it either to chance or silence. Unless Ice T comes up with a better idea. Which, on balance, seems unlikely.

10
THE ART OF DYING
(SLIGHT RETURN)

For the last year or so I've been compiling an ever-expanding Death Playlist on my iTunes, of which I'm unaccountably proud but which has on occasion rather frightened the children as they wander in to investigate the odd noises emanating from behind the door. I can now pick out a reference in a song to murder, suicide, cancer, or nuclear apocalypse blindfold at twelve paces, and no doubt occasionally hear the voice of the Grim Reaper when it simply isn't there. For most people, perhaps mercifully, this is not a useful skill. For them, death is only a low hum in the background, always there but hardly something that makes you want to turn up the dial and tune in. Me, I'm plugged right into the mains.

Over the past hour or so the Death Playlist has been ticking over on the shuffle function and has thrown up "Teen Angel" by Mark Dinning, "Dead" by the Pixies, "We'll All Go Together When We Go" by Tom Lehrer, Paul Robeson's rather stodgy version of "Gloomy Sunday," "Bela Lugosi's Dead" by Bauhaus, "Death Letter Blues" by White Stripes, Bob Dylan's "The Ballad of Hollis Brown," "Six Feet Deep" by Geto Boys, Queen's "Who Wants to Live Forever," Radiohead's "Street Spirit," Gordon Lightfoot's "The Wreck of the

Edmund Fitzgerald," and Tom Waits' "Cemetery Polka."

I'd resort to dusting off my vintage duelling pistols to argue that not one of these songs is, as Mick Jagger argued right at the beginning of this book, "depressing." One of the truths made evident throughout the intervening pages is that plenty of great pop songs have faced up to death with a combination of humor, humility, sentiment, fear, beauty, bravado, lust, and reverence. Above all, they have proved capable of tackling the subject in a way that enriches and entertains rather than deflates.

Although the random selection playing over the last sixty minutes has spanned roughly seven decades of musical history, I can honestly say that at no time while listening did I make any conscious distinction of when or why each song was written. It's become increasingly obvious that the linear view of music history, plotting on a graph the line connecting one great artistic breakthrough to the next, though persuasive and comforting, is unhelpful and unrealistic. Instead, the past meets the future every second of every day, in an untidy, ungainly embrace. Everything happens all at once, all the time, meaning popular music in its broadest sense doesn't so much progress or regress as *expand*. The musical past is always with us, right alongside the present, continually open to reinterpretation, more so than ever in the wider present of the current age, where a considerable portion of its long history is available instantly at the click of a button, arriving without announcing either its intent or its original context.

This long view makes it plain that, although there have been times when mortality has been more obviously on the agenda than at others, the death song from 1961 or 1939 can touch us just as deeply as the one from 2008, whether we are 14, 24, 40, or 64. There is no real reason, after all, why a modern death song would be any more resonant than those of the past; these songs are, in the end, speculative affairs—progress has not yet invented a means of reporting back from the other side.

This being the case, the power doesn't necessarily lie in age or experience but simply in the fine art of communication. Milton Berle, the first great star of the televisual age,

once said, "If you leave 'em like you found 'em, you blew it."
That hasn't changed. Berle's motto still holds in post-digital
times: whether it's the arc of the three-minute pop song,
which needs to speedily take the listener to a different place
than the one in which they were standing when the music
kicked in, or something a little more ambitious, music is all
about the transference of emotion, across genres, across generational boundaries, across eras and continents. Every age
has its trailblazers in this respect.

What has become apparent through examining so many
death songs is that separating the strands of life and death is
like trying to divine precisely where a river ends and the sea
begins. One by necessity spills into the other, and without
one the other loses meaning and substance. Think of George
Jones' immense "He Stopped Loving Her Today," in which
the death of the principal character is used to emphasize the
extent to which he ached his entire life away in "half-crazy"
contemplation of the lost love he swore he'd adore until the
day he died. "The obvious thing to say is that a song about
death is a song about life," says Richard Thompson. "The
sentence has a full stop, without which the sentence wouldn't
be complete and would have no meaning."

It's why many rather specialized off-shoot metal genres,
and much of modern rap and emo, tend not to do the job
—they are stuck in one place and can't or won't offer us the
other half of the picture. "Some days you may feel that the
dark tunnel might engulf you, but I don't think a whole album
of that is going to amuse anyone," as Jagger puts it. "There's
no harm in going there for a moment, but you don't want to
be there all the time. Unless you *are* there all the time, and
then you've got no option." It makes me think of the wearying
repetition of much of My Chemical Romance's music. If mere
death is all a death song has to offer then it is likely to become
a suffocating and grim listening experience; it devalues the
currency. Frankly, it gives death a bad name.

Though the worst culprits are often teen-fixated genres,
using death in a purely isolated way, with little grasp of all
that came before or what may be waiting, it's clear from
what we have seen that the 21-year-old is as capable of writ-

ing meaningfully about death as the pensioner. Sometimes, these two figures turn out to be the same person.

Noting that Dylan is often these days used as an example of a songwriter who is reflecting the realities of his age—67—in his music, Jagger makes another astute point. "I'm a huge fan of Dylan, but he has always been a very dark writer, fixated with mortality. We could talk about this for quite a long time. Stuff like *John Wesley Harding* sounds like the work of a much older man."

It's an important observation. Part of the reason Dylan has aged so well artistically is that he has never worried about the expectations of his audience or written for his age—he has always pleased himself and aligned himself with blues and folk artists, which gives him a wide open remit that is essentially ageless. Mortality has therefore always been one of his recurring themes, right from when he recorded "Let Me Die in My Footsteps" as a callow youth. As Jagger suggests, he was still only 26 when he wrote *John Wesley Harding*, with its fateful songs stuffed with biblical imagery and deathly shadows, not forgetting the poor immigrant "who passionately hates his life and likewise, fears his death." It's one of Dylan's less frequently quoted epigrams, but it positively reverberates with significance in the current age: our inability to face death is a symptom of an increasingly unhappy society.

Johnny Cash, too, perhaps the prime example of an artist who grasped the nettle of his impending death through his music in his advancing years with his remarkable series of *American Recordings*, was hardly bearing away from home territory as he did so. This was a man steeped in the rigors of old-time religious and secular music for the entirety of his life, who had written and recorded literally hundreds of songs on the subject of death before he was swept back into fashion in the nineties. His age and increasing frailty—and the carefully constructed sense of intimacy that defined the sound of these albums—imbued his final recordings with extra layers of emphasis and poignancy, but this was not a man forging a new identity. Instead, it was the logical destination for Cash's long black train of music, and one he had been puffing steadily toward for half a century.

The rather prosaic truth is that most musicians pass the same way dozens of times during their careers, and write the same song over and over again. They hone, they polish, they become more skilful, but they struggle to escape their core preoccupations. Sometimes, often, we forget that there is a real, breathing person behind the songs, worrying away at some very personal business. Van Morrison's main themes —the search for spiritual peace, the depthless horrors of the music industry, the loss of innocence—have remained steadfast for over forty years. The same could be said for everyone from Ice T to Chuck Berry, David Bowie to Ray Davies.

It's often conveniently forgotten that most of the artists cited as prime examples of mature musicians unafraid to address death in their most recent work have been tussling with mortality since they were in their twenties: Dylan and Cash, of course, but also Richard Thompson, Leonard Cohen, Neil Young, Tom Waits, and Lou Reed, among many others. Some artists are never really young—in the same way that some people never really feel any older than 18. I suspect I've been rather fixated with death every since I became aware of what it is, while others I know barely give it a second thought. Who's to say which approach is the most healthy? When it comes to musicians dealing with questions of mortality, these core traits tend only to be re-enforced with age: Dylan gets darker and darker, while Jagger generally prefers to keep things light, describing himself as "an optimistic person. It's rock music, it's supposed to be fun."

He told me that he'd recently been invited to make a stripped-down record in the manner of Cash's later albums, and Neil Diamond's similarly reflective 12 Songs. The tacit understanding with these albums is that the artist is expected to reveal a little more of their core insecurities and the reality of the ageing process, in tandem with the intimacy of the musical arrangements. "I'm not sure if I could keep it up, though," says Jagger. "It might be nice for a few songs but I'm not sure about a whole album. I never play records like that, personally." The fact is, such an undertaking wouldn't be an honest reflection of Jagger's life: he still goes clubbing, he still jet-sets, he still has a keen and active interest in the opposite sex, he can still prance around stage for two hours a night without requiring hospitalization. He is not your average 65-year-old. Or if he is, he is living proof that the 65-year-old in the early twenty-first century is the equivalent of the 40-year-old of only a few decades past.

Ron Sexsmith, on the other hand, though over twenty years younger than Jagger, doesn't think "that there's time for messing around" in these dark days and tends to write accordingly. Richard Thompson now sees "every song as your last song—I think you have to think that way." For Neil Finn, "there's nothing like death to haul things into focus, when it happens close to you." Paul McCartney, meanwhile, reckons death "doesn't make a great song to dance to." You can hear it all spilling out in their music.

On his most recent record, *Memory Almost Full*, McCartney wrote a song called "End of the End" that mused upon his own demise. "I'd heard someone, I think it was James Taylor, use the phrase 'the day I die' in a lyric and it prompted me to think of death as a subject," he says. "So I got into that and found that I was interested in the Irish Wake idea, and jokes being told and stories of old, rather than the solemn, Anglican, doom-laden event."

It's a song about death that nevertheless rather cleverly re-enforces McCartney's innate sense of optimism: "No need to be sad / On the day that I die / I'd like jokes to be told." He even whistles on it. Although it's a rather lovely, uplifting little song, given the choice between writing something chirpy and essentially meaningless such as "Dance Tonight," or a 65-year-old's reflection on his inevitable passing like "End of the End," McCartney will, like most of his peers, still opt for the former every time.

"Death's not a subject that anyone visits that much," he continues. "It's not too jolly, I suppose." It's his own way of admitting that addressing the subject fundamentally contradicts his natural demeanor. Despite the evidence of "Eleanor Rigby," which increasingly seems like the glaring anomaly of his back catalog, McCartney leans toward the optimistic and non-confessional. Meditations on death don't come naturally, and so he doesn't force it.

This is perfectly valid, of course, but does rather discount the idea that creative artists experience a growing desire to get to the bottom of things, down to the emotional nitty-gritty, as they age. More likely, they are trying to find new ways—better ways—of saying the same things they've always said.

In this sense, attempting to trace the evolution of popular music's dealings with death—and even that of an individual artist—is like trying to ensnare a cloud. There is clearly no songwriter's consensus on the subject; how could there be, when ageing is no guarantee of artistic progression—some blossom, some dry up—nor does it bring the intrinsic ability or willingness to begin tackling the grand themes? There is no imperative in pop to be grown up, or indeed to be *anything*. It's a wide open playing field, more so than ever.

"Pop music is a big area, it's not just young people's music, it's not like it was in the fifties and sixties, now it's multi-generational," says Richard Thompson. "It embraces a lot of styles. A lot of the protagonists of popular music are now dead or old—sixty-somethings. I think inevitably and hopefully popular music reflects everything: life, death and everything in-between."

And it's true that some artists, like Thompson or David Bowie, become noticeably more preoccupied with their mortality as they get older, using the ever-shortening distance between the sentence they are writing and the imminent "full stop" as the impetus to reflect upon what their life has amounted to. It takes their writing to interesting places, some of them unsettling and only accessible to those of a certain age. "Kite" by U2, a song about a man fumbling and faltering through a farewell to his family and trying to get to the core of what his life has meant in the face of what he believes is his impending demise, could only have been written by a father and husband who has been around the block a bit and is aware of how much is truly at stake, and yet also how inconsequential he is in the general scheme of things; the same goes for Crowded House's *Time on Earth*. "Death is always getting closer," says Neil Finn. "I was very fortunate, I didn't have to deal with it when I was young, but I suppose that at any age to be reminded of your mortality gets you thinking."

On the other hand, it has sent other musicians scampering as far as possible in the opposite direction, with their fingers in their ears trilling *la-la-la-la-la* until the very end. Where is the sound of Madonna facing up to life in her fifties? Or Michael Jackson? As pop and rock stars get to the age where death is no longer "just a shot away" in some mythical battlefield but is a reality that can be felt in every line, creak, and twinge each morning, and furthermore can be seen striking all around, they are as likely to stop writing about it altogether as to embrace it.

Which means that the next ten years will be very interesting. It's already clear that ageing pop stars are going to continue singing the songs they wrote as youngsters until deep into their twilight years, seemingly without embarrassment or any sense of awkwardness. They have every right to do so. There shouldn't be, I suppose, any creative or moral imperative to address mortality, either as a listener or as a musician. Pop music is entertainment. Showbiz. It need not dirty its hands with death.

I can't help thinking, however, that having the facility to talk about it in a clear and honest way should be part of an artist's arsenal, one of the most basic tools of the trade. Done well, as many of the examples scattered throughout this book have proved, these songs can touch an audience emotionally in a way that few other song subjects rival, as well as casting fresh, clear light on the life being lived.

While Jagger is right in stating that very few people want to hear an artist mired constantly in death and despondency, what is perhaps surprising is how many people lean the other way and remain eager to congregate around these odd little knots of wizened 60-year-olds, still wearing the heroically optimistic hairstyles of their youth and their jeans improbably tight, singing songs that make no acknowledgment whatsoever that they are marching toward the latter stages of their lives. Nostalgia is a powerful, magnetic scent; it can overpower the smell that lingers right under your own nose. But it wears off quickly, and what's left?

Let's not be too stern. I understand that there's something wondrous and magical and funny and heart-warming about the Stones and their ilk puffing on through the decades as though both they and the world are preserved in amber. On one level it is simply a big pantomime, an enormous exaggerated wink, and should be enjoyed as such. A warning shout of "It's behind you!" might even be fitting.

But another part of me believes that there is more to it than that. There comes a time when the act of *not* facing up to the facts becomes in itself a meaningful artistic statement on mortality. There is a tendency to think that as each of us ages we will become more reconciled to the idea of death —that we start mentally preparing for it, readying to face it, and there may be an expectation that popular music should be doing the same. But what if the notion of death becomes more terrifying as it gets closer? What if it is simply too hard to deal with for most of us? This is after all an age, as Arlo Guthrie recently pointed out, intent on singing its songs almost entirely "in the key of me."[1] Perhaps that's why we have become so adept as a society at avoidance tactics, at "generally removing illness and dying from everyday life," as Richard Thompson puts it. "When people get sick or old you stick them in a home or a hospital or on the street."

What was it Joyce said again? "Absence is the highest form of presence." Perhaps, then, the very conspicuous avoidance of death as a subject matter among many of our most venerable pop stars will come to speak far more revealingly about the way most of us feel about mortality in the early part of the twenty-first century than a million songs like Bob Dylan's "Not Dark Yet" or Richard Thompson's "Sunset Song" ever could. Maybe we're not that brave after all. I know I'm not. Could it be, in that case, that the Rolling Stones singing "Jumping Jack Flash," or the last crumbling fragments of the Who still bashing gamely through "My Generation," or Madonna gyrating grimly through "Hung Up," into their sixties, seventies, and eighties will actually turn out to be the most piercingly apt, most unintentionally eloquent death music of all?

EPILOGUE
TO DIE FOR
The Forty Greatest Death Records

In the end, of course, it's all about enjoying the music. But how to distill it all down to an evening's entertainment, the definitive soundtrack to be played on some wind-whipped jukebox at the end of the line; just how do you crack the combination code for the perfect DiPod play list? It's a tricky recipe: we need a sprinkling of humor; a fistful of defiance; pure, unadulterated misery; the undiluted essence of the human spirit; a dusting of tears and sorrow; a shaving of comfort and a soupcon of joy; topped off with the bright red cherry of redemption.

What follows is, naturally, a subjective list, but it's also designed to act as a kind of musical summation of all the ground covered in the previous pages. I haven't even attempted to rank the songs in any order of preference—that way madness lies. Instead, because this is a list of specific recordings of songs, the tracks are ranked chronologically according to the year of release of each particular version. You are more than welcome to plunder this top forty for the purposes of burning a little mix CD for your party of choice: wedding, christening, birthday, graduation, bar mitzvah. It's always good, I find, to throw a few fireworks into the proceedings.

☠

STACK O'LEE BLUES—"MISSISSIPPI" JOHN HURT (1928)

It's virtually impossible to choose just one version of the ultimate murder blues, but in the end Hurt's underplayed acoustic reading is as close to definitive as we're likely to get. It was recorded in New York in 1928, just three days after Christmas, and still culturally close enough to capture the faintest whiff of cordite from the terrible events played out in that St. Louis saloon back in 1895, when Billy Lyons died and a legend was born.

ST. JAMES INFIRMARY—CAB CALLOWAY (1931)

I really do love the 1928 Louis Armstrong version, while Bobby "Blue" Bland's later rendition is vocally peerless, but neither of them are lyrically quite all there. A classic New Orleans funeral blues with its roots stretching back centuries to either Ireland or Scotland, this much-recorded classic recounts the story of a man who discovers his woman has died of syphilis and realizes that he is going to be next. The grandeur and machismo with which he foresees his own funeral ("Now, when I die, bury me in my straight-leg britches / Put on a box-back coat and a Stetson hat / Put a twenty-dollar gold piece on my watch chain / So you can let all the boys know I died standing pat") contains quite startling similarities to some of rap's funeral songs, such as Tupac's "Life Goes On": "Bury me smilin' with G's in my pocket / Have a party at my funeral let every rapper rock it."

GLOOMY SUNDAY—BILLIE HOLLIDAY (1941)

At a time when emo is being blamed for driving our teenagers headlong into the abyss, there is a certain delicious irony in the fact that the greatest, most velvety and seductive suicide song of them all falls well outside the remit of nasty old rock and roll. "Gloomy Sunday," written in 1933 by the Hungarian songwriter Rezso Seress, is quite spectacularly morose in both tune and verse. Though there is precious little hard evidence to support the popular legend that the song directly inspired dozens of real-life suicides, the stories are persuasively colorful nonetheless: like the one about the Berliner who went home and shot himself in the head after hearing a show band playing the mournful melody, or the woman who hanged herself and left a copy of the sheet music to "Gloomy Sunday" lying in her apartment in lieu of a farewell note. Probably apocryphal, but food for thought at least for those who cry sanction when a 17-year-old boy is found hanging in his parents' garage with Blink 182's "Adam's Song" on repeat.

Like the composers of other notable suicide songs, such as "All Apologies" (Kurt Cobain), "Without You" (made famous in Harry Nilsson's 1971 version, but written by Badfinger's Pete Ham and Tom Evans), "Die in the Summertime" (the Manic Street Preachers' Richey Edwards) and "King's Crossing" (Elliot Smith), Seress finally followed through on the threat implied in the song, jumping from his Budapest apartment window in 1968: ironically, he was probably a much happier man back when he had written "Gloomy Sunday," his depression partially the result of never having written anything as popular in the ensuing thirty-five years. Billy MacKenzie of the Associates, who recorded a version of the song in 1982, also killed himself in 1997.

These are neat coincidences for the curse-hungry, but hardly anything more. The fact that the song was marketed as the "Hungarian Suicide Song" when it was first released in the United States would suggest that, even then, there were people who were more than a little aware that death sells and were prepared to nudge the story forward a little. In any case, the song hardly needs any assistance in casting a deathly pall over the listener. The literal translation of Seress' original Hungarian lyrics reveals an almost apocalyptically grim worldview:

> The world has come to its end, hope has ceased to have a
>   meaning
> Cities are being wiped out, shrapnel is making music
> Meadows are colored red with human blood
> There are dead people on the streets everywhere

It is thoroughly depressing but hardly fitting for any musical form outside of death metal. These jagged little lines were smoothed into something a little less crushing by Seress' compatriot, the poet Lazslo Javor. His version established the themes a little more clearly—the singer has lost his lover and, utterly bereft, is now preparing to join her in death—and makes the contemplation of suicide all the more explicit. When it became a hit song in Hungary, popular American songwriters Desmond Carter and Sam M. Lewis each made separate attempts to translate Javor's version of the song into English. Paul Robeson sung Carter's rather over-literal version in 1935, but the effect was a little too stiff and noble.

Lewis' translation, on the other hand, with its brilliant central image of the "black coach of sorrow," had a looser, more poetic bent. The narrator surrenders to and positively luxuriates in the sadness, as well as making the story clearer to follow. This became the definitive English-language translation following Billie Holliday's hugely popular 1941 recording, although Lewis took the precaution of adding a four-line stanza at the end suggesting that it had all been a dream; an attempt to take the edge off the darkness just a little. The song has since been sung by numerous performers, everyone from Mel Torme, Sarah Vaughan, and Ray Charles to Elvis Costello, Diamanda Galas, Sinead O'Connor, Bjork, and Candie Payne. Each of them has found something to identify with in this dark little dance with death.

> *Sunday is gloomy, my hours are slumberless*
> *Dearest the shadows I live with are numberless*
> *Little white flowers will never awaken you*
> *Not where the black coach of sorrow has taken you*
> *Angels have no thought of ever returning you*
> *Would they be angry if I thought of joining you?*
> *Gloomy Sunday*
>
> *Gloomy is Sunday, with shadows I spend it all*
> *My heart and I have decided to end it all*
> *Soon there'll be candles and prayers that are sad I know*
> *Let them not weep let them know that I'm glad to go*

Death is no dream for in death I'm caressing you
With the last breath of my soul I'll be blessing you
Gloomy Sunday

Dreaming, I was only dreaming
I wake and I find you asleep in the deep of my heart, here
Darling, I hope that my dream never haunted you
My heart is telling you how much I wanted you
Gloomy Sunday.

Spell-binding stuff.

FOLSOM PRISON BLUES—JOHNNY CASH (1956)

The great modern American song of death: "I shot a man in Reno just to watch him die" has echoed down through the decades as the bluntest, starkest reminder of the worst a man can do for the most inconsequential of reasons. And delivered in Cash's stentorian baritone, the song carries both terrifying plausibility and fathomless depths of regret. Incidentally, you could substitute "Reno" for almost any geographical location and it might still work as an indication of the universality of banal death, but I suspect if Cash had "shot a man in Lincoln" the song would hold only niche appeal.

KNOXVILLE GIRL—THE LOUVIN BROTHERS (1959)

Still vaguely shocking in its plain depiction of brutal murder in the Appalachians in the 1800s, and Ireland in the 1700s, and . . . Well, you get the picture. It remains the archetype for the damsel-dashed-on-the-rocks murder ballad, and if the way Ira Louvin shrugs/sings "I took her by her golden curls and I drug her 'round and 'round" doesn't give you chills and spine-shivers, then you're made of very strong stuff indeed.

EBONY EYES—THE EVERLY BROTHERS (1961)

No matter how cheesy the premise may sound, there is something unbearably moving in J.D. Loudermilk's song of a man waiting in the darkness at the airport for his lover to come, only to discover that her plane has crashed. Perhaps the emotion really lies in the performance rather than the writing itself. Something in the way Phil Everly slowly recites "The plane was way overdue" makes me really feel the ache of the first stabbing realization that his life is about to be changed forever. Suddenly, we all sense what's coming next . . .

LAST KISS—J. FRANK WILSON & THE CAVALIERS (1964)

This most substantial of all the teen death songs had its roots in a real-life tragedy. Wayne Cochran & the C.C. Rider's original version of the song was dedicated to 16-year-old Jeanette Clark who—alongside two other teenagers—died in a collision with a trailer truck a few days before Christmas in 1962. Recorded in superior form by J. Frank Wilson in the summer of 1964, this version—particularly the vocal—really captures the sense of emotion that first inspired the song. It was later covered by Pearl Jam and, incongruously, gave them their biggest hit single in 1999.

LEADER OF THE PACK—THE SHANGRI-LAS (1964)

Like that soon-to-be-gone fast boy Jimmy, the sob song takes its leave with a bang (preceded by a screech of tires and cries of "Look out, look out, look out!"). The inspiration was a biker gang observed by the song's cowriter "Shadow" Morton in a diner in Hicksville, New York. "Bikers, hot rodders, gum-smacking ladies," recalled Morton with relish. "Not careful at all about their language and what they had to say."[1] The result was a camp, poignant, and sexy view of death as the ultimate bond. And they used a real motorbike in the studio, too.

STRANGE FRUIT—NINA SIMONE (1965)

Still perhaps the most powerful cry for racial equality, much of its force is derived from its unflinching depiction of death, the chilling central metaphor of black lynch-mob victims hanging from blood-stained trees like strange fruit, with their "bulging eyes and the twisted mouth." Adapted to music by Jewish academic Abel Meeropol from his own poem, it may be sacrilege to say that Billie Holiday's 1939 original version could ever be improved upon, but for my money Simone's version, recorded in 1965 at the height of the civil rights struggle, contains a near-perfect mix of sorrow and anger.

PAINT IT BLACK— THE ROLLING STONES (1966)

A veritable orgy of nihilistic grieving, played out over one of the most idiosyncratic, cosmopolitan musical tracks of the sixties. This is the dream of Swinging London flipped over into nightmare; the only swinging that's going on here is from the light fittings.

TOMORROW NEVER KNOWS—THE BEATLES (1966)

For those seeking evidence of how the most mainstream popular musicians of the sixties took the concept of dying a little more seriously than those who came before or have since arrived, there is no greater place to start than this great clattering, pseudo-spiritual drug-induced death trip. It still sounds like a song capable of spanning worlds.

THE BLACK ANGEL'S DEATH SONG—VELVET UNDERGROUND (1966)

The lyrics are abstract and impressionistic to say the least, but it certainly *sounds* like death riding high in the saddle. "Black Angel's Death Song" is what an Elizabethan madrigal would sound like after being mugged by highwaymen, dragged on horseback to a subterranean dungeon, and then beaten about the flesh by the bones of dead pirates for three hundred years. It has a terrible ravaged beauty that recalls nothing before or since. Never mind "Heroin," this is the true sound of the drugged, be-shaded hipster nihilism of Warhol's Factory.

ELEANOR RIGBY—THE BEATLES (1966)

Pop's first unflinching sight of death in all its bald horror, and still perhaps its most unforgiving and austere. A perfect marriage of sound and words, and evidence that the Beatles had both the metaphysical and the prosaic aspects of death well covered.

MY DEATH—SCOTT WALKER (1967)

Consideration of this song descended into an unseemly fist-fight between David Bowie's live twelve-string acoustic version from the Ziggy-era and Walker's more robust, fully fleshed version from his 1967 debut solo album, *Scott*. Walker won. A Jacques Brel number, originally titled "Le Mort" and one of the few that fully survived the translation into English by Mort Schuman and Eric Blau, it is a great barnstorming song that rattles throughout with remarkable imagery. Among leaves, rabbits, dogs, lilacs, magic, and the arms and thighs of pretty girls, death waits like a beggar, a witch, a patient girl, creeping closer and closer with the passing time. "Whatever waits behind the door / There's nothing much to do," sings Walker. Life must be lived in its shadow. "The great [death song] is 'My Death,'" agrees Mike Scott. "The old heaven or hell thing, that deals with the increasing knowledge that our time is short."

ODE TO BILLIE JOE—BOBBIE GENTRY (1967)

Still the knottiest musical murder mystery of them all. Very few songs capture the sheer disorienting atmosphere of lurking evil as Bobbie Gentry's funky little backwater blues. Of course, in the end what matters isn't the means of Billie Joe's death or even why it occurred, but the off-hand way the singer's family react to it over the dinner table. A boy is dead. Pass the salt.

WHO (WILL TAKE MY PLACE?)—DUSTY SPRINGFIELD (1968)

Perhaps the greatest song of pain and regret at what the dying are forced to leave behind, written by none other than

Charles Aznavour. The song taps into the sentiment of the Carter Family's "Will You Miss Me When I'm Gone?" and takes it to even more self-torturing lengths: "Who, when my life is through? Who will know the joy I have known with you? / Who will touch your face? Sleep in your embrace? / Who will take my place when I sleep alone?" Scott Walker also recorded this, but I prefer Dusty's version for the sheer sensual agony she conveys through the late-sixties lounge sounds.

SPIRIT IN THE SKY—NORMAN GREENBAUM (1969)

A three-time British number one in three different versions by three very diverse artists (Greenbaum, Doctor and the Medics, and Gareth Gates) is ample evidence that "Spirit in the Sky" is a bullet-proof song. Written by Greenbaum after hearing Porter Wagoner singing a devotional song on his TV show, it's the lack of any somber observance of the traditional tropes of "spiritual" songs that gives it such an affirming kick. Set to a wonderful fuzz-toned boogie guitar riff and hearty hand claps, the Stovall Sisters, an authentic gospel trio from Oakland, lend the song its audible gospel dimension, but it's really just a great pop single with a sly undertow. It may have been appropriated by Nike, among many others, for the nefarious purposes of selling things to people, but it's the numerous individuals who year after year take solace from the song that really convey its worth.

JOHN BARLEYCORN (MUST DIE)—TRAFFIC (1970)

A beautifully restrained—and simply beautiful—version of the touchstone British traditional song of birth, growth, death, and regeneration. Arranged simply for acoustic guitar and flute, Steve Winwood's vocal floats on the top, pure and sweet as clear air. The sense of unhurried space allows the full pastoral majesty of both the melody and message to shine through.

ART OF DYING—GEORGE HARRISON (1970)

Very much a continuation of a theme for Harrison, this tight, perky little wah-wah-driven rocker from *All Things*

Must Pass is one of his clearest and least didactic statements about his spiritual beliefs, outlining the karmic notion of having to return to earth again and again until we finally learn how to live life and accept death: "Living through a million years of crying / Until you've realized the art of dying."

WILL THE CIRCLE BE UNBROKEN?—THE NITTY GRITTY DIRT BAND (1972)

Adapted in the thirties by A.P. Carter of the Carter Family from the old hymn "Can the Circle Be Unbroken (Bye and Bye)," written in the early 1900s by Ada Habershon and Charles Gabriel, the song recounts the death, funeral, and mourning of the narrator's mother, and finds eventual peace in the notion of a better home a-waiting in the sky. Recorded in literally hundreds of guises by artists as diverse as Jah Wobble, the Wonder Stuff, Pentangle, and the Neville Brothers, the ensemble version recorded by the Nitty Gritty Dirt Band in 1972, featuring such luminaries as Mother Maybelle Carter, Earl Scruggs and Doc Watson, remains the most joyous and expansive interpretation.

SEASONS IN THE SUN—TERRY JACKS (1974)

"Strange," Noel Coward once observed, "how potent cheap music is." He wasn't, but he could have been, talking about "Seasons in the Sun," which is cheaper than chipboard and yet has proved more potent than most. And yet it didn't start off cheap; it had to really *work* at it. Beginning life as a mordant, bitter little work by the great Belgian songwriter Jacques Brel, "Le Moribund (The Dying Man)" was written in 1961. The melody is a rather stricter brother to the one we would later all become familiar with, yet its brisk martial tempo still manages to accommodate a few typically European melancholic flourishes.

Performed by Brel it is a highly theatrical song. The dying man bids his childhood friend Emile, his priest, his unfaithful wife, and his adult friend (and his wife's lover) Tony an ambivalent goodbye, sarcastically but rather dashingly demanding that they all rejoice and have fun when he dies: "All to laugh, all to dance, when they put me in the hole!" It's both a bleak comment on how little he thinks he'll be missed, and a wider comment on the futility and dishonesty of grief, a kind of companion piece to Brel's own "Funeral Tango," another black joke from a dead man.

There is no direct clue in the lyric as to how the singer is dying. Some suggest that he has cancer, but this may be because Brel himself succumbed to the disease in the late seventies. He could well be suffering from an incurable disease, but the song reads like a suicide note to me, or more precisely a theatrical death-scene soliloquy, delivered just after he has plunged the dagger into his chest.

"Le Moribund" was quickly and loosely translated into English by popular poet Rod McKuen and recorded by the Kingston Trio in 1963, to little acclaim. Both the lyrics and the melody were lightened up considerably for a pop audience, and the European sense of laughing bleakly at life's fleeting joys and humiliations in the face of imminent death is stripped away: the deeply Continental, cavalier, Gauloise-puffing fuck-you-all quotient is distressingly low.

In its place arrives the less complicated version of regret recounted by Terry Jacks. "Seasons in the Sun" had already been released in the UK in 1966 by the Coachmen (my next-favorite version: rich, full, and vaguely Beatlesy) and again by the Fortunes in 1968, before Jacks discovered the song and brought it to a Beach Boys session he was producing in the early seventies. The Boys cut a demo but declined to release it, and so Jacks decided to record it himself, scoring an enormous hit.

It's easy enough to argue that "Seasons in the Sun" has endured a process of gradual dilution, from Brel's tough original through Jacks' sappy pop single to the water-weak version recorded by Irish boy band Westlife in 1999. Like a game of musical Chinese whispers, its original intent has been scrambled as it has dripped down through the decades, losing its lustre and mystery with each transmutation. It's a song that is often mocked as mawkish, trite, and teeth-gratingly annoying, and it is indeed not hard to hear how it could be all those things, and yet it's still an extraordinary song: friends are disloyal, wives are unfaithful, fathers are disapproving. To live is to suffer. And still leaving pains him so.

Cover versions by guitar bands like Blink 182 and Too Much Joy have played the song for laughs, mistaking the tinniness of its sound and the sentiment of its poor poetry with a lack of resonance in its meaning. Pah! There will always be those too blinkered, too uptight, to see the real beauty in this kind of song. It was the first record that the 7-year-old Kurt Cobain ever bought and one of the last songs he played with Nirvana before he died; he obviously found something in it that many people miss, but I think I hear it too.

The triumph of "Seasons in the Sun" lies in the fact that it is the anti-"My Way." It faces death not with bravado but with pathos, regret, and self-pity, which is why, to my ears, Terry Jacks' 1974 version—saccharine though it is—pretty much contains the measure of us all. How many of us, when the time comes, will be able to resist a dewy-eyed glance back to childhood innocence, cast an eye around the room of our life and the people in it, and bitterly rue the day we grew up? The song asks: what is the sum total of your life, and how will you face your final days? We can laugh all we want. Brel certainly is. But then he knows that the joke is on all of us.

THEY WON'T GO WHEN I GO—STEVIE WONDER (1974)

Deeper than the grave, wider than the heavens, and one of the most imperial evocations of the world beyond that awaits only a select few. Crucially, the weight, beauty, gravity, and stern rebuke of the words is echoed in the magnificent music.

(DON'T FEAR) THE REAPER—THE BLUE OYSTER CULT (1976)

Not, as is often claimed, a front-page advertisement for a Romeo and Juliet–style suicide pact, but rather an attempt to greet death with acceptance. Despite its heavy rock exterior, the song espouses a very old European view of dying—death is literally depicted as the Grim Reaper, but is not to be feared: the line "seasons don't fear the reaper" plugs straight back into the age-old "John Barleycorn" idea of cycles of loss and regeneration. "I felt that I had just achieved some kind of resonance with the psychology of people when I came up with that, I was actually kind of appalled when I first realized that some people were seeing it as an advertisement for suicide or something," said the song's writer Buck Dharma. "That was not my intention at all. It is not to be afraid of [death], as opposed to actively bringing it about."[2]

LIVE FAST DIE YOUNG—CIRCLE JERKS (1980)

The blunt, over-arching manifesto of US hardcore distilled into ninety-three seconds of pure, righteous teen fury aimed at an adult world that has ruinously fucked its children over. "I don't wanna live to be 34 / I don't wanna die in a nuclear war," sings Keith Morris. And for one-and-a-half minutes, at least, you believe him.

BLASPHEMOUS RUMOURS—DEPECHE MODE (1984)

A simple, effective song, clear, clean, and electronic, making explicit the difficulties in maintaining faith in the face of death, particularly when it picks off the young. In Dave Johnson's band biography *Some Great Reward*, the song's writer, Martin Gore, recalls going to church as a child and hearing a prayer list being read for the seriously ill members of the congregation. Usually, most of them would die, "but still," says Gore, "everyone went right ahead thanking God for carrying out His will. It just seemed so strange." In the same book, singer Dave Gahan insists the song isn't anti-religion but merely "a statement of how everybody must feel at one time or another."[3]

FADE TO BLACK—METALLICA (1984)

Heavy metal's favorite goodbye song, an unambiguous last will and testament before the protagonist commits suicide, sung in the manner of a man ridding himself of a large fishbone wedged in his windpipe. For all its rather lumbering, literal limitations, it's a song that has struck a chord at the very heart of its constituency for over two decades, and it remains an important record for many teenagers. "At that time me and James [Hetfield] spent a lot of time talking about death, obsessing about death," said drummer Lars Ulrich. "And obsessing about the fears that come in the wake of it." "Fade to Black" was one of those songs that put the fear of God into middle America as young male suicide rates rocketed in the eighties, but the band always regarded it as a song of empathy. "Nobody ever talked about the tenfold amount of kids that came up and said, 'I was sitting there with a gun in my mouth. I was sitting out in the car getting ready to gas myself and I wanted to hear 'Fade to Black' one last time and it turned me around. It gave me hope. It gave me inspiration to give it another shot,'" continued Ulrich. "Those were the stories only we heard. We weren't quite prepared for the fact that all of a sudden the lyrics really meant something."[4]

ASLEEP—THE SMITHS (1987)

The suicide song as a lullaby of loneliness, and perhaps the most beautiful thing that Johnny Marr and Morrissey ever produced. "Deep in the cell of my heart, I will feel so glad to go," sings the latter, over simple piano and the sound of the wind whistling outside. The closing, shaky belief in some other, better world is genuinely tear-inducing.

THE MERCY SEAT—NICK CAVE AND THE BAD SEEDS (1988)

As deep and dark as the caverns of the sea, Cave sings as the death row prisoner in the throes of being executed, preparing to meet his maker, and putting what's left of his faith in divine rather than earthly judgment. "And anyway I told the truth, and I'm not afraid to die," he sings, over a block of churning noise that almost disguises the epiphinal final punchline: "But I'm afraid I told a lie." Has he been lying about his innocence all this time? If so, he's about to get found out. Or is he simply lying about his courage in the face of death? If so, again he's been found out. Guilt, sin, faith, redemption, and the measuring of truth. Little wonder

Johnny Cash covered it, with just a stark guitar backing, on *American Recordings III*, but Cave's original still wins out for its sheer biblical blood and thunder roar.

DEATH IS NOT THE END—BOB DYLAN (1988)

An outtake from *Infidels* released on his less than essential *Down in the Groove* record, this song seemingly preaching comfort in the face of life's struggles is more ambivalent and substantial than it first appears. "When the cities are on fire / With the burning flesh of men / Just remember. that death is not the end," sings Dylan. The cumulative effect of the apocalyptic imagery of the verses sitting next to the soothing message of the chorus becomes unsettling. Is death an escape from—a literal end to—earthly horrors, ushering in an afterlife of peace and fulfilment? Or is it a door to another world of infinite pain: there is no end to suffering, either in life or death? Whether you choose to see death as a trip into eternal darkness or the launchpad for the soul's release from earthly chains, Dylan here once again provides plenty to chew on.

HALLOWEEN PARADE—LOU REED (1989)

For a period in the late eighties and early nineties, Reed's music seemed almost entirely concerned with commemorating the dead; entering his forties, he saw friends falling all over the place: drugs, cancer, suicide, AIDS. "Halloween Parade," from his *New York* record, is far from the most explicit of Reed's death songs, but perhaps the most poignant of them all. One of the few songs that captures the impact of death upon a whole community, it conveys the bitchiness, humor, love, loss, and fear felt as New York's gay community confronted the human cost of the AIDS/HIV epidemic of the mideighties, played out against the fantastical backdrop of the city's annual costumed parade: "This celebration somehow gets me down," sings Reed, breaking off from documenting a list of colorful characters to rival his own "Walk on the Wild Side." "Especially when I see you're not around." But it ends on a note of cautious optimism—"see you next year"—and it makes a truly beautiful noise, especially when Dion pops up on harmony vocals at the end.

DEAD HOMIEZ—ICE CUBE (1990)

Cube's second solo single, and one of the first rap songs to really deal with the human price of black-on-black violence. This is a thoughtful, heartfelt eulogy, a funeral song that manages to pay its respects while at the same time seething with anger—"He got a lot of flowers and a big wreath / What good is that when you're six feet deep?"—and almost casually brilliant social commentary: "Why is that the only time black folks get to ride in a limo?" An early and important reminder that rap is capable of adopting a more reflective attitude to death that it's often credited for.

COP KILLER—BODY COUNT (1991)

Beginning with a spoken-world proclamation by Ice T, during which he shares his desire to shoot every corrupt policeman in the face, this tight speed-metal protest song is a visceral, consciously over-the-top reaction to the Rodney King beating, and—seemingly—every other incidence of police brutality anywhere *ever*. A significant piece of steam-letting on behalf of a community that was teetering on the brink, it's worth noting that Ice T started playing a cop on *Law & Order* in 2000, and also played one in *New Jack City* the year "Cop Killer" came out.

TRY NOT TO BREATHE—R.E.M. (1991)

A song sung from the rarest of perspectives: an old woman who has reconciled herself to her coming death and wishes those left behind to do nothing more than remember: "This decision is mine / I have lived a full life." Not only an oddly empowering song for those facing imminent death, but also a song of comfort and strength for the bereaved, espousing the idea that departure is a dialogue, a gentleman's agreement between death and the living. "Are you ready?" asks death, reasonably. "Yes, I am," responds the singer.

EPILOGUE

1952 VINCENT BLACK LIGHTNING—RICHARD THOMPSON (1991)

In many ways simply an adult version of the doomed-love sob song of the sixties, but packing a far mightier emotional punch. Played out over a stunning acoustic guitar figure that harks back to the classic English folk tradition, the tale unfolds of the (fictional) 21-year-old criminal James Adie and his lover, Red Molly, symbolically brought together by their love of the vintage motorcycle of the title. Adie is killed during an armed robbery and Molly visits his deathbed, where he slips her the keys to the bike before he is "carried home" by a fleet of "angels and Ariels in leather and chrome." According to Thompson, "the death is imperative to the story and I'm not quite sure why. That has to happen to make it a satisfying story. There has to be a body. It's the ultimate sacrifice, he's giving everything that he has, which is [his] life."

SEEN A MAN DIE—SCARFACE (1994)

The man who rapped on the Geto Boys' pathologically blood-drenched "Mind of a Lunatic" in 1989 left the Houston crew in 1991 to pursue an often more thoughtful, agonized direction in his solo career. This slow, smoked-out, sinister Southern rap is his masterpiece, a truly haunted song, like some updated biblical parable telling of man's inability to feel empathy with his fellow man—and himself—without first wreaking destruction: "I never understand why / I could never see a man cry, til I seen that man die." Amid all the flash and swagger of most rap depictions of death, this extraordinary, chilling work—words and music perfectly in tandem—stands clear above the rest. A gangsta ballad without an inch of sentiment, it's about as thoughtful and self-questioning as the genre gets in the face of its own obsession with violence.

NOT DARK YET—BOB DYLAN (1997)

To date, the most direct and honest acknowledgment that any of the main players of the original rock generation have made about their inevitable, impending morality. "I was born here and I'll die here against my will / I know it looks like I'm moving, but I'm standing still," sings Dylan near the end. An utterly forlorn piece of work, where the only chink of light allowed—it's not dark *yet*—is snuffed out in the very next breath: "But it's getting there." One of his great songs, from one of his great albums, the twilit, mortally fearful *Time Out of Mind*.

I'M NOT AFRAID TO DIE—GILLIAN WELCH (1998)

Directly contradicting the old Woody Allen adage "I'm not afraid to die, I just don't want to be there when it happens," Welch's marvelously simple country homily sounds almost carefree in its fatalism. "Nobody knows what waits ahead / Beyond the earth and sky / Lie-de Lie-de Lie / I'm not afraid to die." It's the sound of that half-lost old-time world brought bubbling back to the boil; the Carter Family transported into the late twentieth century for one last encore.

O DEATH—RALPH STANLEY (2000)

Has death ever been portrayed in song as a more terrifyingly literal figure, hovering next to the bed, deaf to all entreaties? Singing with a voice that spans centuries, it almost comes as a bit of a shock to learn that Stanley, in his early seventies, only recorded this Grammy-winning version of the song for the Coen Brothers film *O Brother Where Art Thou?* at the turn of the millennium rather than in, say, 1910. The masterstroke was singing the track a capella, letting all that fear and desperation ring out unadorned. "That was my idea," Stanley later said. "I just thought I could put more feeling [into it]. I didn't feel like I could sing it good enough with music, and I thought maybe I could wind it out and put everything I had into it a cappella."[5] It has since sold around ten million copies, a strangely comforting thought.

THOUGHTS OF A DYING ATHEIST—MUSE (2003)

The quintessential twenty-first-century death song, convey-ing a very wobbly atheism indeed. Musically it's robust but emotionally it's leaking blood, indeed almost flat-lining, as it pitches up in front of all that nothingness: "It scares the hell out of me / And the end is all I can see." If the atheist is right, oblivion awaits. If he is wrong, where will his lack of faith throughout his life send him after his death? Neither thought seems to be bringing much comfort in this final tussle between rational thought and the last-ditch attempt to locate a spiritual pulse.

KEEP ME IN YOUR HEART—WARREN ZEVON (2003)

The real thing. The last song on Zevon's final album, writ-ten as lung cancer was killing him and recorded not long before the end. It could so easily be eerie and macabre, but tip-toeing between mawkishness and self-indulgence Zevon succeeds in striking a farewell note that is simple and mov-ing. Crucially, he doesn't ask too much of his lover when he is gone: "When the winter comes keep the fires lit / And I will be right next to you."

Consider it done.

NOTES ON SOURCES

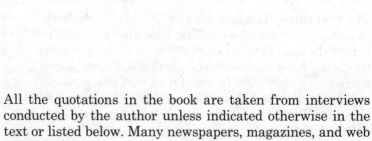

All the quotations in the book are taken from interviews conducted by the author unless indicated otherwise in the text or listed below. Many newspapers, magazines, and web pages have been enormously helpful in the writing of this book but, alas, they are too numerous to individually list here. All direct quotations from specific publications are referenced below.

PROLOGUE

1   *The Word*, October 2007

CHAPTER ONE

1   *You Wrote My Life: Lyrical Themes in Country Music*, Melton Alonza McLaurin and Richard A. Peterson (G&B Arts International, 1992)
2   Interview by Daniel Redwood, published on www.healthy.net
3   Lost Highway press release for *Jerusalem* by Steve Earle, 2002

CHAPTER TWO

1   "Death as Portrayed to Adolescents Through Top 40 Rock and Roll Music," Bruce L. Plopper and M. Ernest Ness, *Adolescence*, Vol. 28, 1993

2 *American Hardcore: A Tribal History,* Steven Blush (Feral House, 2001)
3 *England's Dreaming,* Jon Savage (Faber and Faber, 2005)
4 Interview with Gerard Way by Jonah Weiland, CBS News—*The Comic Wire,* July 2007
5 "From Her to Maturity," *Melody Maker,* May 1997

CHAPTER THREE

1 *The Many Lives of Tom Waits,* Patrick Humphries (Omnibus Press, 2007)
2 "From Her to Maturity," *Melody Maker,* May 1997
3 Mute press release for *Murder Ballads* by Nick Cave, 1996
4 *Johnny Cash at Folsom Prison: The Making of a Masterpiece,* Michael Streissguth (Da Capo Press, 2005)
5 *Songs,* Bruce Springsteen (HarperCollins, 2005)
6 Ibid.
7 Mute press release for *Murder Ballads* by Nick Cave, 1996

CHAPTER FOUR

1 *Revolution in the Head,* Ian MacDonald (4th Estate, 1994)
2 *Tomorrow Never Knows: Rock and Psychedelics in the 1960s,* Nick Bromell (University of Chicago Press, 2000)
3 *The Beach Boys,* Keith Badman (Backbeat Books, 2004)
4 From the liner notes of the remastered recording of *Forever Changes* by Love (Rhino)
5 *The Word,* February 2007

CHAPTER FIVE

1 *The Best of Everything Show,* with Dan Neer
2 Joan Smith, the *Independent,* December 4, 2005
3 *Helter Skelter—The True Story of the Manson Murders,* Vincent Bugliosi and Curt Gentry (W.W. Norton & Co Ltd, 2002)
4 *Love All the People,* Bill Hicks (Constable, 2005)

CHAPTER SIX

1 Mute press release for *Murder Ballads* by Nick Cave, 1996
2 "Death as Portrayed to Adolescents Through Top 40 Rock and Roll Music," Bruce L. Plopper and M. Ernest Ness, *Adolescence,* Vol. 28, 1993
3 *Harp* magazine, January/February 2007
4 Ibid.

CHAPTER SEVEN

1 *Ruthless: A Memoir*, Jerry Heller with Gil Reavill (Simon Spotlight Entertainment, 2006)
2 "OGs in Post-Industrial Los Angeles: Evolution of a Style," Robin D.G. Kelley, published in *Cultural Resistance Reader*, Stephen Duncombe (Verso Books, 2002)
3 *Stagolee Shot Billy*, Cecil Brown (Harvard University Press, 2003)
4 Ibid.
5 *Mystery Train*, Greil Marcus (Faber and Faber, New Ed., 2005)
6 *Stagolee Shot Billy*, Cecil Brown (Harvard University Press, 2003)
7 "OGs in Post-Industrial Los Angeles: Evolution of a Style," Robin D.G. Kelley, published in *Cultural Resistance Reader*, Stephen Duncombe (Verso Books, 2002)
8 "Hip-Hop Flop: The Failure of Liberal Rap," Stephen Rodrick, published in *Rap on Rap: Straight-up Talk on Hip-Hop Culture*, Adam Sexton (The Windrush Press, 1996)
9 "OGs in Post-Industrial Los Angeles: Evolution of a Style," Robin D.G. Kelley, published in *Cultural Resistance Reader*, Stephen Duncombe (Verso Books, 2002)

CHAPTER EIGHT

1 Via email to author
2 "The Irish Origins and Variations of the 'Ballad of Molly Brown,'" Jennifer J. O'Connor (*Canadian Journal for Traditional Music*, 1986)
3 "Death as Portrayed to Adolescents Through Top 40 Rock and Roll Music," Bruce L. Plopper and M. Ernest Ness, *Adolescence*, Vol. 28, 1993
4 *Observer*, April 7, 2002
5 *New York Times* via Guardian Unlimited blog, published January 23, 2008

CHAPTER TEN

1 *International Herald Tribune*, August 8, 2007

EPILOGUE

1 *Rolling Stone*, December 2004
2 http://www.learningfromlyrics.org/Don'tfear.html
3 *Some Great Reward*, Dave Johnson (St. Martin's Press, 1995)
4 Interview on *MTV Icon*, 2003
5 "Ralph Stanley Roams On," Jeffrey B. Remz, *Country Standard Time*, July 2006

SELECTED BIBLIOGRAPHY

American Hardcore: A Tribal History, Steven Blush (Feral House, 2001)

The Beach Boys, Keith Badman (Backbeat Books, 2004)

Black Folktales, Julius Lester (Grove Press/Black Cat, 1970)

Bob Dylan: Performing Artist 1974–1986, Paul Williams (Omnibus Press, 2004)

Country Music Culture: From Hard Times to Heaven, Curtis W. Ellison (University Press of Mississippi, 1995)

Cultural Resistance Reader, Stephen Duncombe (Verso Books, 2002)

Death Discs, Alan Clayson (Sanctuary Publishing, 1997)

Dylan: Behind the Shades, Clinton Heylin (Viking 1991)

England's Dreaming, Jon Savage (Faber and Faber, 2005)

Helter Skelter—The True Story of the Manson Murders, Vincent Bugliosi and Curt Gentry (W.W. Norton & Co Ltd, 2002)

Johnny Cash at Folsom Prison: The Making of a Masterpiece, Michael Streissguth (Da Capo Press, 2005)

John Peel: Margrave of the Marshes, John Peel and Sheila Ravenscroft (Corgi, 2006)

Last Train to Memphis: The Rise of Elvis Presley, Peter Guralnick (Abacus, 1994)

Love All the People, Bill Hicks (Constable, 2005)

The Many Lives of Tom Waits, Patrick Humphries (Omnibus Press, 2007)

Mystery Train, Greil Marcus (Faber and Faber, New Ed., 2005)

Nothing Feels Good: Punk Rock, Teenagers, and Emo, Andy Greenwald (St. Martin's Griffin, 2003)

Our Band Could Be Your Life: Scenes from the American Indie Underground 1981–1991, Michael Azerrad (Little, Brown, 2001)

Rap on Rap: Straight-up Talk on Hip-Hop Culture, Adam Sexton (The Windrush Press, 1996)

Revolution in the Head: The Beatles' Records and the Sixties, Ian MacDonald (4th Estate, 1994)

Ruthless: A Memoir, Jerry Heller with Gil Reavill (Simon Spotlight Entertainment, 2006)

Some Great Reward, Dave Johnson (St. Martin's Press, 1995)

Songs, Bruce Springsteen (HarperCollins, 2005)

The Sound of Stevie Wonder: His Words and Music, James E. Perone (Praeger Publishers Inc., 2006)

Stagolee Shot Billy, Cecil Brown (Harvard University Press, 2003)

Teenage: The Creation of Youth Culture, Jon Savage (Viking Books, 2007)

The Third MOJO Collection, edited by Colin McLear and Jim Irvin (Canongate, 2003)

Tomorrow Never Knows: Rock and Psychedelics in the 1960s, Nick Bromell (University of Chicago Press, 2000)

Unforgettable Fire: The Story of U2, Eamon Dunphy (Viking, 1987)

You Wrote My Life: Lyrical Themes in Country Music, Melton Alonza McLaurin and Richard A. Peterson (G&B Arts International, 1992)

INDEX

INDEX